Constitutional Futures

Constitutional Futures

A History of the Next Ten Years

Edited by
Professor Robert Hazell

The Constitution Unit

OXFORD
UNIVERSITY PRESS

OXFORD

UNIVERSITY PRESS

Great Clarendon Street, Oxford ox2 6dp

Oxford University Press is a department of the University of Oxford
It furthers the University's objective of excellence in research, scholarship,
and education by publishing worldwide in

Oxford New York

Athens Auckland Bangkok Bogotá Buenos Aires Calcutta
Cape Town Chennai Dar es Salaam Delhi Florence Hong Kong Istanbul
Karachi Kuala Lumpur Madrid Melbourne Mexico City Mumbai
Nairobi Paris São Paulo Singapore Taipei Tokyo Toronto Warsaw

with associated companies in Berlin Ibadan

Oxford is a registered trade mark of Oxford University Press
in the UK and in certain other countries

Published in the United States
by Oxford University Press Inc., New York

British Library Cataloguing in Publication Data

Data available

Library of Congress Cataloging in Publication Data

Data available

ISBN 0-19-829801-3

1 3 5 7 9 10 8 6 4 2

Printed in Great Britain
on acid-free paper by
Biddles Ltd.,
Guildford & King's Lynn

Contents

Contributors

Richard Cornes is a New Zealand public lawyer currently working as a Senior Research Fellow at the Constitution Unit, School of Public Policy, University College London. His primary research interest is intergovernmental relations, both domestic and international.

Paul Craig is Professor of English Law at the University of Oxford and a fellow of St John's College, Oxford. He has written extensively on EC, constitutional and administrative law. Recent publications include *EC Law, Text, Cases and Materials* 2nd edition (Oxford: Oxford University Press, 1998) with G de Búrca, *Administrative Law* 3rd edition (London: Sweet and Maxwell, 1994), and *Public Law and Democracy in the UK and the USA* (Oxford: Oxford University Press, 1990).

Ann Dummett has worked as Research Officer for the Joint Council for the Welfare of Immigrants, Director of the Runnymede Trust, and consultant to the Commission for Racial Equality on its European policies. She has written extensively on nationality and immigration law, race relations, and minorities in Europe.

Conor Gearty is Professor of Human Rights Law and Director of the Civil Liberties Research Unit at King's College London. He is the author of numerous books and articles including *Freedom under Thatcher. Civil Liberties in Modern Britain* (Oxford: Clarendon Press, 1990) with K D Ewing, *The Future of Terrorism* (London: Orion, 1997) and *European Civil Liberties and the European Convention on Human Rights: A Comparative Survey* (The Hague, Boston: Kluwer Law International, 1997).

Robert Hazell is the Director of the Constitution Unit and Professor of Government and the Constitution in the School of Public Policy, University College London. Originally a barrister, he spent most of his working life at the Home Office. He left Whitehall to become director of the Nuffield Foundation and founded the Constitution Unit in 1995.

Richard Macrory is Professor of Environmental Law at Imperial College, London and a practising barrister with a particular interest in European Community environmental law. He is a member of the Royal Commission on Environmental Pollution, and a specialist adviser to the House of Commons Select Committee on Environment, Transport, and the Regions. He is editor in chief of the Journal of Environmental Law, and was the first chairman of the Environmental Law Association.

Jeremy Mitchell is currently Director of the Masters Programme in the Faculty of Social Science at the Open University. He has written extensively on elections and British politics. His recent publications include *Reforming the Lords* (London: IPPR, 1993) with Anne Davies and *Governance in the Asia Pacific* (London: Routledge, 1998), edited with Richard Maidment and David Goldblatt.

Bob Morris was a Home Office official from 1961–97. He has worked variously in enforcement, public control and constitutional areas, and has had experience with both the preparation and operation of international instruments, as well as being at the receiving end of judicial review.

Brendan O'Leary is Professor of Political Science and Convenor of the Department of Government at the London School of Economics. He has advised and written extensively on Northern Ireland and is the author of numerous books and articles on national and ethnic conflict. Recent books include *The Politics of Antagonism: Understanding Northern Ireland* (London: Athlone Press, 1996) and *Explaining Northern Ireland: Broken Images* (Oxford: Blackwell, 1995), both written with John McGerry.

Ben Seyd is Senior Research Fellow at the Constitution Unit, School of Public Policy, University College London, where he is responsible for the programme of research on elections, democracy and parties. Prior to joining the Unit, he worked at the Confederation of British Industry, specialising in higher education policy and regional economic development.

Frank Vibert is co-founder and director of the European Policy Forum, an independent London-based think tank. He has written extensively on British and European constitutional issues.

Helen Wallace is Professor of Contemporary European Studies and Director of the Sussex European Institute at the University of Sussex. She is also Director of the ESRC programme 'One Europe or several'. Her recent publications include *Policy-making in the European Union,* edited with William Wallace (Oxford: Oxford University Press, 1996) and *The Council of Ministers of the European Union*, with Fiona Hayes-Renshaw (New York, NY: St Martin's Press 1996). In 1996 she was made a Chevalier de l'Ordre National du Mérite.

List of Figures

Foreword

This is the most ambitious project the Constitution Unit has yet undertaken. The Unit has made its name for its detailed studies of individual reforms: devolution to Scotland and Wales, reform of the House of Lords, human rights legislation, introducing freedom of information, the conduct of referendums, changing the electoral system. In this book we have tried to view the Government's reform programme as a whole, to forecast the cumulative impact of all these different constitutional changes, and to explore the interactive effects between them.

We do so at a time of extraordinarily rapid constitutional change. In all, the new Government has introduced twelve constitutional bills in the first session of the new Parliament; with more reforms to come. They will transform the political landscape and reshape the British state in ways that are not fully understood. We do not pretend to full understanding ourselves, nor to perfect knowledge in our forecasts; but we hope that the book enables people to see the linkages between the different elements in the constitutional reform programme, and to have a better sense of where the programme as a whole may be taking us.

This study is the first systematic attempt to foresee the full effects of the new Government's constitutional reform programme. Because of the scale of the project, all the members of the Unit have been involved in a collaborative venture, together with experts from six other universities: Professor Paul Craig (Oxford), Professor Conor Gearty (King's College, London), Professor Richard Macrory (Imperial College, London), Jeremy Mitchell (Open University), Professor Brendan O'Leary (London School of Economics), Frank Vibert (European Policy Forum) and Professor Helen Wallace (Sussex). They kindly came to regular meetings of a Steering Group to discuss draft chapters as the book gradually took shape. The result is more than a collection of essays by individual authors. Although each contributor is responsible only for the chapter against his or her name, it has been a collective effort, in which the chapters have benefited greatly from the collective comments of the Steering Group and from individual comments from outside experts.

We owe special thanks to Conor Gearty and Helen Wallace, for commenting on successive drafts, even though they do not feature as individual authors; and to Ann Dummett, for contributing an excellent chapter at short notice. Others who have kindly commented on draft chapters include Alison Barry, Frank Cranmer, David Farrell, Justin Fisher, Philippa Helme, Simon James, Peter Lynch, James Mitchell, Roger Phillips, and Richard Rose. Within the Unit, members and associates who have contributed to the project include Richard Cornes, James Cornford, Katy Donnelly, Julia Fox, Graham Leicester, Bob Morris, Sara Northey, Mads Qvortrup, Meg Russell, David Sinclair and Nicole Smith.

The book was edited and put together with great speed and efficiency by Judith Ayling and David Sinclair. Thanks also go to John Louth and Nigel Sleight at OUP, for publishing it in record time.

Finally, we owe a special debt of gratitude to the UCL Friends Programme and to the Gatsby Charitable Foundation, who both made generous grants to this project, and who have shown great interest in the book as it has appeared.

Robert Hazell   School of Public Policy
November 1998   University College London

1

Introduction

ROBERT HAZELL AND RICHARD CORNES

THE NEW CONSTITUTIONAL SETTLEMENT

Tony Blair has described the Government's programme of constitutional reform as 'the biggest programme of change to democracy ever proposed'.[1] This view is echoed by the Lord Chancellor, Lord Irvine of Lairg, the Minister who is presiding over the Government's constitutional reform programme. He has also commented that the reforms while addressing universal problems are 'tailored to the particular needs of the British constitution'.[2] The programme will transform the political and legal landscape, in ways not yet fully understood. Twelve constitutional bills have been introduced in the first legislative session of the new Government, and eleven have been passed which are set out in Figure 1.1 below.

This raft of constitutional legislation amounts to a new constitutional settlement, which will be looked back on as the major achievement of the new Blair Government. The consequences of the reform programme will be cumulative and reveal themselves gradually over the next decade or more. This book sets out to predict the main consequences of constitutional reform, both those currently under way and those that are likely to ensue over the next five to ten years.

It does so against a background of major constitutional change not only in the UK but also in Europe. The European Union (EU) is the source or inspiration of some of the constitutional changes in the UK[3] and an important backdrop to the remainder. Chapter 4 shows how the EU is grappling with some of the same issues: trying to remedy the democratic deficit, reversing excessive centralization, finding the right balance between uniform standards and diversity. The labels are different: 'flexibility' and 'multi-speed Europe' for the EU, and a 'rolling programme of devolution' in the UK. But the challenges are essentially the same—to construct a framework which is broad

---

[1] Speech to Labour Party Conference, 4 October 1994.

[2] Irvine, 1998 National Heritage Lecture, 'Constitutional Change in the UK: British Solutions to Universal Problems'; delivered to the US Supreme Court, 11 May 1998.

[3] Evidenced in the first year legislative programme, where two of the constitutional bills emanate from the EU.

and flexible enough to allow for asymmetrical development, at different speeds, but not so flexible that the system flies apart.

Figure 1.1. Constitutional Bills in the first-year legislative programme 1997–8

Devolution
- Referendums (Scotland and Wales) Act 1997
- Government of Wales Act 1998
- Scotland Act 1998
- Northern Ireland (Elections) Act 1998
- Northern Ireland Act 1998
- Regional Development Agencies Act 1998

Europe (Amsterdam Treaty)
- European Communities (Amendment) Act 1998

Incorporation of the European Convention on Human Rights
- Human Rights Act 1998

Independence of the Bank of England
- Bank of England Act 1998

Electoral Reform
- European Parliamentary Elections Bill 1997[4]
- Registration of Political Parties Act 1998

Elected Mayors
- Greater London Authority Referendum Act 1998

Strictly only ten of these bills count as first class constitutional measures, in the sense that their Committee stage in the House of Commons was taken on the floor of the House.[5] They are set out not chronologically but thematically. Six of the bills were on devolution. Of these three were relatively minor—the bill to authorize the referendums held in Scotland and Wales in September 1997, the bill to authorize the elections in Northern Ireland held in June 1998, and the bill to establish Regional Development Agencies as the first tentative

---

[4] The European Parliamentary Elections Bill fell right at the end of the session because the House of Lords refused to accept closed party lists, even though the bill was sent back from the House of Commons five times. The government is likely to reintroduce the bill in the second session, but without the co-operation of the Lords, the new voting system may not take effect until 2004.

[5] The two bills which went upstairs to Standing Committee for their Committee stage were the Regional Development Agencies Act and the Registration of Political Parties Act.

step towards regional government in England. But three are very major—the three big devolution bills to Scotland, Wales and Northern Ireland. Their impact is discussed in Chapter 3.

Next come four bills influenced by Europe. There was the bill to implement the Amsterdam Treaty, and the bill to introduce a proportional voting system for the European Parliament elections, which (if passed) will bring us into line with the rest of the EU. The Bank of England Act was introduced to bolster the central bank in part to prepare for Economic and Monetary Union (EMU), whether the UK goes in or stays outside. Independence of the central bank is not one of the constitutional changes discussed in this book, but EMU is discussed in chapter 4. The Human Rights Act comes from another part of Europe, the Council of Europe in Strasbourg, and brings us into line with most of the Council's other member states, which in different ways guarantee the European Convention on Human Rights in their domestic law.[6]

The Registration of Political Parties Act is a consequence of the new party list system of voting, in the European elections and in the new electoral systems for Scotland and Wales. It is the first time political parties in our system will have been subject to direct regulation, but not the last: the Neill Committee's recommendations on the control of party funding would represent a much larger regulatory step.[7] Lastly, the Greater London Authority Referendum Act authorized the referendum held in May 1998, as the first step towards the new Greater London Authority and directly elected Mayor.

Twelve constitutional bills in one session has to be a parliamentary record. In particular, the passage of the three big devolution bills in a single session was an extraordinary achievement. It was not an overstatement when the Scottish White Paper described these as 'the most ambitious and far reaching changes in the British constitution undertaken by any government this century'.[8] Taken together they will amount to a new constitutional settlement, but one whose features will not become fully apparent for some years to come.

THE PURPOSE OF THIS BOOK

The Constitution Unit has made a name for its detailed studies on the implementation of individual constitutional reforms: devolution, reform of the House of Lords, human rights legislation, introducing freedom of information,

---

[6] See The Constitution Unit, *Human Rights Legislation*, 1996, paras 36-40. In 1995 the only countries which had not incorporated or otherwise guaranteed the ECHR were Ireland, Poland and the UK.

[7] Committee on Standards in Public Life, *The Funding of Political Parties in the UK*, Cm 4057-I, October 1998.

[8] *Scotland's Parliament* Cm 3658, July 1977

referendums and electoral reform.[9] This book is something much more ambitious: a forecast of the cumulative impact of these different constitutional changes, and an explanation of the interaction between them. Many of the changes being introduced will be irreversible: while repeal of the Scotland Act or the Human Rights Act may be legally and constitutionally possible, politically such a step would be inconceivable. And in time, if the reforms endure, the legal position may come to match the political reality. There may be Acts of Parliament which are regarded as organic laws and which become entrenched. These are fundamental alterations in the constitutional arrangements of the United Kingdom, which amount to a reshaping of the British state.

Constitutional reform is likely to release dynamics in politics and the law which will take on their own directing force. The cumulative impact of increased openness of government, a rights culture and devolution will work together to produce a dynamic whole that is greater than the sum of its constituent parts. Further, this constitutional change occurs at a time of rapid change in international law and politics, both at European and global levels. Interactive effects will occur at this level too. The European Communities Act 1972 and the Single European Act 1986 introduced profound constitutional changes, as will Economic and Monetary Union (EMU), whether the UK joins or remains outside. European law has shaped our political and legal institutions and thinking in ways that few would have predicted when the UK first joined the European Community.

But the flow need not be all one way. Constitutional reform is badly needed in Europe as well. There is the prospect that constitutional reform at home may put the UK in a position to be a constructive contributor in the development of European constitutionalism. Constitutional models may flow upwards as well as down. A UK more certain of its own institutions could propose the model of its own asymmetrical union, based on the rule of law, representative democracy and respect for human rights, as a possible guide to the EU; a more flexible model to set against the conceptual dominance of a 'federal' Europe modelled on the lines of the German federation.

The following chapters draw out the links between the components of the reform programme and consider their cumulative impact. They are based on prediction, not prescription. We do not necessarily advocate the changes we foresee. We are trying to forecast what the world will look like as a result of the constitutional changes now in train. Some aspects of that world will be welcome, others not. Constitutional reform does not deliver unmixed blessings.

---

[9] *Delivering Constitutional Reform* (1996); *Reform of the House of Lords* (1996): *Scotland's Parliament* (1997); *An Assembly for Wales* (1997); *Regional Government in England* (1997); *Human Rights Legislation* (1997); *Report of the Commission on the Conduct of Referendums* (1997); *Introducing Freedom of Information* (1997); *Changing the Electoral System* (1997).

What is undeniable is that the world will be different, and we seek to forecast what the main differences will be. We have tried to avoid other forms of forecasting, driven by economic, social, technological or cultural factors, and to concentrate on what we know about, which is the political and legal effects of constitutional change.

We do not assert what is likely to happen simply by peering into the future; but by studying carefully what has happened elsewhere. Although for the UK constitutional change of this kind may seem a bold experiment, other countries have been here before, including countries with political, legal and administrative cultures similar to ours. To study the impact of incorporating the European Convention on Human Rights (ECHR), we can look at the effect of New Zealand's Bill of Rights Act 1990, or the Canadian Charter of Fundamental Rights and Freedoms 1982, as well as those European countries which have recently incorporated the Convention (Denmark, Norway, Sweden). To study the impact of freedom of information we can look at Australia, Canada and New Zealand, all of which legislated in 1982, and more recently at Ireland (1997). For the impact of PR on a Westminster Parliament we turn again to New Zealand (1996). And for devolution we can look at our own history, in the experience of the Stormont Parliament (1922–72), at the operation of federal systems (Australia, Canada, Germany) and at the other major countries of Western Europe which have introduced a regional tier of government (France, Italy, Spain). The experiences of these countries are set out in case studies in the chapters which follow. Comparative studies are endlessly fascinating, for the differences they throw up as well as the similarities. For those who are fearful that the UK is taking a wild leap in the dark, they offer some beacons to guide us. Whether beacons of hope or beacons of warning is for the reader to judge.

THE BOOK'S STRUCTURE

The book has four parts. Chapters 1 and 2 introduce each of the main items in the constitutional reform programme, and their likely effect. The effects of some changes are more readily predictable than others. To accommodate a range of forecasts, we posit two broad scenarios, one minimalist and one maximalist, which are described in Chapter 2. In Chapters 3–12 the authors draw on these scenarios to launch more detailed discussion and to consider the possible effects of the reform scenarios in particular areas. Chapters 3–9 consider general questions, such as the effects on Whitehall or the political and party system. Chapters 10–12 are case studies of the effects of the reform programme in selected areas of policy.

Finally Chapter 13 collects the conclusions of the authors under five themes: first an assessment of how the UK is developing a more overtly constitutional form of government, with greater checks and balances and greater separation of powers; second, how popular sovereignty is replacing parliamentary sovereignty as the fundamental principle underlying the new constitutional settlement; third, how devolution will lead to a form of quasi-federalism, with some of the characteristics of a federal system, but some important differences (asymmetry, no parliament for England); fourth, the tighter rule of law, with ECHR incorporation and devolution giving the courts important new roles; fifth, the growth of a more pluralist, consensual politics with more coalition governments and more minority parties in place of the adversarial two-party system.

The final chapter identifies some of the gaps in the constitutional reform programme. These are not items to be added to the agenda, but elements necessary to underpin the existing programme. In the main they are changes required of central government, in Westminster and Whitehall. The energy in the first year of the new Government has been on driving the legislation through, and on the design of the new institutions in Scotland, Wales and Northern Ireland. But those institutions will significantly change the balance of power within the Union, and require a re-balancing at the centre if the new constitutional settlement is to be built on sure foundations.

2

The Shape of Things to Come: What Will the UK Constitution Look Like in the Early 21st Century?

ROBERT HAZELL

This chapter seeks to sketch the changes to the UK political landscape which may result from the current programme of constitutional reform. It sets to one side developments in Europe, which are explored in Chapter 4, and focuses on the domestic agenda. Two scenarios of how the constitutional reform programme may unfold are taken for the purposes of assessing the position in around ten years' time, one minimal, one maximal (see Figure 2.1.).

Figure 2.1. Minimal and maximal scenarios for constitutional reform		
Area	**Minimal**	**Maximal**
Devolution	Scottish Parliament with legislative power, not exercising its limited tax raising powers	Scottish Parliament exercising legislative and tax raising powers. Independent Scotland?
	Northern Ireland Assembly with legislative but no tax raising power	Northern Ireland Assembly with legislative and tax raising powers
	Welsh Assembly with secondary legislation making powers only	Welsh Parliament with legislative and tax raising powers
	Regional Development Agencies in England appointed by central government	Elected Regional Assemblies in some English regions; Regional Chambers elsewhere
	Elected mayors in a few cities with limited powers	Strong elected mayors in the major cities
	Joint Ministerial Committee on Devolution meeting infrequently; fire fighting only	Joint Ministerial Committee as strong part of the devolution settlement
	Council of the Isles as token consultative body	Council of the Isles developing wider functions

Area	Minimal	Maximal
Parliamentary reform	Limited reform of the House of Lords, involving removing the hereditary peers and re-balancing party numbers. House of Lords remains a nominated body	A predominantly or solely elected House of Lords representing the nations, regions and cities. Some changes to strengthen its functions and powers
	Referendum rejects electoral reform for House of Commons	House of Commons elected by proportional representation
	Closed list PR for elections to the European Parliament, enabling voters only to choose between parties	Open list PR for EP elections, enabling voters to choose between individual candidates
A rights culture	ECHR as part of UK statute law but no Human Rights Commission to promote a new rights culture	ECHR as part of UK law, Human Rights Commission, domestic Bill of Rights either in preparation or already in the statute book
Openness	Restricted Freedom of Information regime, focused mainly on access to personal files	Liberal Freedom of Information Act enabling access to general government information
Judicial structure	Appellate Committee still sitting as members of the House of Lords. The Privy Council adapted to hear 'devolution' disputes	A new supreme court for the United Kingdom, separate from the House of Lords
Inter-governmental relations	Informal intergovernmental consultative processes based on Whitehall concordats	Formalised Council of British Isles with full time secretariat

The actual position may be any range of combinations between the two. For the purposes of domestic forecasting the mini and maxi scenarios can be used to draw two possible sketch maps of Westminster and Whitehall, and of the wider political system. The effect of the changes will be analysed separately, and in terms of their cumulative impact.

DEVOLUTION

Devolution is a process, not an event. In France and Spain it has taken ten to twenty years to introduce regional assemblies, and they have not reached a stable equilibrium. Nor will they: even in federal systems state/federal relations are continually evolving. So it will be in the UK, even on a maxi scenario, which otherwise might be seen as an endpoint. In ten years' time devolution in the UK will still be unfolding. This is explicitly recognized in Northern Ireland, where the Northern Ireland Act plans for the transfer of power for the Northern Ireland Assembly to be linked to progress in the implementation of the Belfast Agreement.[1] There may be a once-for-all transfer in formal terms, or a transfer in several stages; but in either case devolution and the balance of power between Westminster and the Assembly will be a continually evolving process.

In Great Britain there is likely to be a process of leapfrog whereby the slower English regions seek to catch up with those which have established regional assemblies; and Wales seeks to emulate Scotland. This may lead the Scots to press for further devolution to keep one step ahead. For the nationalist parties the demands for devolution will never be satisfied: national and regional political parties will use the devolved assemblies as a political platform to attack central government, and to demand greater powers and autonomy. There is nothing unusual in this: it is commonplace in federal systems, where provincial politicians (the Reform Party of Western Canada, the CSU in Bavaria, the Premiers in Australia) use attacks on the federal government, whether of their own party or not, as one strategy in various intergovernmental games. It is an expression of the tension which exists between the centre and the provinces in all polities; a tension partly suppressed within the UK's unitary system, which will find more overt expression under devolution.

Apart from certain symbolic issues (language in Wales, nuclear power or fishing in Scotland) the tensions will be strongest over finance. The strengthening role of national government in the supply of local finance is unlikely to be reversed: the trend worldwide is for taxes to drift to the centre. Even in federal systems the states raise only a small proportion of their own revenue: in Australia the proportion is around 20 per cent. In other countries the proportion is higher; but given the current starting point in the UK, and traditional Treasury nervousness allied to politicians' nervousness about devolving revenue-raising power, devolved assemblies will continue to rely on central government for the bulk of their budgets. EU requirements for monetary discipline, whether or not the UK joins the single currency, will mean that central government needs to retain tight control over all public expenditure, including spending by devolved assemblies and local authorities.

Tight control of central government contributions need not feed into control of how regional budgets are spent; although it often does. It requires great self restraint by central government to distribute block rather than specific grants; but the current Scottish and Welsh blocks show it can be done. Significant decentralisation of both the provision and the supply of public services can be achieved without there necessarily being any increase in the proportion of finance raised locally. But if devolved governments are to have genuine

---

[1] Northern Ireland Act 1998, s 3.

responsibility for making choices about the level and nature of public spending, rather than simply administering aggregate public spending decisions reached by central government, they will need to have some tax revenues under their own control. This is explored further in Chapter 11.

The formula for distributing central government funding to the nations and regions will be the subject of sharper debate and controversy, because the levels of government support to the different regions will be much more exposed and transparent. Greater autonomy will lead to greater variability and may lead to greater inequity. The poorer regions (Northern Ireland, Wales, the North of England, *not* Scotland) will continue to press for equalisation. The growing fiscal pressures on central government may lead it, despite any policy instincts to the contrary, to devolve functions in order to devolve expenditure: as has happened with local authorities and community care.

There will also be tensions between the devolved assemblies and local government, which again will centre on the distribution of functions and of finance. That is unlikely in Northern Ireland, where local government has relatively few functions; but in Scotland and Wales (and England, if Regional Assemblies are created) tensions may quickly become apparent.[2] The hostility of local government to the Scottish Office and Welsh Office will transfer to the devolved administrations, especially if they embark on a further review of the new local government structure. On the mini scenario the Welsh Assembly will find that its only room for manoeuvre financially lies in its ability indirectly to precept upon local authorities. In the English regions, the requirement for a predominantly unitary structure before the creation of directly elected regional assemblies may mean that regional assemblies only emerge after a further local government review which involves the extinction of the counties. One of the key central government functions which might then be devolved to regional government is the distribution of revenue support grant to local authorities. This could lead to more various redistributive outcomes, because distributions would no longer follow a single formula.

A key function for devolved assemblies will be regional economic development. In the mini scenario Regional Development Agencies will be established in each of the English regions which will compete against the Scottish and Welsh Development Agencies and the Northern Ireland Development Board (which in turn may have entered into partnership with its Irish counterpart in the South). They will be in competition with each other for inward investment, for European funding, and for promotional opportunities abroad. Central government will come under pressure to intervene to prevent

---

[2] To defuse these tensions the Welsh Assembly is required by the Government of Wales Act to establish a Partnership Council with local authorities; and in Scotland a Commission on Local Government and the Scottish Parliament was established in 1997, chaired by Neil McIntosh, former chief executive of Strathclyde Regional Council.

them outbidding each other with investment incentives and to ensure a level playing field.

Both the mini and maxi scenarios posit a rolling programme of devolution, with 'variable geometry' in terms of the different degree of power devolved in different parts of the UK and at different moments. Another form of the variable geometry which may be difficult to manage is that between different services: between those services which are likely to remain centralized (like broadcasting) and those which are devolved (education, arts and culture). Tensions may also arise where a devolved matter (environment in Scotland) covers the same area as a policy development in a reserved matter (e.g., the Westminster Government exercising its foreign affairs power to enter into international commitments concerning the environment). This is dealt with further in Chapters 8 and 9.

This account has focused on the tensions which will emerge as the devolution process unfolds. Paradoxically, the tensions may prove greater in the mini scenario, because that would imply greater hesitation by central government about the devolution project. The account would not be complete without a brief mention of the potential benefits: the reduction in the workload of Westminster and Whitehall; greater political participation in the regions, and stronger local accountability; a higher profile for the regions, both within the UK and the EU; a better understanding of regional economies; and generally a redirection of political energy away from the hothouse of Westminster.

These benefits will emerge more strongly in the maxi scenario. The political parties will also need to change, to compete with new political parties at regional level (and at UK level if there is PR): the parties will become national coalitions, ceding greater autonomy to their regional branches. These changes are explored further in Chapter 6.

A REFORMED HOUSE OF COMMONS AND HOUSE OF LORDS

On the mini scenario the referendum would lead to no change in the voting system for the House of Commons. The House would not be immune to other changes (the impact of regional politics); but first past the post would ensure the continuing domination of major parties. On the maxi scenario, with a House of Commons elected by PR, the major change would be the increase in the number of MPs from minority parties; and the expansion of the number of minority parties. This would lead to a dynamic series of changes, which might include the fragmentation of one or more of the major parties, as happened in New Zealand during the period leading up to the introduction of PR (also discussed further in Chapter 6).

The minimum impact of PR can be demonstrated by 'static' modelling done on the 1997 general election results, showing the different party strengths resulting from different voting systems. Extrapolating from current party strengths, the main difference would be the number of Liberal Democrats. Instead of the 46 MPs elected in 1997, the Liberal Democrats would have had twice that number of MPs in a House of Commons elected by the 'AV Top-up' voting system recommended by the Jenkins Commission.[3] The Conservatives and the Labour Party would less often have an outright majority, and would rely more frequently on Liberal Democrat and/or other minority party support to form a government. The Liberal Democrats would move centre stage, if they maintained their share of the popular vote, and would often determine which of the major parties formed a government. The nationalist parties would also have more seats, but from a lower base: extrapolating again from the 1997 election figures, the SNP and Plaid Cymru might have had 15 instead of 10 seats between the two parties. Here, too, dynamic modelling would produce more dramatic results.

Whatever assumptions are made about individual party strengths, coalition governments are likely to become more frequent. The Monarch would more often be faced with a delicate choice of whom to invite to form a government. The protocol developed between the private secretaries in the Palace, Number 10 and the Cabinet Secretary might harden into constitutional conventions about the consultation process, as has happened in the constitutional monarchies of Europe (and for other European heads of state) where PR often throws up no outright winner.[4]

Flowing from the changes in its composition, a House of Commons elected by PR would also have a different political culture. It would probably contain more women, and it would be less adversarial, at least in the two-party sense: more a place of shifting coalitions. The lack of an outright government majority would be reflected not only on the floor but also in committees. Party discipline would be harder to maintain; with the growing number of parties, and possible fragmentation of major parties, the efficient management of business through the Whips' offices would be harder to achieve. Governments might suffer more frequent defeats, but might no longer be expected to regard every major legislative or policy defeat as one requiring a vote of confidence. There might be more log rolling as a result of the presence of regional parties. At its worst this more fluid kind of Parliament based on shifting coalitions could degenerate into the politics of drift and stagnation evident during much of the post-war period in Italy, or glimpsed in the travails of the 1970s Labour Government

[3] Report of the Independent Commission on the Voting System (Cm 4090) October 1998, para 157.

[4] See Bogdanor, V., *The Monarchy and the Constitution* (Oxford: Oxford University Press, 1995), ch. 6.

once it had lost its majority. At its best such a Parliament could become a stronger check on the executive, scrutinising legislation more effectively, and through more open and consultative processes gaining wider public and professional support.

In the House of Lords, the minimalist scenario would see the removal of the hereditary peers, but with reform stopping at this point. The second chamber would then consist simply of life peers, all appointed by the current and previous governments; and the bishops and law lords. This might provoke a further bout of questioning about the legitimacy of the second chamber, and a further debate about its functions: is it simply a revising chamber? Is it a House of experts, or of corporate and professional interests? Should it be seeking to call the executive to account, when that is one of the primary functions of the Commons? Should it assume new functions: human rights watchdog; stronger scrutiny of Europe (perhaps co-opting MEPs); or representing the nations, regions and local government (which it could do by a system of nomination as well as by election)?

Similar questions about functions arise on a maximalist scenario. If the House of Lords became (wholly or partly) an elected chamber, what would be the basis of the franchise? To preserve its complementary role it would need to be elected on a different franchise from the House of Commons. But it need not be directly elected. It could consist of politicians already elected to lower tiers of government. Indirect election might form part of a wider devolution settlement, tying the newly devolved governments into the centre by enabling them to be represented in the Westminster Parliament, rather as the Länder governments in Germany are represented in the Bundesrat. But the Bundesrat is not the only model. The regional representatives could be appointed by central government (as with the Canadian Senate); or the regional *assemblies* could be represented rather than their governments, as in the Indian upper house, the Council of States (Rajya Sabha).

A RIGHTS CULTURE

The mini scenario would stop at incorporation of the European Convention of Human Rights (ECHR). This would formalize the arrival of a stronger rights culture into politics and public administration; although the emergence of such a culture has been evident for some time. Up to now, the rapid growth of judicial review and the impact of EC law have been more important than the flow of judgments coming from the European Court of Human Rights. The main difference following incorporation will be that challenges in the British courts will be much swifter than the five-year wait for a decision from Strasbourg; and the Government and Parliament will need to be more vigilant in ensuring that laws and practices comply with the ECHR/Bill of Rights before introduction, rather than rectifying matters afterwards. The ECHR will be available before all domestic tribunals as well as the courts.

The process of adjustment may be difficult as politicians come to terms with the new and immediate vigilance of the British courts, as opposed to the more remote and occasional interventions from Strasbourg. The growth of legal challenges may provoke a reaction against the whole idea of rights; or against the cost and delays involved in litigation, similar to the periodic outbursts against the rise in judicial review. There may be pressure to develop cheaper and speedier means of resolving such disputes, through ombudsmen, tribunals and mediation as alternatives to litigating in the courts.[5] A Human Rights Commission may be introduced, to monitor compliance and promote good practice, but it is unlikely to stem the flow of litigation. And ombudsmen, mediation and other means of alternative dispute resolution may prove more difficult to utilize because of the need for such schemes themselves to be consistent with the Human Rights Act, with its strong emphasis on the right to a fair and public hearing (ECHR Article 6).

The maxi scenario would involve the development of a British Bill of Rights, which might include some basic economic and social rights as well as the further development of civil and political rights. If a new Parliamentary Human Rights Committee is established to scrutinize compliance with the ECHR it is likely at some stage to conduct an enquiry into the adequacy of the ECHR as a statement of human rights for the 21st century. Development of a British Bill of Rights could have a much deeper impact on the emergence of a rights culture, because it is hard to see how a native Bill of Rights could be drafted without an extensive process of public consultation. Consultation could lead to the project being abandoned, because of failure to establish any popular consensus; or it could develop a ground swell of popular support for the Bill of Rights, as happened with the major consultation exercise undertaken before the introduction of the Canadian Charter of Rights and Freedoms.[6]

OPENNESS AND TRANSPARENCY

A Freedom of Information (FOI) Act would only be part of a trend towards greater openness in government, which has grown over the last twenty years. On its own it would not be the panacea which its proponents sometimes suppose. Overseas experience suggests the major area of demand will be for access to personal files; with relatively slight interest in policy papers, at least initially, and requests coming more from business than from journalists or

---

[5] On the Ombudsman and ECHR see the Constitution Unit, *Human Rights Legislation* (1996), paras 227-230.

[6] Penner, R., 'The Canadian Experience with the Charter of Rights: Are There Lessons for the United Kingdom?', *Public Law* (Spring 1996).

pressure groups. Whether FOI leads to a greater culture of openness depends on the strength of the Government's commitment, and whether it has strong ministerial champions to lead the charge. If, as in Canada, FOI claims some early ministerial scalps, the Government's commitment may quickly wane. FOI does not on its own lead to greater public participation in policy making. Rather it is a small check on the integrity, fairness and accuracy of government information, especially when dealing with individuals.

Other pressures may also contribute to a more open policy-making process. The lack of a parliamentary majority may force the Government to seek allies for its legislative proposals, instead of simply relying on the Whips. This may involve the publication of Green and White Papers; the publication of bills in draft; pre-legislative scrutiny hearings; publishing the responses of other consultees, or making them available on the Internet. All these developments would increase the opportunities for participation by interested parties and public interest groups; but they would also lead to a slower and more diffuse legislative process. Consultation and deliberation take more time than legislating with the security of a compliant parliamentary majority. This may make it harder to adopt ideologically driven policies (the poll tax); on the other hand it risks the kind of stalemate on major issues such as welfare or tax reform which was evident in Germany before the 1998 election.

A stronger rights culture will also make for greater openness—as will devolution. Government will be expected to publish more of its own pre-legislative scrutiny (human rights impact statements); and to publish reasons for its decisions.[7] With devolution, interdepartmental consultation and negotiations which previously took place behind the Whitehall curtain will now be conducted between governments, and so be much more in the open; as will the regional flows of finance. This is explored further in Chapters 9 and 10.

INTEGRITY OF THE DEMOCRATIC PROCESS

Another check on the integrity of government will be the growing number of Commissions and Commissioners who act as guardians for different aspects of the democratic process. The main ones already in existence are the National Audit Office; Audit Commission; Parliamentary Commissioner for Administration (the Ombudsman); and the Boundary Commissions. Then there are the more recent bodies associated with Nolan: the Committee on Standards in Public Life; the Commissioner for Public Appointments; and the Parliamentary Commissioner for Standards. To these the constitutional reform programme could add a Human Rights Commission; Judicial Appointments

---

[7] Freedom of Information White Paper, *Your Right to Know* (Cm 3818) , December 1997, para 2.18.

Commission; Electoral Commission (to regulate campaign expenditure) and/or Referendum Commission; an Information Commissioner; and a Territorial Grants Commission, to advise on the distribution of government funding to the nations and regions. Similar issues (of a *Quis custodiet?* kind) arise in relation to these bodies as have been asked of the public utility regulators: there is a difficult balance to be worked out between their independence and their accountability.[8]

THE EFFECT ON WHITEHALL

The main impact on Whitehall will come from devolution. The roles of the Secretaries of State for Scotland, Wales and Northern Ireland will change. Most radically their roles could revert to the Home Office; the Cabinet Office; a senior minister without portfolio; or a new Secretary of State for Territorial Affairs, heading a small central department. Day-to-day co-ordination would fall to the other Whitehall departments but will be more time-consuming than at present; consultation and negotiation will require higher level input than when they took place between civil servants serving the same administration. There will also be a need for consultation between the devolved administrations *inter se*: the equivalent of the Council of Australian Governments (COAG) process in Australia, the Conference of Minister-Presidents in Germany or the Council of Ministers and the Committee of Permanent Representatives in the EU. The kind of machinery which might develop is described in Chapter 9.

The impact of regional government in England will initially be less marked. On a mini scenario, the Regional Development Agencies will have few significant consequences for Whitehall, because they will be appointed by central government, and Whitehall has retained control of the major regional budgets (e.g., the Training and Enterprise Councils' budget in the Department for Education and Employment, Regional Selective Assistance in the Department of Trade and Industry). Whether control gradually shifts to the regions will depend on the evolution of Regional Chambers, which could emerge as bodies to whom the RDAs and the Government Offices for the Regions could be made accountable: but only in the sense of giving an account—they would still be called to account by Ministers, who would be their political masters.

Only on a maxi scenario, with the creation of Regional Assemblies, would central government functions come into play, and the impact on Whitehall would vary in proportion to the functions devolved. At the outside the functions could include all those functions devolved to the Scottish and Welsh Offices, leaving central government responsible for defence, national security, foreign

---

[8] Explored further in the Constitution Unit Briefing on *Constitutional Watchdogs* (1996).

affairs, economic and monetary policy, taxation, transport, social security, the legal system, the criminal justice system, and broadcasting. But even if service delivery was devolved Whitehall would need to retain a policy interest and capability in agriculture, environment, natural resources, industry, economic development, training, education, health, social services, planning, arts and culture: both to set and monitor UK standards in these fields, and to represent UK interests in the EU. In practice a much more modest package is likely, at least initially, with devolution to Regional Assemblies of some of the functions currently performed by the Government Offices for the Regions. These might include overseeing the distribution of resources, such as lottery funding and the single regeneration budget; supervising the Regional Development Agencies; drawing up the regional development plan, together with some planning and transport functions.

Other constitutional reform will require a stronger role for the centre in Whitehall. The Cabinet Office will need to be strengthened to hold the ring on devolution; to scrutinize legislation for human rights compliance; and to give a firmer lead on negotiations with Europe, which currently falls between Number 10, the Cabinet Office, the FCO and the lead subject departments. The Cabinet Office may also be reorganized as the locus of responsibility for constitutional matters themselves. At present these are scattered between half a dozen different Whitehall departments, visible as the lead departments in the 1997–8 constitutional legislative programme (Home Office, Lord Chancellor's Department, Foreign and Commonwealth Office, Scottish Office, Welsh Office, Northern Ireland Office, Department of the Environment, Transport and the Regions). On a mini scenario that division of responsibilities would continue, and the Cabinet Office would simply provide a co-ordinating Secretariat. On a maxi scenario the Cabinet Office would take a stronger lead, starting with those subjects which have no obvious parent department, such as Lords reform. Whether it consolidated this lead would depend on wider changes at the centre, in particular on changes in the role and perception of the Cabinet Office following Sir Richard Wilson's review.[9] But even with a stronger Cabinet Office the constitution is likely to remain a footloose subject, with responsibility divided between half a dozen departments. One of the lesser difficulties of having an unwritten constitution is that no government department is obviously responsible for it.

EUROPEAN DEVELOPMENTS

Europe properly belongs to Chapter 4. The primary test of domestic constitutional reform is whether it improves the process and outputs of

---

[9] Hansard HL deb WA 186, 28 July 1998.

government within the UK; but an important secondary test is whether it enables the UK to be a more effective player internationally. This could break in one of two ways. Constitutional reform could lead to the development of a less adversarial, more tolerant and inclusive political system; and the development of a more consensual domestic politics could enable the UK to be more flexible and astute in its international relations. Or the cumulative impact of devolution, PR and other checks and balances could be deadlock, policy drift and loss by central government of financial discipline and control. These are issues to which we return in the final chapter.

JUDICIAL SYSTEM

The reform programme, whether mini or maxi, will draw the courts more obviously into constitutional issues and into politics. The vigorous development of judicial review over the last 20 years prepares some of the way. However, incorporation of the ECHR will take the courts into a realm of rights discourse that has largely remained either in Strasbourg or the extra-curial writings of a select band of judges. Judicial appointments will come under sharper focus, with continuing pressure for a Judicial Appointments Commission or nomination hearings by Parliament.[10] The devolved governments will also take a keen interest in the appointment of judges, because of the role of the courts in adjudicating the respective competencies of the parliaments and governments operating within the UK. Full reform of the House of Lords may provide the spur to consider the need for a supreme or constitutional court for the whole UK, which is properly resourced and more clearly independent from any of the UK's constituent governments. The Canadian Supreme Court and the High Court of Australia are possible models. It is less likely that we will see the development of a separate constitutional court, as in Germany and South Africa.

INTERGOVERNMENTAL RELATIONS

More governments mean more relationships between governments; greater need for consultative mechanisms to facilitate policy development; and greater potential for conflict, both legal and political. The new sub-national UK governments will relate not only to each other, their local governments, and to Westminster, but also to the EU. There will be areas of overlap where a legitimate exercise of a power reserved to Westminster impinges on a devolved

---

[10] As an example of such pressure, see the front page coverage on 21 July 1998 and campaign for more open appointments procedures in *The Guardian*, 5 August 1998, following the appointment as law lords of Sir John Hobhouse and Sir Peter Willett.

policy area. This will be especially pronounced in the Westminster government's use of the foreign affairs power as more and more policy becomes globalized/internationalized. And it will happen in reverse, with the devolved governments lobbying around EU negotiations: the Scottish Parliament, the Northern Ireland Assembly and the Welsh Assembly will have their own offices in Brussels, which may not always support the Westminster line. If devolution is to lead to a stronger Union, not a fragmenting one, new consultative intergovernmental relations regimes and mechanisms need to be developed along the lines described in Chapter 9. In this area the UK will need to learn from the experience of countries like Australia, Canada, various federal or quasi-federal EU member states, and the EU itself, with its mix of intergovernmental and supra-national structures.

CONCLUSION: THE CUMULATIVE IMPACT OF THESE CHANGES

Each of these changes on its own will have a significant impact; but because of dynamic and interactive effects the overall impact will be greater than the sum of the individual parts. Two examples will suffice to show how interaction between different elements in the programme will bring this about. Fragmentation of the party system is a well known consequence of the introduction of proportional representation. Less well known is the likely impact of devolution. As Chapter 6 shows, this will also fragment the national parties, and spawn new regional political parties. The interactive effects are demonstrated in Figure 6.1. Taken together, devolution and PR will work to fragment the party system more effectively than either change would working on its own.

Another example is the way the courts will be drawn into political disputes. This is a frequently expressed concern in relation to the ECHR. One of the reasons why incorporation has been opposed is because it is feared that it would drag the judges into political controversy. But so will devolution. Intergovernmental disputes about the validity of Scottish legislation or the powers of the Northern Ireland Assembly will carry a high political charge and draw the judges directly into the political arena. The two changes taken together will ensure that the judges have a much higher political profile, and become known for their political and moral beliefs. In helping to shape the devolution settlement and applying the ECHR the courts will be seen to adopt a policy stance in a way which is unfamiliar in the UK, and which many politicians and judges will find uncomfortable.

These are but two examples of interactive effects. Others will be mentioned in subsequent chapters, and the final chapter attempts to summarize the overall impact of the constitutional reform programme. Even on the mini scenario outlined at the beginning of this chapter, the cumulative impact will be profound, because the constitutional reforms already set in train will unleash a political and legal dynamic which the government will not be able to rein back. On the maxi scenario the impact would be greater still. The individual reforms would go further: but in addition the government's implementation of those reforms would imply a whole-hearted commitment to change the political culture which would itself be an important influence in helping to shape the new constitutional settlement.

3

A Rolling Programme of Devolution: Slippery Slope or Safeguard of the Union?

ROBERT HAZELL AND BRENDAN O'LEARY

The Union will be strengthened by recognising the claims of Scotland, Wales and the regions with strong identities of their own. The Government's devolution proposals, by meeting those aspirations, will not only safeguard but also enhance the Union.

White Paper *Scotland's Parliament*, Cm 3658, July 1997, para 3.1.

INTRODUCTION

In its first year in office the Labour Government has unleashed five separate initiatives in devolution, each with a different dynamic, whose cumulative effect will be to transform the nature of the UK as a multi-national state. Each initiative has been planned with little obvious regard to the other elements in the devolution package (save for some read-across between Scotland, Wales and Northern Ireland); and with no sense of the package as a coherent whole. But as devolution is implemented in this piecemeal fashion there may be a growing need to develop a coherent framework, if only after the event, for practical and political reasons. Coherence need not mean symmetry or even federalism by another name; but it should imply, where appropriate, the development of common solutions to common problems, and a common institutional framework to cement the devolution settlement. The chapter begins by describing each of the elements in turn, and then stands back to forecast what a devolved UK might look like in ten years' time. It also contains a couple of comparative case studies: one on devolution in Spain, the other on the lessons to be learnt from the Nordic Council.

SCOTLAND

Scotland will have the most devolved power, though Northern Ireland will have the greatest freedom to expand the range of devolved functions and powers, and intergovernmental co-operation (Belfast Agreement: paras 3 and 27). The Scotland Act 1998 provides for the Scottish Parliament to be able to legislate in all matters except for the UK constitution, foreign policy, defence and national security, immigration and nationality, macro-economic, monetary and fiscal policy, regulation of markets, employment and social security. The Scottish Parliament will regard itself as being in the devolution vanguard, and will want to retain that position; and with a population of five million it will be the largest of the devolved units, except London, but with far greater powers and a much bigger budget.

Interestingly the Parliament will only just be the largest in terms of its own size. It will start with 129 members: 73 constituency members, based on the existing Westminster constituencies, and 56 additional members from eight regional lists to ensure proportionality. But in recognition of Scotland's current over-representation at Westminster, the Scotland Act provides (s 86) for the number of Scottish MPs at Westminster to be revised in line with the electoral quota for England at the time of the next Parliamentary Boundary Commission review. The next review is due to be completed by around 2005. It will mean a reduction from 72 to around 57 MPs—with a corresponding reduction of some 15 constituency MSPs in the Scottish Parliament, because Schedule 1 to the Scotland Act provides for the Scottish Parliament to share the same constituencies as the Westminster Parliament. The Scottish Parliament will have four-year terms, so in its first two terms (elected in 1999 and 2003) it will have 129 members; but for its third term in 2007 it is scheduled to go down to just over 100 members. This is because Schedule 1 requires the Boundary Commission to maintain the ratio between constituency and additional members.

Polling forecasts are presently highly volatile. At the time of writing they suggest that Labour, to govern, would have to form a post-election coalition with the support of the Liberal Democrats; or that the Scottish National Party (SNP) might even win a plurality of the seats in the Scottish Parliament. Although this appears to have taken Labour in Scotland by surprise, it should not surprise observers of territorial politics in other countries. Chapter 6 shows how regional parties typically perform better in elections to regional assemblies than they do in national elections: in Catalonia the main regional party dominates the regional elections, but comes second or third in general elections, and similar differential patterns of voting are found in Quebec. The voting surveys reported in Chapter 6 suggest such differential voting may also occur in the UK.

The Scottish Parliament will give the SNP a much stronger platform from which to broadcast their independence message. With only six MPs at Westminster their voices are drowned amongst the louder noise. In Edinburgh they look likely to be the main opposition party; and may form the first government. To compete against the SNP electorally the Scottish Labour Party will have to emphasize its Scottishness, and distance itself sharply from the British Labour Party. The occasion in June 1996 when Tony Blair reversed overnight the Scottish Labour policy on the need for a referendum is likely to be the last time that the leader of the national party can tell the Scottish Labour Party what to do. A Labour First Minister of the Scottish Parliament will be judged by his ability to stand up to the UK Prime Minister, and not by his loyalty to his former Cabinet colleagues, or to the national Labour Party.

Indeed Scottish politics increasingly are likely to resemble Quebec politics. The unionist Labour Party in the UK, like the federal Liberal Party in Canada, is likely to face double tensions. It will have to contest with the nationalist SNP as the Canadian Liberals do with the nationalist Parti Quebecois, and it will have to manage the consequences within its own party structures. As Chapter 6 explains, the Labour Party will increasingly 'federalize' or it will suffer predictable electoral consequences.

What if the SNP do win a majority, and the Scottish Parliament then votes for independence? Legally such a vote would have no effect, because the Scottish Parliament has no powers to alter the constitution of the UK, and indeed no power to alter its own constitution as set out in the Scotland Act (see s 29(2) and Schedule 4). However, the SNP has plainly signalled in advance that it will seek a mandate to hold a referendum on independence within the European Union rather than treat a plurality victory in Scottish Parliamentary elections as a mandate to secede from the Union. Moreover, Donald Dewar, the Secretary of State for Scotland, has recognized that politically such a resolution could not be ignored if it was supported by a majority of the Scottish people voting in a referendum. It might also be difficult to deny the principle of self-determination to the people of Scotland, when it appears long to have been accepted in relation to Northern Ireland. But the self-determination offered by the UK Government to the people of Northern Ireland is not for full independence, but the right to rejoin the Republic of Ireland. It is a more limited right of reunification, not a right of unconstrained self-determination.[1]

Will it come to this? Is devolution, as Tam Dalyell has said, 'a motorway without exit to an independent state'?[2] Not necessarily. Autonomy is two-edged. It can be a stepping stone to secession, but it can also invigorate an existing union. Other countries such as Spain and Italy have granted devolution to parts of the territory without it leading to independence, and Germany and Austria have been stable federations in the post-war years. In Spain secessionist sentiment is still vigorous in the Basque country and Catalonia, but so far secessionist parties have not won mandates to negotiate independence. Indeed their support has declined since the grant of regional autonomy over the last 15 to 20 years. In evidence to the Scottish Affairs Select Committee Professor Paul Heywood put it this way:

[1] See the Belfast Agreeeement, (Cm 3883), Constitutional Issues, para 1(ii).
[2] Hansard HC deb 4 Mar 1998 Col 1081.

There is less demand for independence and separatism in Spain now than there was 15, 20 years ago. Opinion polls show this quite clearly, voting patterns show it quite clearly. Voting for parties which stand for independence or separatism has declined ... In Catalonia the only party which calls out for independence won eight per cent at the last national elections for the Spanish Parliament and slightly less than that in the regional elections for the Catalan Parliament. In the Basque country the main [separatist] party, Eri Batasuna, the equivalent of Sinn Fein, the political wing of ETA, has never scored more than 15 per cent in any election and rarely now can expect to get more than about 11 per cent.[3]

Figure 3.1. gives a brief account of the devolution process in Spain.

Figure 3.1. Spain's rolling programme of devolution[4]

Regionalism has been described as the 'single most important issue in Spanish politics'.[5] The regions' demands for autonomy was the main cause of the Spanish civil war in the 1930s. It also proved to be the most divisive problem facing the authors of the democratic constitution after the death of Franco in the 1970s. A compromise had to be struck between those who feared the break-up of Spain (especially on the Right) and those who actively pursued this as their ultimate political goal (the nationalist parties in the Basque country and Catalonia).

The Government's proposal for a federal constitution was unacceptable to unionists and separatists alike. In the case of the former this was because federal structures were seen as a slippery slope to independence; in the case of the latter because a federal constitution implied that the so-called historical nations (the Basque country, Catalonia and Galicia) were no different from regions like Valencia, Rioja and Andalusia.

The uneasy compromise reached in the negotiations resulted in Art. 2 of the Constitution which states:

'The Constitution is based on the indissoluble union of the Spanish nation, the common and indivisible motherland of all Spaniards, and recognizes and guarantees the right to self-government of the nationalities and regions of which it is composed...'

This principle was developed in the Constitution's section on the 'Territorial Organisation of the State' which outlined alternative routes to autonomy, and led to the creation of seven 'high autonomy' regions out of a total of 17 autonomous regions:

• an inside track, used by the historic nations of the Basque country and Catalonia in 1979;
• a fast route (Article 151) used by Galicia (1981) and Andalusia (1981) following endorsement in regional referendums, and soon after by Valencia, the Canary Islands and Navarre;

---

[3] Select Committee on Scottish Affairs, *Minutes of Evidence*, February 25, 1998, 105–7.

[4] This part of the chapter has been contributed by Mads Qvortrup who was during 1998 a Senior Research Fellow in the Constitution Unit.

[5] Ortega y Gasset, J., *La rendención de las Provincias y la decencia nacional* (Madrid: Revista de Occidente, 1931), 1.

• an ordinary route (Article 143), used by the remaining ten regions, which required agreement by all the provinces and three quarters of the municipalities in the region.

This is a highly condensed account of a complex evolutionary process with several unexpected twists and turns. The regions have legislative and executive powers in the following areas:

Economic	**Social**	**Education and Culture**
Public works	Health	Education
Railways and roads	Spatial planning	Regional language
Ports and airports	Environmental protection	Sport
Agriculture and forests	Social assistance	Museums & libraries
Water		
Mineral resources		
Hunting and fishing		
Economic development		
Research		
Tourism		

The degree of autonomy varies considerably between regions. Those with high autonomy run their own health and education systems with minimal involvement of the central government (national minimum standards, and comparability of educational awards).

This variation in the powers of the different regions is a product of each region drafting and negotiating its own constitution for self-government with the centre. Some regions have demanded special powers in education, others in policing, and yet others in powers of taxation. Catalonia has been granted considerable powers in educational and cultural matters, whereas the Basque country has been granted tax-raising powers. Yet other regions (Andalusia, Galicia and Valencia) have been granted powers to establish regional police forces. All the regions have single chamber parliaments, a supreme court, a regional president (elected from among the members of the regional parliament), and their own civil service.

Leap-frog or equilibrium?

It has been argued that Spanish devolution has been characterised by a process of leap-frog, in which the historic nations have reacted to increased powers for the other regions by demanding further powers for themselves. This assertion gained prominence in 1992 when the Catalan president Jordi Pujol created the post of commissar for foreign relations, suggesting that Catalonia intended to remain one step ahead. Yet it is difficult to find continuing support for the leap-frog thesis. Catalonia has not called for tax-raising powers although this right has been granted to Navarre – a region with a considerably smaller degree of national self-consciousness. Nor have the historic nations responded in a leap-frog manner to the granting of additional powers to the other regions (e.g. special policing powers granted to Andalusia).

Spanish devolution has moved from a process of conflict between the central Government and the regions, to one of competition between richer and poorer regions.

The autonomous regions remain dependent on central Government transfers for more than 80 per cent of their revenue.[6] This system has been criticized by Catalonia and the Basque country, two wealthy regions, who are net contributors to regions like Galicia and Andalusia. The regional parties (which exist in most of the regions[7]) have sought to use their influence in the national parliament to strengthen their own economic interests at the expense of other regions. This battle between the regions has thus far been won by the richer regions. This was most recently shown in 1996 when the conservative *Partido Popular* Government decided to transfer 30 per cent of the income tax revenue to the regions, thus allowing the richer regions to keep a larger share of the taxes raised in their area at the expense of the poorer regions.[8]

Spain's rolling programme of asymmetrical devolution has not resulted in the chaotic scenarios predicted by opponents of devolution, nor has the process led to greater demands for independence in the historic nations. The 1980s were, to be sure, characterized by conflicts between the regions and the Madrid Government, the most tangible consequence being a drastic increase in the number of appeals to the Constitutional Court. At its peak 56 per cent of central laws were being challenged by one or more regional governments in 1988, and 11 per cent of regional laws were being challenged by the central Government. This barrage of court challenges fell rapidly, to proportions of zero and 1.8 per cent respectively by 1991.[9]

There has also been a decline in the calls for independence. Opinion polls suggest that only 8 per cent of Catalans, and 17 per cent of Basques support independence. This has prompted one observer to conclude that there is 'a strong indication that the new regional state has reached a point of equilibrium and stability'.[10] This assessment is a far cry from the denunciations that the new constitution in the late 1970s would lead to the breakup of Spain; and from criticisms in the early 1980s that the open-endedness of the constitutional provisions for autonomy was a recipe for constitutional chaos. It might well be that this vagueness and lack of direction in the devolution process has been a positive advantage as it left room for improvisation and compromise. The Spanish devolution process may not have reached a steady state but it has led to an accommodation between the centre and the regions, and between the national and regional political parties. This is no mean accomplishment in a country which once fought a civil war over this issue.

What will undoubtedly happen as a consequence of devolution is that there will be greater and more public intergovernmental bargaining between Edinburgh, Cardiff, Belfast and London (for the machinery which will be required see Chapter 9). Devolution will bring out into the open parts of the political system which have remained relatively hidden—the distribution of

---

[6] Heywood, P., *The Politics and Society of Spain* (London: Macmillan, 1995), p.152.

[7] Esteban, J., and Lópes Nieto, L., *Los partidos políticos en España actual* (Madrid: Planeta, 1992).

[8] *El Mundo*, 27 March 1996.

[9] Zaldivar, C. A., and Castells, M., *Spain beyond Myths*, 1992.

[10] Newton, M., *The Institutions of Modern Spain* (Cambridge: Cambridge University Press, 1997), p.143.

resources to the different regions, of inward investment, of gains from European policies, and the attitude of Whitehall Ministers and departments to central and regional issues. This public bargaining may exacerbate tensions between different parts of the country. It may lead the Scots—spurred on by the SNP—to question how good a deal they get from the Union. It may also lead the English to question whether they are being short-changed. In short, the Union may increasingly rest on constant recalculations of the balance of advantage rather than on a willingness unquestioningly to cross-subsidize between one part of the country and another.

It is true that some of the original factors which led the Scots to join the Union in 1707 no longer apply, or not so strongly. Scotland no longer needs the UK for access to European or world markets. The European Union (EU) and the World Trade Organisation now guarantee that. And Scotland no longer necessarily needs the UK for defence. That is now guaranteed under the umbrella of NATO. But Scotland still benefits substantially from UK Government spending, with comparable public expenditure per capita some 20 to 30 per cent higher in Scotland than in England (even though many English regions are now significantly poorer). The spending differences are discussed in Chapter 11. The Treasury Select Committee has argued (HC 341, 17 December 1997) that it is time for a fresh needs assessment, to show whether the Barnett formula remains the appropriate method of allocating changes in expenditure to the four parts of the Union. The formula was originally devised in the late 1970s, as part of Labour's first attempt at devolution. The Government stoutly maintains that the Barnett formula has delivered satisfactory spending settlements for Scotland (which indeed it has) and is not up for review—or at any rate not yet. If devolution has a price, that is something the Scots will only discover in due course.

But the Union does not rest simply on financial calculations. There is still a sense of being a single national community which underlies the willingness to subsidize the poorer members. There has been, and still is, a great deal of migration between England, Scotland, Wales and Ireland, and a great deal of intermarriage, as well as close sporting, cultural and other links which help bind the different parts of the UK together. But as Chapter 12 explains, the symbols of national identity which help to express the ties which bind us together lie largely in the past. Britain as a national community, in which the Scots and others could share a common monarchy, a common Protestantism, a common enemy (the French) and pride in shared national institutions was forged in the eighteenth and nineteenth centuries—in particular in the common project of the Empire. National identity and even laws of citizenship became bound up with the Empire, and it has proved difficult to find a common focus since. Until the Second World War, indeed until the 1960s most Scots seemed content with the Union, and with their dual identity as Scots and Britons. What the devolution settlement will decisively test is whether the shared identity of being British will survive the passing of the historic interests which brought the Union into being, and be able to express itself in new forms. This is explored further in Chapter 12.

NORTHERN IRELAND

The Union with Ireland took place later than the Union with Scotland. Formally it dates from the Acts of Union of 1801, when the Irish Parliament in Dublin was abolished, and Irish MPs first began sitting at Westminster. Ireland also offers all the history we have to date of devolution within the UK. Gladstone's attempts and failures to re-establish an Irish Parliament in the Home Rule Bills in 1886 and 1893, and Asquith's in 1912, helped prompt the break of the Union of Great Britain and Ireland. The 50 years of the Northern Ireland Parliament which ruled from 1922 to 1972 by contrast showed that legislative devolution was possible within the framework of the sovereignty of the Westminster Parliament (expressly preserved in s 75 of the Government of Ireland Act 1920); and that it was possible to have asymmetrical devolution within one part of the kingdom without extending it to others.

The reasons for Stormont's failure are debated. Some claim it had too much devolution, others too little. What is undisputed is that its devolutionary arrangements lacked adequate protection for minority rights. Using a miniature version of the Westminster system, the Unionist majority was able to trample on the rights of the nationalist minority; and Westminster was incapable or unwilling to intervene until forced to do so by the civil rights movement and growing unrest and disorder in the late 1960s. The Northern Irish experience dramatically demonstrated the deficiencies of the Westminster model in the presence of deep national, ethnic and communal tensions; its one-party rule a salutary reminder that local 'democracies' can engender communal tyrannies.

This weakness in the devolutionary arrangements emerged very early in the 1920s, when Craig changed the voting system for local government in Northern Ireland, and effectively defied Westminster to stop him. The British Government, faced with a threat by Craig to dissolve Stormont and force an election on the issue, was forced to back down. This step was accompanied by a gerrymandering of local government boundaries, and followed by the abolition of the single transferable vote (STV) system of proportional representation for elections to the Northern Irish Parliament. (These are salutary warnings for those who think the Scottish Parliament will meekly do Westminster's bidding; or who assume that any dominant party in Scotland or Wales can be trusted to exercise its hegemony lightly).

Now Northern Ireland is set to make devolutionary history again. In many respects the new institutions in Northern Ireland, and across Ireland, are unique, being tailored to the special circumstances of Northern Ireland; but some of the wider aspects, and the wider machinery put in place to buttress the political settlement will have important implications for devolution in the rest of the UK.[11]

The Northern Ireland Assembly will have 108 members, elected in six-member constituencies by STV. The constituency boundaries will be the same as the 18 Westminster constituencies. The Assembly will exercise full legislative and executive authority in respect of the matters currently devolved administratively to the six Northern Ireland government departments. It will thus have powers similar to the Scottish Parliament; a Cabinet (the Executive Committee) with up to 12 Ministers; and it will have the capacity, by local agreement, and subject to Westminster approval, to expand its autonomy.

There are, however, special safeguards to ensure that all members of the community can be effectively represented in the Assembly, its committees and the Executive. This means that—unlike in Scotland and Wales—the Executive will always contain Ministers representing the minority community, in proportion to their parties' strength in the Assembly. (At present the nationalists are the minority community; but if demographic trends continue the Unionists may find themselves in the minority). The Northern Ireland Executive Committee, as currently envisaged, will be broadly inclusive and operate without conventional collective cabinet responsibility. This plan will be strengthened by the creation of a novel dual premiership. The First and Deputy First Minister of Northern Ireland, who will have identical powers and capacities despite their different titles, will be elected in a manner that will require the endorsement of both Unionists and nationalists, and therefore both First Ministers will need to be broadly acceptable as well as nationally representative.

Other safeguards include:

- **Qualified majority voting** (QMV) to ensure that key decisions are taken on a cross-community basis. These are the election of the First Minister, Deputy First Minister and Chair of the Assembly; approval of the Standing Orders; and annual budget allocations. These must be approved by a majority in the Assembly, including a majority of both the nationalist and Unionist groups in the Assembly (parallel consent), or by 60 per cent of the Assembly and 40 per cent of both the nationalist and Unionist groups (weighted majority).
- **QMV** can be triggered for other decisions by a petition of concern, which can be brought by a significant minority of members of the Assembly (30/108).

---

[11] For a further analysis of the British-Irish agreement of 1998 see O'Leary, B., *The British–Irish Agreement: Power-Sharing Plus*, Constitution Unit, June 1998.

- **The European Convention on Human Rights** (ECHR) and any **Bill of Rights** for Northern Ireland which the Assembly is expected to introduce to supplement it, backed by a Human Rights Commission.
- **A North/South Ministerial Council** to develop co-operation with the Republic of Ireland. To underline its importance the Belfast Agreement declares:

> Participation in the Council to be one of the essential responsibilities attaching to relevant posts in the two Administrations (Strand Two, para 2);

and

> The North/South Ministerial Council and the Northern Ireland Assembly are mutually inter-dependent, and one cannot function successfully without the other (para 13).

- **An implicit model of double protection** in which both Unionists and nationalists are protected as national and ethnic majorities and minorities, whoever holds the sovereign power in Northern Ireland. That is to say, it is intended that Northern Irish nationalists be granted now the same rights and protections that will be granted to Ulster Unionists if they ever find themselves in a unified Ireland. As the Agreement phrases the idea:

> The power of the sovereign government with jurisdiction ... [in Northern Ireland] ... shall be exercised with rigorous impartiality on behalf of all the people in the diversity of their identities and traditions and shall be founded on the principles of full respect for, and equality of, civil, political, social and cultural rights, of freedom from discrimination for all citizens, and of parity of esteem and of justice and equal treatment for the identity, ethos, and aspirations of both communities.

It also recognises

> the birthright of all the people of Northern Ireland to identify themselves and be accepted as Irish, or British, or both, as they may so choose ... [and their] right to hold British and Irish citizenship is accepted by both Governments and would not be affected by any future change in the status of Northern Ireland.[12]

The wider aspects of the Agreement, which have significance for the rest of the UK, include:

- **The principle of national self-determination**, which had already been recognized in the Joint Declaration for Peace of December 1993, and in the Framework documents agreed by the British and Irish Governments in February 1995. It is repeated in these terms in the 1998 Agreement:

---

[12] The Belfast Agreement, Cm 3883, para 1(v), 1(vi).

it is for the people of the island of Ireland alone, by agreement between the two parts respectively and without external impediment to exercise their right of self-determination on the basis of consent, freely and concurrently given, North and South, to bring about a united Ireland, if that is their wish, accepting that this right must be achieved and exercized with and subject to the agreement and consent of a majority of the people of Northern Ireland
(Constitutional Issues, para 1(ii)).

Irrespective of the legal niceties, this principle is likely to be invoked by both Scottish and Welsh nationalists.

- **A British-Irish Council.** This body will provide a forum for all the devolved governments throughout the UK—and the UK's adjacent dependent territories. Its membership will comprise representatives of the British and Irish Governments; the devolved governments in Northern Ireland, Scotland and Wales; 'if appropriate, [devolved institutions] elsewhere in the United Kingdom'—anticipating possible regional government in England; and representatives of the Isle of Man and the Channel Islands (Strand Three, para 2). It is too early to say how such a body might evolve, but it could provide one means of underpinning devolution throughout the UK; and a basis for fostering intergovernmental relations which is one of the keys to making devolution work (see Figure 3.2 and Chapter 9).
- **The wholesale endorsement of principles of power-sharing and proportionality** in electoral, legislative, executive, and policing arrangements—with possible repercussions for the political objectives of national and ethnic minorities in Great Britain.
- **A Civic Forum**, to comprise representatives of the business, trade union, voluntary and other sectors, which will act as a consultative mechanism on social, economic and cultural issues (Strand One, para 34), and may acquire some of the traits of a second chamber. The Scots have been hunting for a body which might represent some of the wider elements in civil society that came together in the Scottish Constitutional Convention, recognising that the Parliament will be dominated by the political parties. The Northern Ireland Civic Forum, and its all-Ireland counterpart, might provide a possible model.

Figure 3.2. The Nordic Council and the British-Irish Council (or 'Council of the Isles')[13]

The Nordic Council was created as an informal body of parliamentarians from the Nordic countries (Denmark, Finland, Iceland, Norway and Sweden) in 1952. It was subsequently joined by three autonomous territories: the Faeroe Islands (part of

---

[13] Based on Constitution Unit, *The Nordic Council: Lessons for the Council of the Isles*, November 1998.

Denmark) and Åland Islands (Finland), in 1970, and Greenland (part of Denmark) in 1984.

The Council was initially established to consult on a range of practical issues. A shortage of doctors, nurses and teachers led to agreements about validation of educational qualifications for health professionals and teachers. This reform led to the establishment of a common labour market (1954), equal treatment in social security (1955), and finally a passport union in 1957. These developments, which in some cases reached beyond those agreed by the European Economic Community under the Treaty of Rome, were formalized in the Helsinki Treaty signed in 1962.

Brief history of key dates in evolution of the Nordic Council

1952	Nordic Council formed as inter-parliamentary body
1954	Common labour market
1955	Equal treatment in social security
1957	Passport union
1962	Treaty of Helsinki
1971	Nordic Council of Ministers established
1974	Helsinki Treaty amended to include environmental policy
1995	Sweden and Finland join the EU
1995	Treaty amended to include co-ordination of policies in the EU

The Nordic Council inter-parliamentary body has 18 representatives from the four largest countries (Denmark, Finland, Sweden and Norway), 6 members from Iceland, and 1 representative from each of the autonomous territories. They are chosen by party groups to reflect the party balance in their domestic assemblies, and in the Nordic Council they join party groupings (much as in the European Parliament) and divide on party lines. They can question ministers from other countries about issues of common interest. During the 1997 session the Danish representatives thus grilled the Norwegian health minister for failing to address the shortage of places in Norwegian medical schools, which had led to a 70 per cent increase of Norwegian students at medical schools in Denmark. The issues raised in the Nordic Council are mainly low salience issues in areas like education, culture, the environment and transport.

A significant change took place with the development of the Nordic Council of Ministers in 1971. The Nordic Council sits in plenary session as a parliamentary body only two full weeks each year. The Nordic Council of Ministers meets as frequently as its EU counterpart, with specialist meetings of Transport Ministers, Environment Ministers, etc. Day to day business is conducted by the Committee of Permanent Representatives, corresponding to COREPER in Brussels. The Nordic Council of Ministers shares a joint secretariat with the Nordic Council of 80 civil servants, and administers a budget of around £65m. Most of the proposals put before the Council of Ministers still originate in the parliamentary body of the Nordic Council, or one of its three committees. Proposals before the Council of Ministers must be carried by unanimity, and are then binding on member Governments.

The Nordic Council has evolved to become a regular part of Nordic cooperation, and it now meets to co-ordinate the Nordic line in EU negotiations. It is an encouraging precedent for the new British-Irish Council, but the starting point here is not the same.

In some respects British-Irish co-operation is further advanced than the Nordic countries were in 1952; in others less so. There has long been a common travel area between the UK and Ireland, with free movement of people and a free labour market between the two countries. Both countries grant each other's citizens reciprocal voting rights. Inter-parliamentary cooperation is less well-developed, with the British-Irish Inter-parliamentary Body meeting only since 1990, and being less well known than its Nordic counterpart.

Other differences are as follows:

• six of the members of the British-Irish Council will be dependent territories of the UK. In the Nordic Council the balance is reversed, with five sovereign states instead of just two, and three dependent territories;
• the members of the Nordic Council wished to co-operate and have developed institutions, bottom up, for that purpose. The British-Irish Council is more top down. The dependent territories were not consulted: it was imposed upon them;
• the British-Irish Council risks being dominated by the UK. In the Nordic Council there is much nearer equivalence in size between the major partners;
• the inter-parliamentary body in the Nordic Council is still the primary body and the source of most initiatives;
• the Nordic countries share a close political ideology and a common religious background. There is less congruence between the political parties in Great Britain and Ireland, North and South; and a greater religious divide.

Lastly, there are many devolution issues which it would not be appropriate to raise in the forum of the British-Irish Council. Major issues such as the representation of Scotland, Wales and Northern Ireland at Westminster, or the funding of the devolved territories through the Barnett Formula, are issues internal to the UK and could not be discussed in the presence of a foreign Government. The British-Irish Council will only be able to discuss issues which have an Irish dimension.

Northern Ireland will above all be a test case for bi-nationalism. On the one hand it may see the reconstruction of 'Britishness'. The reformed Ulster Unionist Party may build a more inclusive conception of British identity and break decisively from the Orange supremacism of the past—an identification that the British of Great Britain no longer understand or care for. On the other hand the new institutions unequivocally endorse the equality and parity of esteem of both national and political traditions in Northern Ireland and the island of Ireland as whole. If they work, they will accommodate both equality and diversity in a pattern that may yet find imitators at home and abroad. Over the next ten years, and probably as early as the next UK general election, we will definitely know whether these new institutions, or variations on them, have taken root. If they have they will be weathering the consequences of the present underlying demographic shift, as cultural Catholics draw near to equality with cultural Protestants in numbers of residents of the region (though not yet of numbers of adult citizens or voters).

WALES

Although culturally distinct, Wales was never a separate, integrated political unit, and has been an incorporated part of the Union for much longer than Scotland or Northern Ireland. Its conquest and legal assimilation into England goes back to the Middle Ages, and was completed in the Tudor Acts of Union of 1536 and 1543. That history, and a longer history of migration into the principality from all parts of these islands, may explain the lesser demand for devolution in Wales: the 1979 referendum for a Welsh Assembly was defeated by four to one; and the 1997 referendum was carried by the narrowest majority, of 50.6 per cent, on a turnout of only 50.3 per cent. The opposition was able to claim that only one Welsh voter in four supported the Assembly.

This lack of enthusiasm can be attributed to a number of factors: the greater assimilation of much of Wales into British identifications and institutions; the continuing split within the Welsh Labour Party over devolution; the absence of a body like the Scottish Constitutional Convention to generate proposals, give leadership and build cross-party support; a lack of national self-confidence; the absence of a strong Welsh elite; the small base of the historic Welsh-speaking and historically indigenous Welsh population; and the divisions within Wales, between North and South, East and West, and between the Welsh-speaking and English-speaking communities.

The Welsh language has proved a divisive rather than a unifying factor, although the Welsh Language Act 1993 has taken some of the heat out of the issue. More important it has proved a diversion for Plaid Cymru as the standard bearer for Welsh nationalism. For much of its history Plaid Cymru has been a movement to preserve the Welsh language, a cultural conservation society as much as a political party. This has tended to confine Plaid's appeal to Welsh-speaking Wales, and it does not attract the same broad support across the country as the SNP does in Scotland. (At the 1997 general election Plaid won 10 per cent of the total vote in Wales, while the SNP won 22 per cent). Because of its localized support it is much harder to envisage the possibility of Plaid Cymru winning a majority of the seats in the Welsh Assembly, or even forming the main opposition party. Labour is likely to form the first Government in Wales, and to face three opposition parties with the seats divided fairly evenly between the Conservatives, Plaid Cymru and the Liberal Democrats.

What will the situation look like in ten years' time? Devolution itself may no longer be an issue. The referendum decided that in 1997, however narrowly, and Conservatives and Labour dissidents alike will quickly learn to live with the result. Nor will independence loom very large: certainly nothing like as strongly as in Scotland and Northern Ireland. The main issue may be the nature of the devolution settlement itself, which in Wales is unstable and liable to change. For what has been chosen is a weak form of devolution which represents a compromise position between the pro- and anti-devolution wings of the Welsh Labour Party, but which is not supported by either of the other pro-devolution parties, Plaid Cymru and the Liberal Democrats.

The Government of Wales Act 1998 creates a National Assembly for Wales with 60 members: 40 constituency members, elected from existing Westminster constituencies, and 20 additional members to provide a measure of proportionality. The Assembly will have executive power and powers of secondary legislation only, operating within a framework of primary legislation laid down by Westminster, and entirely dependent upon Westminster for its annual block grant.

This model of executive devolution has been criticized on a number of grounds:

- The Assembly will be dependent upon the degree of discretion conferred by the Westminster Parliament. A well intentioned Westminster might confer broad delegated powers; but sometimes Parliament will leave little or no room for local discretion or choice.
- Schemes for future legislation will be prepared in Whitehall by officials who are no longer responsible for their administration in Wales.
- Welsh legislation will have to take its chance each year in the long queue of measures put forward by Whitehall departments, only one quarter of which find space in Westminster's legislative programme.
- There will be no capacity to amend existing statutes except through Westminster, which will have other priorities.[14]

If the Welsh Assembly had legislative power it would be able to get round the Westminster log-jam. Without it, it won't. It will be dependent on the legislation passed at Westminster and prepared by Whitehall, where the Government will have a different agenda and other priorities. An Assembly with executive powers only risks incurring the worst of both worlds. It will create high hopes in Wales of independent action which the Assembly may not be able to fulfil; but will be a permanent supplicant in Whitehall, leading to continuous tension between London and Cardiff.

But aside from these intrinsic difficulties there will be powerful external factors at work. The Scottish Parliament and the Northern Ireland Assembly will both have significant legislative power. The opposition parties in Wales will be able to point to their achievements and to contrast them with the subordinate position of the Assembly in Wales. It might be different if there were some quid pro quo that the leader of the Assembly could point to as an advantage of remaining tied to Westminster; but there is none. Wales does not

---

[14] See The Constitution Unit, *An Assembly for Wales,* June 1996.

appear to do particularly well out of the territorial distribution of public expenditure. With identifiable public expenditure in Wales only 12 per cent higher than the UK average, the Welsh benefit a lot less than the Scots and the Northern Irish, even though Wales is significantly poorer than Scotland in terms of GDP per capita (see Chapter 11).

The Welsh Assembly will not only feel like a poor relation in its powers and status; with just 60 members it will also look like one. The small size is another product of Welsh Labour's ambivalence about having an Assembly; but it is beginning to look increasingly anomalous. Northern Ireland, with less than half Wales' population, will have an Assembly almost twice the size. The low ratio of additional to constituency members will make it difficult to achieve full proportionality, and has been criticized by electoral reform bodies. Just as seriously, the Assembly will find it very difficult to man the number of committees envisaged for it, especially now that it is to have regional as well as subject committees. The Institute of Welsh Affairs has estimated that it might need as many as 20 committees, which looks impossible from an Assembly with only 60 members.[15]

The former Secretary of State for Wales, Ron Davies has often said that devolution is a process and not an event. He would not be averse to the Assembly having legislative powers; but believes that it must first prove to the people of Wales that it can make a difference before asking Westminster for more. In Wales as in Scotland electoral competition may drive Labour further than it currently wants to go. Plaid Cymru and the Liberal Democrats will continue to campaign for an effective Assembly, with legislative and tax raising powers; and will portray the Labour leadership in Cardiff as the puppets of Labour in London, or as doubtful managers of local patronage. The Labour leader in Wales may find that the only way to establish sufficient credibility will be to break with the model of executive devolution; but the Assembly will be reliant on Westminster to pass the legislation to cut the knot.

THE ENGLISH REGIONS

In opposition, Labour's policy on regionalism in England developed in two separate streams, which appeared in separate chapters in Labour's election manifesto. Jack Straw was charged with looking at regionalism in the context of a wider programme of devolution, and proposed a two-stage approach to developing a regional tier: first, to establish indirectly elected Regional Chambers of local authority representatives, which could move on, where there

---

[15] Institute of Welsh Affairs, *Making the Assembly Work*, Cardiff, The Stationery Office, Novermber 1997.

is demand, to directly elected Regional Assemblies.[16] John Prescott meanwhile established a Regional Policy Commission which recommended the creation of a Regional Development Agency (RDA) in every English region, on the lines of the successful Scottish and Welsh Development Agencies, and suggested they should be made accountable to the Regional Chamber.[17]

The separate chapters of the manifesto record these policy commitments as follows:

We will establish one-stop Regional Development Agencies to co-ordinate regional economic development, help small business and encourage inward investment. Many regions are already taking informal steps to this end ... (Chapter 3, on business);

and

The Conservatives have created a tier of regional government in England through quangos and government regional offices. Meanwhile local authorities have come together to create a more co-ordinated regional voice. Labour will build on these developments through the establishment of regional chambers to co-ordinate transport, planning, economic development, and bids for European funding and land use planning.

Demand for directly elected regional government so varies across England that it would be wrong to impose a uniform system. In time we will introduce legislation to allow the people, region by region, to decide in a referendum whether they want directly elected regional government. Only where clear popular consent is established will arrangements be made for elected regional assemblies. This would require a predominantly unitary system of local government, as presently exists in Scotland and Wales, and confirmation by independent auditors that no additional public expenditure overall would be involved. Our plans will not mean adding a new tier of government to the existing English system (Chapter 9, on politics and government).

Early in the life of the new Government it was decided to legislate for RDAs but not for Regional Chambers.[18] The RDAs will be appointed by Ministers and accountable through Ministers to Parliament; their budgets will come from Whitehall, and even though their members will be chosen from the region, the RDAs will be agencies of central Government. But Regional Chambers have not been wholly written out of the script, although they will have to operate on a voluntary, non-statutory basis. The White Paper on RDAs says:

---

[16] Labour Party, *A Choice for England,* July 1995; *A New Voice for England's Regions,* September 1996.

[17] Regional Policy Commission (chair Bruce Millan), *Renewing the Regions,* Sheffield Hallam University, June 1996.

[18] The decision was very early. It appeared in the discussion paper on Regional Development Agencies published by the DETR on 11 June 1997, only six weeks into the life of the new government.

These proposals will also build on the arrangements for Regional Chambers which are being established by the regions themselves on a voluntary basis. We are proposing broad principles as to the composition of voluntary Regional Chambers to ensure that their input to RDAs is properly representative.[19]

Nor have Regional Assemblies been written out of the script. In his introduction to the White Paper John Prescott wrote:

The Government are committed to move to directly-elected regional government in England, where there is demand for it, alongside devolution in Scotland and Wales and the creation of the Greater London Authority. But we are not in the business of imposing it. There is a lot we believe we can do within the present democratic structure to build up the voice of the regions. Local authorities are already coming together with business and other partners, to form voluntary regional chambers and to create a more integrated regional approach ...

where there is popular demand, we are committed to further consultation on directly-elected regional assemblies. This may take time, just as the developments in Scotland and Wales have come about over time and with the growing support of the population.

Where might all this lead in 10 years' time? On a maxi scenario, we might see the emergence of one or more directly elected Regional Assemblies, starting in the North of England, where the Campaign for a Northern Assembly has already run up its flag. In emulation of the Scottish Constitutional Convention's Claim of Right, in 1997 the Campaign issued a Declaration of the North, which called for 'a directly elected Assembly representing the people of the North', and asked for a referendum 'as early as possible' in the lifetime of this Parliament.

A referendum in this Parliament looks highly unlikely; and even in the next the North of England Assembly will face some high hurdles. For under the evolutionary policy proposed by Jack Straw a Regional Chamber would have to satisfy four conditions before it could become a directly elected Regional Assembly:

- a predominantly unitary structure in local government
- approval by Parliament
- approval in a region-wide referendum
- auditors' confirmation that no additional public expenditure overall is involved.

---

[19] *Building Partnerships for Prosperity—Sustainable Growth, Competitiveness and Employment in the English Regions*, Cm 3814, December 1997, para 1.3.

The first hurdle is particularly high: local government has no appetite for a further round of structural reorganization, and in most areas the creation of a 'predominantly unitary structure' in effect requires the remaining counties to be abolished—something which they will not accept without a fight. Nor will many Regional Chambers necessarily wish to move to directly elected Assemblies: the local government representatives in the Chamber may not willingly cede authority to an Assembly which they will not control and which will have an independent electoral base.

A minimalist scenario would see little change beyond the introduction of the RDAs, which would operate as national quangos appointed by Ministers and led by businessmen, with the Regional Chambers left to wither on the vine. This is quite possible; Regional Chambers will not flourish without more encouragement from Government, and will find it difficult to operate on a voluntary and non-statutory basis. They may quickly be dismissed as talking shops by the businessmen, who will concentrate on the RDAs.

But more likely is a midi scenario in which the Regional Chambers gradually come to be accepted as necessary partners in the business of regional development, and are given statutory recognition and statutory powers. This may come about for a variety of reasons:

- The RDAs have been given limited budgets and limited powers. They also run the risk of being dismissed as talking shops. It is difficult to envisage an expansion of their role without an expansion of Regional Chambers.
- Regional bodies have come together in the English Regional Associations, which are 'committed to the development of democratically elected regional government in England', and have been lobbying that 'RDAs should be accountable to statutory Regional Chambers'.[20]
- The Local Government Association (which has been very muted so far) may start to campaign more effectively for Regional Chambers to be put on a statutory basis.
- The greater voice given to Scotland, Wales and London by devolution may lead to growing demands from the English regions.

This last may prove to be the most important factor. Having been given RDAs in imitation of the Scottish and Welsh Development Agencies, the English regions may find they are still losing out because they do not have political leaders to promote the region—they do not have anyone to compete with the First Minister in Scotland and the directly elected Mayor in London. Moving to a directly elected Assembly would be the logical response, but may

[20] English Regional Associations, *Regional Working in England: Policy Statement and Survey of the English Regional Associations*, June 1998.

prove too much for both central and local government. Breathing new life into the Regional Chambers might seem a sensible first step for all parties.

ELECTED MAYORS

In one part of England the Regional Development Agency will be accountable to a directly elected Regional Assembly, and that is in London. The Government's plans for a new Greater London Authority (GLA) include a London Development Agency, which will have broadly the same powers as RDAs in the rest of England; but instead of being appointed by Ministers it will be appointed by the new directly elected Mayor. The Mayor is intended to be a strong voice, speaking up for the whole of London, and exercising all the executive powers of the new Authority (including running a new transport authority, as well as the London Development Agency).

The Mayor will be accountable to a 25-person Assembly, also directly elected, with 14 area members and 11 additional members to ensure proportionality. This is a revolutionary new model for city government in the UK, with a powerful elected Mayor answerable to an Assembly whose prime duty is to hold the Mayor to account. The Assembly will approve the Mayor's budget and strategic priorities; scrutinize his performance, and that of all the executive agencies under his control; and also initiate scrutinies of other issues of importance to Londoners, such as health, even though these fall outside the GLA's responsibility. The Mayor and the GLA will be expected to take an interest outside their direct responsibilities, and this will help to compensate for the Mayor's limited sphere of operation, and relatively small budget; because of his direct election by such a large electorate the Mayor will be a figure of national standing, and have an authority which goes much wider than his formal powers.

In time other cities may follow London's example. A Private Member's Bill introduced by Lord Hunt of Tanworth in 1997 would have allowed local authorities to experiment with elected mayors, and other forms of separate executive, but despite Government support it was blocked in the Commons. However the Government are planning to introduce their own bill in 1998–9 which may include measures to revive local democracy.[21]   When the first elections are held for the Mayor in London in 2000 other cities will be watching with interest, and some may be encouraged to follow suit.

If in time cities like Manchester, Liverpool, Newcastle and Birmingham have elected mayors, it will not only impact on the government of the city, but of the surrounding region. Big provincial cities are the hub of their region and the

---

[21] Set out in the White Paper, *Modern Local Government: In Touch with the People*, Cm 4014, July 1998.

centre of the regional economy. They could offer an alternative model for regionalism in England, based on some 30 to 40 city regions, which may not sit easily alongside the more top down structure of nine Regional Development Agencies covering a much wider area.[22] And at regional level there may not be room for two political leaders claiming to be the voice of the region, one as leader of the Regional Assembly and the other as the Mayor of the largest city. Which model wins through may depend upon who occupies the political space first. At present the elected mayors look likely to get there first. The enabling legislation may be in place from 1999, the Government wants to see more, and other cities could opt for elected mayors from 2000 onwards. Regional Assemblies are some way further back, and must first pass through the antechamber of indirectly elected Regional Chambers representing the local authorities and other main stakeholders in the region. Elected mayors as the leaders of the biggest local authority in the region may prove to be one more voice that discovers little interest in moving on to a Regional Assembly, once they realize that it would be a countervailing source of power over which they would have less control. Conversely, local authorities outside the major conurbations may prefer the Regional Chamber/Assembly route, for fear of domination by the cities. The outcome will depend on which model is able to muster decisive political support at the centre.

THE DEVOLUTION SETTLEMENT IN TEN YEARS' TIME

Talk of a 'settlement' may be misleading. It should be clear from the description of the individual elements in the devolution programme that there is no coherent pattern which binds the different elements together; and that devolution is unlikely to have reached a steady state in ten years' time. But some conclusions can be drawn about the nature of devolution in the UK, how it might evolve, and how some coherence might be thrown around it.

A rolling programme: Some academic experts and politicians have proposed the immediate introduction of a federal system for the UK, but the different starting points and different degrees of enthusiasm around the country suggest that a rolling programme best fits the political realities. The motivations for devolution in Scotland, Wales, Northern Ireland and the English regions are all different. A rolling programme of devolution will allow different parts of the UK to move at their own speeds, depending on local demand (and central interest). Scotland, Wales and Northern Ireland will set the pace; interest in the English regions will pick up as the bandwagon starts to

---

[22] The idea of city regions goes back a long way. For a recent exposition see Partridge, S., *Building a New Britain,* City Region Campaign, London, March 1996.

roll. In Spain a bandwagon effect was clearly evident (see Figure 3.1); in England the pace will be set by the Campaign for a Northern Assembly. Westminster will have least concern about the autonomy of Northern Ireland, and indeed its possible departure from the UK. By contrast, we can expect a much more vigorous interest in the nature of Scottish-UK relations.

A long time-scale: In France and Spain it has taken 20 years to introduce a regional tier of government, and the process is still evolving. France had indirectly elected Regional Chambers for over 10 years before moving to directly elected Regional Assemblies. In the English regions we may need to think in terms of a similar time-scale. So long as the principle continues to be one of devolution upon demand, the process will be allowed to evolve at its own pace.

Never a steady state: Devolution may never reach a stable equilibrium. It is in the nature of territorial politics that the balance of power between the centre and the regions is being continually renegotiated: even in federal systems, where the formal division of powers is laid down in the federal constitution. So it will be here: the devolution settlement will be the subject of continual adjustment through intergovernmental negotiations, litigation, funding flows and external relations (e.g. with the EU).

Asymmetrical devolution: Devolution need not and will not be uniform. Although the principle of equal political rights for all throughout the UK is attractive it is breached in practice already through different degrees of administrative devolution in the UK and different civil rights in Northern Ireland. Other European countries live with lopsided devolution, with Spain the best known example (Figure 3.1); and the UK did so for 50 years with Stormont. Devolution will need to embrace different settlements for Scotland, Wales, Northern Ireland, and as between the different regions of England. The trick will be to identify and understand what items need to be held in common throughout the kingdom as constants of UK citizenship; and what items can be allowed to vary. This is explored further in Chapter 12.

A union not a unitary state: In grappling with different degrees of devolution it is helpful to understand that the UK is a union, and not a unitary state; and we can learn a lot from other multi-national union states, like Canada and Spain, which allow varying degrees of asymmetry. Michael Keating has described the union state as a pact or contract, which since the parties have generally acceded on different terms, is often asymmetrical in origin.[23] But this territorial variation needs to be adapted and renegotiated in each generation, in order to meet contemporary needs and continue to legitimize the state and its authority. With the devolution legislation we are going through a major renegotiation; but the process of adaptation between the centre and the territories will continue post-devolution—it is ongoing, never finished business.

The risk of leap-frog: We can also learn about some of the difficulties involved in trying to hold the nation state together as a whole, while allowing greater devolution to some parts than others. One is the risk of leap-frog. In Spain and in Canada a ratchet effect has been suggested by some observers, whereby the low autonomy regions are trying to catch up the leaders, which provokes the leaders (Catalonia and the Basque region, and in Canada Quebec) to seek yet further autonomy to keep one step ahead (see Figure 3.1). A rolling programme of devolution is likely to stimulate similar demands here: from the English regions for a piece of the action granted to Scotland and Wales; from Wales for legislative powers on a par with Scotland and Northern Ireland; will Scotland then demand more to stay one step ahead of Wales? The risks of leap-frog, of course, will be discounted for Northern Ireland itself: Westminster and Whitehall will happily oversee whatever is agreed to in Northern Ireland, including maximum devolution or reunification with the rest of Ireland. The interest of Northern Ireland may rather lie in its use by nationalist parties in Scotland and Wales to press for similar autonomy, if further devolution is granted to Northern Ireland.

One possible factor which may rein in the process is our high expectations of equity. In hospitals, local authority housing or schools we expect the same standards of service throughout the kingdom. This goes deep in our political culture, is reinforced by the UK's strongly national media, and further reinforced by performance measurement and national league tables. In this respect our expectations are those of a unitary state. Soon we will have our first state-wide charter of civil and political rights, once we have incorporated the ECHR.[24] It may be that we will also need to develop a baseline statement of social and economic rights, to give expression to our deeply felt expectations of equity; and that statement may help to define one set of boundaries beyond which devolution cannot go.

---

[23] Keating, M., 'What's Wrong with Asymmetrical Government?', paper presented to ECPR Newcastle conference, February 1997; *Nations Against the State: the New Politics of Nationalism in Quebec, Catalonia and Scotland*, (London: Macmillan, 1996).

[24] The new Northern Ireland Human Rights Commission will be invited to advise on rights supplementary to the ECHR to constitute a Bill of Rights for Northern Ireland; but to be defined in Westminster legislation. Belfast Agreement, Strand Three, para 3.4.

Demands on the centre: In this and other respects devolution will impose major demands on central Government, to articulate a vision and give leadership to the process, to hold the ring, to lay down the basic rules, and itself to adapt in terms of its structures and its style.   Both Whitehall and Westminster will have to adopt a more hands-off approach, and develop a new style for governing what will be a quasi-federal system. This is explored further in Chapters 7 (Westminster), 8 (Whitehall) and 9 (Intergovernmental Relations).   In Whitehall the first structural move might be to bring together the rump offices of the Secretaries of State for Scotland, Wales and Northern Ireland.   They will be left with only a dozen or so officials each, who would benefit from coming together in a single unit; and it would enable Whitehall to have an overview of the devolution process, and to develop common solutions to common problems as they arise.   It could also be a precursor to an eventual merging of the separate Secretaries of State; but that is a political development which, although functionally driven, will have to take place at the right political moment.   This will always be difficult in Northern Ireland where nationalists would interpret it as an integrationist measure.

In terms of style, departments will have to reorient themselves from top down policy making, to policy observation, co-operation and co-ordination. The same will be true of Westminster: Parliament will need to develop a more hands-off approach, to enact more framework legislation (especially if the Welsh Assembly is to have sufficient headroom), and to be willing to legislate for the devolved Assemblies with their consent.   There will be occasions when it makes sense to legislate for a common standard or a common approach throughout the UK, but in a subject matter which has been devolved.   In Germany the Länder pass a lot of common legislation in this way, by pooling their legislative powers in the Bundesrat. At Westminster the role would come more easily if a reformed House of Lords contained representatives of the devolved governments or assemblies who could similarly give their consent to a common approach.   It would be another respect in which Westminster became a quasi-federal Parliament: a role for Westminster (to legislate sometimes on devolved matters) which is acknowledged in the Belfast Agreement[25] but not in the Government's published thinking about Scotland and Wales.

Finance: Financial arrangements will be crucial to making devolution work. The specific financial arrangements will need to reflect the functions of the different assemblies. Chapter 11 sets out three basic principles:

- The principle of equalization according to need should continue to apply in the allocation of public resources across the UK. This has led to regional

---

[25] Strand One, para 26(e). On reforming the Lords to help underpin the devolution settlement, see Osmond, J., *Reforming the Lords and Changing Britain* (Fabian Society, August 1998).

transfers throughout the UK, governed in Scotland, Wales and Northern Ireland by the Barnett formula. But the formula applies only to incremental changes in expenditure; it is not related to any recent assessment of need; and it could not provide a basis for financing regional government in England. As the formula comes under increasing scrutiny and pressure, the time will come when the Government is forced to concede a fresh needs assessment, as the Treasury Select Committee has already recommended.[26] It may not command sufficient credibility for that assessment to be conducted in-house by the Treasury; the devolved governments will want to be consulted, and the task may have to be given to a commission or task force on which they are represented.

- The devolved assemblies should be able to raise a proportion of their own revenue. This has been recognized in the case of Scotland and London; but not for Wales and Northern Ireland. Without revenue raising power the assemblies will have political accountability to their local electorates but no fiscal accountability. They will constantly blame central government for restricting their finances, whilst central government will constantly blame them for overspending (as we have seen with local government). The element of own revenues need not be large to give some ability to vary spending decisions at the margin.
- The assemblies should have freedom to allocate the spending according to their own priorities. This is accepted for Scotland and Wales, but denied to London, where 85 per cent of the GLA's expenditure will be predetermined by central government.

A new sense of national identity: Devolution could either strengthen or weaken or simply change the overall government of the UK. It releases political forces which have been quietly but firmly suppressed in Scotland and Wales under our centralized system of government, and neither quietly nor successfully suppressed in Ireland this century. Left to themselves, the forces are centrifugal; they do represent a slippery slope which could lead to the breakup of the UK. It will require some imaginative re-engineering of the centre, and a spirit of trust and generosity on both sides, to make the devolution settlement work.

As Chapter 12 shows, it will also require a shared sense of national identity and of citizenship. This is not within the control of government in quite the same way as the other levers of power discussed above; but it is a matter on which the Government needs to give a lead, in its actions and its words, to bind the Union together in order to counterbalance the centrifugal political forces of devolution. The Government needs to understand and allow political space to those forces, and the regional and national loyalties which underpin them; but

---

[26] Report on the Barnett Formula, HC 341, 15 December 1997.

it also needs to understand and articulate clearly a sense of the wider loyalties which bind us together at the level of the nation state, and to foster a sense of loyalty to the Union. This is not an easy task, because of the confused national identities which people have as a result of the UK being a multi-nation state (particularly the English). It will require an acceptance of multiple identities, and indeed a celebration of them, as the Government has shown itself ready to accept in Northern Ireland (in the preamble to the Belfast Agreement the Government 'recognize the birthright of all the people of Northern Ireland to identify themselves and be accepted as Irish or British, or both ...'). And it will require a clear statement of the common core of rights and responsibilities shared by all UK citizens. This goes much wider than formal statements of rights and responsibilities, such as the ECHR, because national identity needs to convey a sense of the mutual obligations which go with being members of the same national family: mutual obligations between communities as well as between individuals, including a willingness to cross-subsidize between one region and another. Here too the Belfast Agreement captures some of the common core of civic values and mutual obligations which must bind together the peoples of the UK when it speaks of the principle of 'parity of esteem and of just and equal treatment for the identity, ethos, and aspirations of [all] communities', and of the need for the Government to exercise 'rigorous impartiality on behalf of all the people in the diversity of their identities and traditions'. Not in themselves resounding words; there is a project here for the Government's speech writers and the team who worked on 'rebranding Britain' to capture in more ringing language the values and the mutual obligations which bind us together, wherever we come from—English, Scots, Welsh, Irish, Asians, West Indians—to express the common values we hold in being British, and the values which make the UK a state which is still worth belonging to.

4

British Constitutional Reform and the Relationship With Europe

FRANK VIBERT

This chapter explores the influences affecting the possible evolution of European political union over the next decade and the interplay with the UK's own constitutional changes. It suggests that at a fundamental level there are reasons for hoping that constitutional changes in the UK will help bring about a convergence of attitudes and approaches towards the way in which politics is conducted. If these hopes are fulfilled, they promise a period of much greater harmony between Britain and Europe. A relationship which has generated almost constant stress and upset for the last 20 years, both within the British political system and between Britain and its European partners, may now be entering smoother waters.

The chapter also outlines two different scenarios for Europe. Under one scenario, European political integration has reached some kind of 'high water mark'. This scenario provides a reassuring background to the UK's own changes and is conducive to the more harmonious relationship which is promised. The other scenario involves considerable further change in Europe's procedures and institutions. This latter scenario, on the whole the more likely one, has the potential for re-awakening the difficulties between the UK and its European partners on the shape of political union. It will test whether the principles and experience underlying constitutional renewal inside the United Kingdom can find their place in the rethinking about the characteristics of the enlarged European Union getting under way.

THE EUROPEAN CONTEXT

The Challenges Ahead

Over the coming decade the European Union will be facing a number of formidable policy challenges. They include:

(i)   **Enlargement**: Six countries (Cyprus, Hungary, Poland, Estonia, the Czech Republic, and Slovenia) are currently negotiating for membership. Views differ as to when the first of these applicants might achieve membership and for the purposes of planning the European Union's (EU) financial framework the Commission has chosen 2002 as an illustrative date. In addition, negotiations with further applicants will need to start (possibly concurrently). Once again views diverge as to how quickly this should be done. The process not only needs to be managed well but a Union of 25 or more members will have major implications for its policies, procedures and institutions.

(ii)   **The Single Currency**: On 1 January 1999 conversion rates will be set and banking in the Euro will become possible. The immediate priority will be to establish the single currency area as one of low inflation, and for the European Central Bank (ECB) to establish its credibility as a manager of a currency that maintains its value. In the medium term, a framework will be needed for the Euro to build its role as an international currency—a joint responsibility of both the ECB and the Council of Ministers.

(iii)   **Developing A Common Foreign Policy**: The Union and its Member States are rightly criticized for their inability to think and act strategically on important issues—whether it be on relations with Turkey or Russia or elsewhere in the world. One problem is the incoherence of policy in some Member States. Another has been the tendency of some Member States to wish to define the Common Foreign and Security Policy in terms of projecting an 'identity' and in particular a negative identity of 'not the United States'. A more productive approach might be to develop common principles. In one way or another, greater coherence needs to be achieved.

(iv)   **World Trading Rules**: New world trade talks will be starting in 1999. Their scope and focus remain to be defined. Nevertheless they will mark a new and more difficult stage in the global trade regime since tariff barriers have been largely removed. The substance of the negotiations will thus need to focus on such non-tariff issues as regulatory barriers and competition rules which are inherently more intrusive and intractable matters (particularly when cultural issues are involved). Dispute settlement mechanisms—particularly in services —may also be central. The Union and its Member States will have a key role in these talks, particularly if trade agreements remain difficult for the United States administration to conclude.

(v)   **Cross Border Crime**: In the past decade it has been the single market programme which has provided much of the impetus behind Union activities. Over the next decade it could be that matters related to what the Treaty of Amsterdam refers to as an area of 'freedom, security and justice' assume a much greater importance—particularly in respect of cross border crime and the cross border movement of people.

(vi)   **Security and Defence**: Some observers feel that developing a common European defence policy and capability remains as the big new challenge for the Union after the start of the single currency area and the completion of the single market. With NATO still in the process of redefining its role as well as absorbing the lessons of Bosnia, the way in which Europe develops its defence capacity in relation to the revamped NATO will be of key importance. EU

Member States are divided about the role of the EU in relation to the new NATO. Regardless of these differences, the Union has to press ahead with the reshaping of forces in all European countries to meet new post cold war tasks. It must also address the fact that European technology lags behind the technology available to American forces.

A High Water Mark?

One of the difficulties with the agenda described above is that several of the items may seem remote from the everyday concerns of people. From this perspective the Union may have continued difficulties in building popular support.

The Amsterdam Intergovernmental Conference (IGC) (1996–7) tried to address this problem by including a chapter on employment in the revised Treaty (the Treaty of Amsterdam 1997). The particular problem of high unemployment may anyway begin to diminish as economic recovery in Europe gathers steam. But the underlying problem of finding a European agenda that is relevant but not meddlesome (and not the responsibility of other organizations such as NATO) remains.

In some key areas of public policy, common EU policies are neither feasible nor sensible and the role of the EU will be consultative—that is providing a system of peer review and identifying best practice. The more complicated nature of the relationship between public policies in Member States and policies of joint concern in the Union can be illustrated by the example of welfare reform, which, driven by both demographic trends and public finance concerns, is probably the most critical item on the public policy agenda within the Member States. So far, the role of the EU in this area is seen to be limited. The current focus is on trying to eliminate quantitative investment barriers in the Single Market and establishing a new, qualitative regulatory framework. This is extremely important for fund managers but it leaves the primary task of reshaping welfare provision with the individual Member States. The fiscal discipline demanded of the eleven members of the Euro zone will provide continuing impetus behind reform efforts but, unfortunately, this may lead Member States to scapegoat the Union rather than to give it credit for much-needed budget discipline.

Another item which may rise in importance is any evidence of a growing high technology lag between Europe and the United States. While there is evidence of such a lag when the size of high technology sectors and the uptake of high tech equipment are compared, nevertheless it is not clear that it is continuing to grow. In so far as the underlying problems involve a lack of entrepreneurship and poorly performing education systems within Member States, once again the role of the EU will seem less clear and the tough reform decisions will rest with the Member States themselves.

Items such as welfare reform, which is central to popular concerns, or any technology gap which is capable of catching the public imagination also illustrate the importance of adapting 'best practice' from around the world. While there are some who argue that Europe's approach to these and other issues must be distinctively European, nevertheless the day of launching new common policies with an exclusively European flavour seems to be over (for example 'welfare to work' schemes being tested in a number of European countries inevitably draw to some extent on American experience). This is not necessarily a disadvantage. Europe has much to gain from a more systematic approach to comparing public policies of the different Member States instead of launching common legislation.

The emphasis on making Europe more 'relevant' and on emphasizing techniques such as the peer review of policies rather than new legislation, is consistent with the view that in certain respects Europe has reached some kind of 'high water mark' in its current efforts at integration. Again this should not necessarily be seen as a negative. Perhaps public opinion needs time to digest what has been achieved. The idea that European integration is like a bicycle that overbalances if it is not constantly kept on the move is a metaphor that should be questioned. On the contrary, popular support for Europe might benefit from a quieter phase where the Union becomes part of everyday life, rather than being seen as a venture requiring the continued setting of ambitious new objectives in order to acquire new sources of legitimacy.

If European integration is to move into a phase involving consolidation of existing policies rather than bold new initiatives to follow on the single currency, then it is tempting to suggest that there will be a similar period of rather modest institutional and procedural developments as far as political union is concerned. In other words, the 'high water mark' view means that what we have now in the form of Treaties and political arrangements is broadly what we will have 10 or more years from now.

A further reason underlying the sense that some kind of 'high water mark' has been reached is the perception that the public mood across Europe is against more initiatives from 'Brussels'. In part, this seems to reflect a reassertion of local and regional identities. Whatever the reason, it adds a layer of complication to further institutional and procedural change and will possibly make the governments of the Member States more inhibited in contemplating additional pooling of competences at the European level.

If some kind of 'high water mark' has indeed been reached then the inter-relationship between the constitutional development of the UK and the constitutional development of Europe might be best expressed by suggesting that Europe will cease to be the divisive issue in British politics that it has been over the last decade. A pause in the European agenda would provide a tranquil backdrop against which constitutional changes in the UK can be bedded down. Europe would thus become a more widely accepted part of the UK's institutional and procedural scenery, but there would be no new departures in the relationship.

Yet, for good or ill, there are reasons which have nothing to do with bicycles that suggest that the 'high water mark' scenario is unlikely to play over from the area of policies into the area of European institutions and procedures. That is to say, we may not see great initiatives on European public policy but this does not mean that institutional and procedural change may not be required.

The first and most important of the reasons for anticipating further change is enlargement. A Union of 25 or more simply cannot work in the same way as a Union of 15. While a Union of 25 may still be a rather distant prospect, there are a number of existing governments that would like key arrangements for any enlargement to be put in place before it happens, simply because of the increasing difficulty of getting unanimous consent to Treaty changes in a growing Union. At the moment there is no consensus on what needs to be done or on the timing of reforms, and public opinion is also divided about the ramifications of enlargement. Nevertheless, there does appear to be a growing recognition at recent meetings of heads of Government (at Cardiff and in Austria) of the need for fresh thinking on European structures in the light of enlargement.

Secondly, the idea that some kind of high water mark has been reached in European integration is far from being a generally prevailing view. On the contrary, the more widely held view is perhaps that the start of the Euro area may drive forward much closer co-operation between participants on the whole range of associated economic policies—whether they relate to taxation and budgets or labour market practices. This is because the Euro zone will operate with one interest rate policy and one exchange rate so that members of the zone will have to rely on adjusting other policies if their relative performance lags or gets out of step. If new areas of common policy do emerge within the Euro zone, this could in turn lead to further procedural and institutional developments with consequential frictions between the 'ins' and the 'outs'. Moreover, in the case of the UK the referendum on whether or not to join the Euro area means that what otherwise might be a calmer period in UK relationships with the EU will almost certainly not be so. The 'no' campaign is likely to focus on the shortcomings of Europe as a political union as much as or more than on the economics of the single currency.

Thirdly, there are external pressures on Europe which could also drive policy and institutional change. Here the most commonly cited factor is 'globalisation'. Put in no doubt over-simplified terms, the argument is basically that global developments ranging from the need for Europe to see its competitiveness in global terms to the need to frame its foreign policy in terms of accepting a role as a global power, means that there will be a renewed impetus for a continuing transfer of functions from Member States to the Union, an urgency to streamlining procedures and a major effort required to strengthen the role of EU institutions. From this perspective, the impetus behind 'more Europe' is not one of creating a European identity on the world stage, but a reactive and defensive one in the face of external pressures.

According to some, the follow-up to the single currency and the need to take account of the Union's global role involves an emphasis on more centrally co-ordinated policies and stronger central institutions. For others the message is more ambiguous. Greater centralization certainly runs counter to the desire of some of Europe's political leaders to see greater 'subsidiarity' in the Union so that the Union will not impinge unnecessarily on other jurisdictions. Greater centralization also runs counter to the view that an enlarged Union will have to allow for greater differentiation between the Member States. But the upshot of putting these conflicting views together means that there could be a desire from all sides to have a further review of 'who does what' in the Union.

This leads finally to the view of some observers (such as the European Constitutional Group) and political leaders (such as former Chancellor Kohl) that the time has come for some kind of constitutional 'settlement' in Europe. This settlement would incorporate the changes needed for an enlarged Union, provide a political 'hat' for the Euro zone and bring greater clarity and reassurance about 'who does what'. It would also set out constitutional principles in a way that makes the Treaties intelligible rather than impenetrable as at present.

Under this alternative scenario, reforms in Britain would not be bedded down against a background of less intrusion from European arrangements, but instead the changes in UK arrangements could be fast overshadowed by debate about fundamental changes in the nature of European political union. Both systems need to adapt, but the question is whether the adaptations will work in the same direction or at cross purposes.

Sources of Division

As an economic union the history of European integration has been one of great success as internal market barriers have come down and Europe has had the confidence to open up to the global market. As a political union the story has also been one of great success. The Franco–German relationship has been transformed to the enormous benefit of the rest of Europe, the prospect of membership has provided a powerful incentive for newly democratized countries to turn their backs on their past, and enlargement now holds out the promise of cementing a united rather than a divided Europe. At the same time, it would be unrealistic to pretend that all is sweetness and light between Member States. In fact there are sources of tension that need to be recognized. These have been contained in the past and there is every prospect that they will continue to be contained in the future. Nevertheless, there are frictions in Europe that will colour the institutional and procedural development of the

Union and they will need to be actively managed in order to prevent them becoming disruptive.

The possible sources of friction that need to be taken into account are between:

Small and Large Member States: Europe consists of a large number of small countries and a few substantially larger ones. Germany is the predominant power and the Franco–German relationship has been a critical force in promoting change in the Union to date. This historical setting and the different lessons drawn about the nature of integration not only affects relationships in the Council of Ministers, particularly voting arrangements, but also the role of the Commission (which is often presented as the protector of the interests of the smaller Members) and arguably the composition of the European Parliament (EP).

Rich and Poor: Political economists pay particular attention to the divide between higher income and lower income Member States of the Union. This is because such differences can and do affect a wide range of policy preferences. For example, attitudes towards environmental standards may differ with populations in higher income countries wishing to pay more for environmental protection. This has an impact not only on the more obvious areas of policy such as budget transfers but also on approaches to procedures such as subsidiarity and voting, because these procedures allow for differences to be expressed.

North/South and East/West: Until recently income differences in the European Union could be roughly characterized in North/South terms. With enlargement to Central and Eastern Europe the axis has changed and at the same time the Baltic has gained in strategic importance alongside the Mediterranean. Geography stands for more than income differences. It stands also for different ways of looking at a broader range of Europe's interests including trade and foreign policy and also how Germany perceives its interests.

Euro Ins and Euro Outs: As already indicated, another possible source of division within Europe is marked by those countries that participate in the Euro zone and those that do not. Just how important this distinction will prove to be is unclear but the dispute between members over the role of the Finance Ministers of the Euro participants (the Euro X Committee) in relation to the Finance Ministers of the membership as a whole (ECOFIN) is heralded as indicating the potential for the creation of an inner circle with possibly far-reaching impact. If this were to happen, Britain's relationship with the Union could become more fraught rather than more relaxed.

Language: English is becoming *de facto* the common working language of Europe as indeed it is in the world at large (for example it was the working language at the Amsterdam IGC while it had not been at the Maastricht IGC). This development arouses tensions between transactional efficiency and cultural sensitivities that can have side-effects on topics ranging from the efficiency of proceedings in the Council (where interpretation could be avoided) to trade policy (for example in attitudes to the Internet).

Religion: Despite having an established church, the British political tradition is broadly speaking a secular one in comparison with most other countries in Europe. Religion plays a more prominent role in a number of other European political cultures, with effects ranging from party formation to attitudes towards basic human rights or indeed the nature of Europe itself.

Anglo-Saxon Attitudes: The day when General de Gaulle vetoed British entry to the Common Market on the grounds that Britain was not sufficiently European but belonged to a different transatlantic 'Anglo-Saxon' world has faded in history. But assertions about the presence in Europe of different conceptions of civil society, the conduct of politics and the role of government remain—not just as assertions but as indicators of real differences in underlying attitudes and approaches towards public policy and the practice of politics.

None of these real or alleged sources of division in Europe appear to have the Union-breaking potential of the North/South divide in the early United States. But they have had and will continue to have a real impact on the way in which the Union, its procedures and its institutions evolve. They will in addition continue to affect the British relationship and the UK's ability to build majority coalitions on policy and institutional questions of importance to it.

A 'Comprehensive Review of the Institutions'?

The Amsterdam Treaty calls for a 'comprehensive' review of the institutions before membership in the Union exceeds 20 countries. Argument about when and how to implement this provision is likely to bring to a head differences about the scenario for the European Union outlined above. Some Member States (including France, Belgium and Italy) would like to see this comprehensive review take place as soon as possible so that major adaptations can take place. Others, perhaps feeling that some kind of 'high water mark' has been reached, look to making the necessary adjustments on a more piecemeal basis, perhaps as individual negotiations with potential new members take place. The critical areas where reforms will need to be considered can be identified in any event, regardless of whether they are handled as part of a comprehensive review or as part of a more ad hoc adjustment process. These are outlined in the next section.

DEVELOPMENTS IN THE EU—PROCEDURES AND INSTITUTIONS

Key Debates—Procedures

At the time of the Maastricht negotiations (1991), debate over procedures centred on the 'pillars structure' of EU arrangements and 'subsidiarity' (both explained below). By the time of the Amsterdam revisions to the Treaty, both had become less prominent topics but two new areas of debate had risen in importance—'flexibility' and questions relating to 'rights'. Over the coming years developments can be expected in each of these areas, both in terms of practice and in terms of possible Treaty developments. The questions relating to each are summarized briefly below.

The Pillars Structure: the so-called 'pillars structure' of the Treaties was devised at Maastricht to distinguish between the procedural and institutional arrangements in three broad areas of public policy – the Single Market, including 'flanking policies' such as social and environmental policy, the Common Foreign and Security Policy (CFSP), and Judicial and Home Affairs. Economic matters in the Community pillar, particularly the Single Market programme, involved a role for EC institutions (such as the Commission) and for procedures such as qualified majority voting, which were not felt to be appropriate in the case of the other two areas, each of which had their own characteristics. These distinctions were controversial at the time since they appeared to attack traditional EC ways of doing things and were also felt likely to cause practical difficulties since, for example, the Single Market programme involved the free movement of people where responsibility lay uneasily divided between the Community pillar and the home affairs pillar.

The Amsterdam revisions have tended to blur these distinctions. On the one hand arrangements within the Community pillar have become more diverse. On the other hand, arrangements in the other pillars have become less distinctive (for example with the European Court of Justice given a larger role in what remains of the third pillar dealing with police and judicial co-operation in criminal matters).

It is possible that the pillars structure will be further eroded in practice and possibly disappear in future Treaty revisions. This is not because it did not reflect important differences but because the recognition that different areas of policy merit different procedures and institutional arrangements has grown. Experience suggests that greater differentiation can possibly be achieved throughout the Treaty without depending so heavily on the distinctions offered by the original Maastricht pillars.

Subsidiarity: subsidiarity was introduced as a general principle (Article 6) into the Maastricht Treaty as an attempt to guide the exercise of powers by the Union so that it did not intrude unjustifiably on matters better left to the Member States and their regions. It was introduced in part because the measures under the Single Market programme were being seen in some cases as over-prescriptive. In order to give operational sense to the new provisions of the Treaty the European Council agreed on guidelines which have since been incorporated as protocol 30 under the Amsterdam Treaty.

The general principle of subsidiarity was less of an issue in itself at Amsterdam. This may in part have reflected that the bulk of Single Market initiatives were coming to an end but there were other factors as well. Awareness of the costs of regulation had also grown and acted as an independent constraint on new legislative initiatives. Several aspects related to subsidiarity were taken up in different contexts at Amsterdam, notably in the discussions about flexibility. At the same time, the limitations of the provisions were becoming apparent. Subsidiarity did not in itself provide an answer to poor quality legislation; a test case (*United Kingdom* v. *Council: the Working Time Directive*)[1] showed it did not protect a Member State in a minority view about the limits of Community powers. It could not demarcate powers clearly because the distinctions it borrowed from German constitutional practice about exclusive, shared and reserved powers could not carry over with precision when there was no clear enumeration of powers between different jurisdictions in Europe's Treaties (see for example the discussion in Chapter 10 on the difficulty of distinguishing between layers of responsibility on environmental matters).

Thus, the underlying questions that the Maastricht provision on subsidiarity tried to address have not gone away. On the contrary, politicians are even more aware of the need to relate Europe to the people and to avoid the perception that Europe is a project of the elites imposing a remote and distant form of government. Dissatisfaction with the way subsidiarity is working was expressed at the June 1998 meeting of the European Council in Cardiff. As a result it is likely that the subsidiarity provision itself will be the subject of a new review (starting at the special summit in Austria in October 1998) and it is also likely that any such review will go well beyond questions simply of the exercise of powers in order to consider afresh the division of powers between the Union and Member States as well as the institutional questions posed by the devolution of powers within Member States.

---

[1] C-84/94, 12 November, 1996.

Rights: Discussions about rights, both civil and social, took on greater importance at Amsterdam. This was because with the change in British Government, most Member States saw an opportunity to stress the social dimension of the market-place in Europe by strengthening the reference to social rights, and because it was recognized that enlargement would bring in countries where the commitment to respecting civil rights is new. In addition, for reasons of legal principle as well as for more technical legal reasons arising from potential differences in the way similar cases are adjudicated by the European Court of Justice and the European Court of Human Rights, there seemed to be a need to clarify the status of the European Convention on Human Rights and the relationship between the two Courts. At the same time there were constraints on what could be done. Declarations of rights have far-reaching implications for powers and jurisdictions and there was a general agreement at Amsterdam to try to keep the agenda of change within manageable limits. As a result, the changes did not go as far as some advocates of declarations of rights had wished (see Chapter 5 for an interpretation). The Council is empowered to legislate in the area of certain rights (such as racial discrimination) by Article 13 of the Treaty on European Union, but it remains unclear whether use will be made of this enabling provision. The question of how to handle rights remains one of the largest open questions in the evolution of the Treaties towards constitutional status, and the one with the most profound implications for the relations between the powers of the Union and the powers of the Member States. Its importance will continue to grow and it will inevitably form a key part of any comprehensive review of the Treaties.

Flexibility: 'Flexibility' became the most important procedural issue addressed in detail at Amsterdam and the one with an outcome that has left almost all protagonists dissatisfied—other perhaps than those who were against such provisions in the first place. The issue was approached from two very different perspectives. Some Member States felt that there was a need to be able to pioneer new areas of common policy, for example on taxation policy, and to be able to use Community institutions and procedures for this purpose, even if not all Member States wanted to go along—a sense better conveyed by the French term 'co-opération renforcée'. From this perspective flexibility was designed to overcome a situation where just one country (possibly the UK) could block all others in what they wanted to do. Other Member States felt that in an enlarged Union, policies and procedures would have to become more differentiated, since one size could not fit all and they saw flexibility as a way of enshrining this principle.

The protagonists of the first approach had to reconcile their desires to be free to pioneer with the principle that the Treaties express limits on what is to be done collectively. They therefore had to accept the provision that any use of flexibility procedures had to be 'within the limits of the Treaty'. The protagonists of the second approach had to define core functions which were to be subscribed to by everyone, and outside of which flexibility would be permissible. The problem for this group was to define the core functions. In addition, both groups had to provide for the relationship between 'ins' and 'outs' to be handled in situations where some, but not all, Member States had decided to co-operate more closely in one area or another. This involved procedural aspects (for example, defining the processes under which a non-participating country could later join). It also involved tough institutional questions, such as whether the European Court of Justice as a whole could consider a legal issue raised by a more closely co-operating group of countries or whether only those justices from participating states could be involved in adjudication.

The outcome has been that general provisions of doubtful utility have been added to the Treaties. But at the same time there has been a substantial growth in arrangements to handle specific and case-by-case differences. A striking example of the use of flexibility arrangements is their adoption for the incorporation into the Treaty of the Schengen agreements which covers arrangements to manage the external borders of the Union and to make free movement possible inside the Union (the arrangements exclude the UK and Ireland but include a non-Member State, Norway). The clearest outcome has been the introduction of another layer of uncertainty, complexity and unintelligibility into the Treaties. On a more optimistic note the arrangements allowed for the introduction of a number of new procedural and institutional departures, and these may help in the transition from a Treaty suited to 15 members to a Treaty suited to 25 or more. But whatever can be said either for or against the Amsterdam provisions it seems inevitable that the issue will have to be addressed again at the next Treaty revision. In the meantime some of the provisions will be tested in practice.

One insight to be gained from this review of key Union procedures is the extent to which they still represent not settled principles or approaches so much as work in progress where further change is both inevitable and desirable. The downside of the present state of affairs is the lack of clear, consistent and understandable principles; the upside is that proponents of all viewpoints have everything still to play for in trying to bring about improvements.

KEY QUESTIONS—INSTITUTIONS

If it is true to say that key procedures in the EU remain far from settled, so too it is true to say that institutional roles continue to evolve and currently lack the clear definition desirable in constitutional settings.

Policy Making and the Council

Jostling between the Council and the Commission over the setting of the policy agenda and calling the shots on public policy in the EU have existed since the start of the Community. The way in which the relationship evolves depends partly on working procedures in the Council which involve practical matters rather than constitutional procedures (for example, eliminating formal statements made for the record, which can take up inordinate time at meetings). But there are other aspects which are constitutional in their nature, such as voting arrangements and the weighting of votes of Member States. At the same time there are now several different formulae in the Treaties for expressing the relationship between Council and Commission in addition to the original Community formula giving the Commission the exclusive right of initiative. Both bodies face questions about their 'accountability' or lack thereof. It is possible that certain of the questions relating to each body can be sorted out in the context of enlargement negotiations with individual applicants (for example the scope for more majority voting in the Council). But it is difficult to see progress on fundamental issues such as accountability without the respective roles of the Council and Commission being defined more clearly.

Legitimacy and the European Parliament

Unlike the parliaments in the Member States (but like the Congress of the United States) the composition of the European Parliament does not reflect the choice of voters for a party of government. This is a liberating influence in one sense because it means that the EP can amend measures and criticize Council and Commission without bringing down a Government. But its ability to increase its powers and role in this direction is constrained both by the sense that it is 'representative' only in a weak sense (in the absence *inter alia* of a pan-European public opinion and pan-European parties) and by the reassertion by national parliaments of their continuing role. Protocol 9 (recognizing the scrutiny role of national parliaments and a role for their joint body (the Conference of European Affairs Committees of national parliaments and the European Parliament, known by its acronym COSAC) was included in the Amsterdam Treaty. These developments can be seen as an embryonic form of bicameralism. Bicameralism in a quite different form is proposed by those who see the Council developing as a second chamber (see Chapter 7). In one way or another the perception that 'Brussels' suffers from a 'legitimacy deficit' or 'democratic deficit' continues and will have to be resolved.

Administration and the Commission

In the same way that enlargement will force changes on the Council so too it will force changes on the Commission. Part of the responsibility for good administration rests with the Member States but the way in which the Commission acts as network manager leaves much to be desired. One area of growing importance concerns the administration of competition law and policy as well as the development of regulatory mechanisms in those areas where there is not full competition, such as where utilities are being privatized. There is a strong case for an independent competition authority at arms length from the political hot-house of Brussels, while the approach to regulation could involve a variety of different models. In terms of their impact on people, the actions of competition authorities and regulators can seem much more direct (because their actions are reflected in weekly bills) than the actions of other parts of Government. Thus it is important for the Union to get right what otherwise might seem a rather secondary aspect of European Government.

The European Court of Justice and Constitutional Oversight

Because the Treaties represent an evolving framework for political union, Member States have been careful to try to keep the main lines of their development in their own hands. This has had certain drawbacks—not least, the process of revisions through periodic Intergovernmental Conferences has been unsatisfactory as a means to explore and resolve basic issues. In addition another body, the European Court of Justice, has asserted a role in developing the basic framework of the Union. This too has had its drawbacks since it relies on a process of acquiescence by governments to judgments that pioneer in new areas, and it departs from the principle that new rules of basic constitutional importance should receive majority (and possibly a super-majority) approval through the body politic (instead of unanimity to overturn). The consequence is that at present the Treaties contain a mixture of provisions for judicial oversight by the European Court of Justice and political oversight by governments which add to the questions surrounding the legitimacy of the arrangements. The dilemma is that the political route will become more and more problematic as membership in the Union grows, but at the same time it seems vital for the fundamental rules of the Union to have the basic support of the people.

In the UK, referenda are being used to try to ensure that fundamental changes are rooted in popular support and that change is seen as a bottom-up rather than top-down process. It is important to recognize that in a number of European countries referenda are viewed with great suspicion because of their historical misuse by governments to manipulate opinion. This illustrates the fact that there cannot be one single approach to rule-making and rule-changing in the EU, but it also points to a different dilemma. The issue is that some observers feel that traditional styles of 'representative democracy' no longer provide the kind of responsive systems of government that people want. The suggestion is that more 'participative' styles of democracy are needed. While there are a number of different components of participative democracy, referenda are one potentially important part. What this means is that for historical reasons, the divide (between those who stress the need for more participative styles of government in Europe and those who stress the virtues of representative government) is not an easy one to bridge. Yet if the Union is to overcome continual questioning of its 'legitimacy' there has to be a consensus on the underlying approach to styles of government. Differences between 'participative' and 'representative democracy' are not the only relevant divides. As already mentioned another potential tension is between those stressing the importance of 'rule-based' systems of government and those emphasising 'rights-based' approaches to systems of government.

This brief synopsis suggests that the Treaties contain arrangements in vital institutional areas as well as procedural areas which seem unstable and will be in need of thorough review.

THE UK CONNECTION

In trying to pin down the relationship between the UK's constitutional renewal and the evolution in the EU it is tempting to try to look for similarities and borrowings in the 'hardware' of the arrangements—the institutions. It is in fact a mistake to search for this kind of connection. Transpositions are rarely likely to succeed and arrangements for a Union of 15 or 25 are inherently unlikely to be able to borrow institutional forms directly from any one Member State or to provide institutional models for any Member State to borrow back. (One or two exceptions to this general principle are mentioned later). However, it is fruitful to look for connections in the 'software' of the arrangements—in the approaches to key procedures and principles. In this more fundamental and important sense a number of connections can be seen.

A change in political style?

First, the changes taking place in the UK involve a change in the style of British politics. British public opinion will over time be getting used to:

- more devolved structures;
- more consensual politics;
- an independent central bank;
- a greater role for constitutional law and law related to 'rights'.

As described in other chapters, these changes unleash their own dynamic. A similar need to look at the dynamics of change exists within the wider context of the European Union. Yet there is considerable ambiguity about the dynamics involved. For example, some view the arrival of the European Central Bank and the Euro zone as clearly centralizing and likely to lead to the further centralization of other areas of economic policy including taxation. Others would argue that the single currency makes it even more important for participating states to be able to try out different approaches in their domestic labour markets and different approaches to welfare reform and related taxation structures.

At a very broad level of generality there is one sense in which the European Union promotes centrifugal forces. In the absence of external security threats and under the umbrella provided by membership in a club which provides rules of behaviour and a sense of security in a non-military sense, then it is possible for smaller political units to become more articulated within the larger whole. 'Independence within Europe' is a symptom of this. By contrast, in other senses the Union is centralizing—its institutions want more power rather than having to face competing centres of power, and the questions being raised about the lack of impact of 'subsidiarity' provisions are just one illustration of the way in which procedures remain fundamentally centralizing. The importance of 'getting it right' hardly needs emphasis. At its crudest, the danger is that 'Brussels' or 'Frankfurt' will provoke a nationalist backlash rather than provide the setting within which national diversities can find peaceful expression.

A Different Habit of Mind?

Secondly, the changes taking place in the UK are likely to foster a different habit of mind in thinking about politics. There will be less parroting about the importance of parliamentary 'sovereignty' and a greater willingness to place the role of a reformed Westminster in the context of a wider set of rules governing politics. There is already less tolerance for claims of executive discretion and a desire for greater accountability. In more general terms there is a departure from seeing politics as an ad hoc activity to one which is better placed within more formal arrangements. It is not yet possible to claim that these more formal arrangements are underpinned by a consistent constitutional logic, or that there is a 'constitutional mindset' in the UK as there is for example in the United States. Nevertheless muddling along with the great unwritten constitution is already an inaccurate description of the British approach.

It is ironic that despite the uniquely British doctrine of the sovereignty of Parliament, a 'black hole' at the centre both of revised arrangements in the UK and in Europe concerns the role of Parliaments. Chapter 7 describes how, in the UK, the House of Commons appears likely to remain essentially unreformed and the relationship between it and the 'reformed' House of Lords does not appear to have been thought through. In Europe some still have aspirations for the European Parliament to emulate national parliaments in having a composition and role which reflects the making and breaking of governments, rather than looking to a different model of separation of powers between governments and parliaments where the representative assembly is free to criticize and amend without bringing down a government. Traditionally, representative assemblies are thought of as playing a vital role in the legitimation of the processes of government. Another way of trying to express the role of representative assemblies is to focus on their 'integrative' functions—the bringing together of opinions and interests from across jurisdictions. As mentioned earlier, uncertainty about the role of parliaments in Europe (as well as in the national contexts such as the UK) is one of the factors underlying unease about the legitimacy of the European constitution. To express this in a more positive way—there is a need to achieve a more effective relationship between the role of national parliaments and the European Parliament as one way in which constitutional systems can link up. Other link-ups may also be important, for example between the European Court of Justice and the constitutional courts of Member States.

Mirrorings

These changes in political 'style' in the UK and the development of a rather different and more constitutionally oriented 'habit of mind' are being accompanied by a number of parallel developments in both the UK and the EU. In both there is a search to find a new relationship between central and devolved powers and in both there is an unsettled aspect to present arrangements for expressing this relationship, even after the reforms in the UK and after the Treaty revisions in Europe. In the politics of both the EU and the UK there is a growth in the importance of 'rights-based' politics, and uncertainty as to how to incorporate a greater role for rights within the framework of the basic rules. In both the arrangements for the EU and the UK there is a search for new approaches to hold the executive to account and a need to refresh the role of parliamentary democracy, including bringing new life to different forms of bicameralism. In both, the form of constitutional 'guardianship' is under experiment.

As mentioned above, in both the UK context and in Europe, dynamics are at play that are conducive at one and the same time both to the fragmentation of existing political units and to centralization. Thus there is a need to find both procedures and institutions that can contain the resulting tensions and provide a sense of 'settlement' rather than continuing flux. As also outlined above, in the European context this issue has begun to be addressed under the rubric of 'flexibility'. Amsterdam made some progress in defining the minimum features of membership (Article 6 was added to the Treaty insisting that Member States must be democratic) but there was less progress in defining 'core' policies on which all Member States agree to act collectively. There was agreement on the need to avoid policies that set up barriers to trade within the single market but other aspects of the core look to be much less settled. The term 'single market' itself does not have a unanimously agreed definition because it is not clear what range of policies are included in it (for example, should it include social policies?). Although common rules for agriculture are needed, even the need for a system of budgetary transfers looks less than rock solid when half of the existing EU budget goes to just one producer group (farmers).

The Amsterdam discussions on flexibility also revealed considerable confusion over institutional roles. One quite important possible distinction in the European context is between bodies that act collegially for the membership as a whole (for example the ECJ and the Commission) and those that do not (the Council and the Parliament). The inference is that collegial bodies could develop an essential role in holding the Union together across different policy groupings while the Council and Parliament could divide between different policy groupings. But this distinction, important in theory, does not apply so neatly in practice (for example the public perception of the European Parliament might be damaged if its members participated along the lines of 'ins' and 'outs' among different countries in different policy groupings). A similar point about the difficulty of distinguishing between institutional roles can be made about arrangements in the UK. In the abstract it seems possible to think of the reformed Upper House performing a role for the Union as a whole, while the House of Commons might become more divided between its English and other members (for example, holding an 'English day' to conduct its English business). These possibilities are discussed further in Chapter 7.

Borrowings

As mentioned above, direct institutional borrowings in either direction between the UK and the European Union are unlikely. The most glaring exception to this in the case of the EU is the direct borrowing of the German model of Central Bank independence. This model is a source of difficulty for some Member States and, as also mentioned above, a different borrowing from German constitutional practice—the way in which subsidiarity is expressed—already looks in need of revision. Against this general background, there is one area where British practice may have some potential for transferability: in the case of administrative reform Britain has gone further than most Member States in the reform of the central civil service and in the creation of agencies.

CONCLUSIONS—HARMONY RESTORED?

This brief review of the way in which the EU is developing and how UK reforms connect—not in terms of 'hardware' but in terms of the 'software' of politics—suggests that the relationship should become more harmonious. The changes underway in the British style of politics, the development of a more constitutional habit of mind, and the importance of mirroring and parallel developments in key areas such as devolution, all give grounds for hoping that a gradual process of convergence in basic political approaches is under way. In other words, the adaptations under way in the UK and the adaptations likely in the EU could be working in the same direction and in a complementary manner.

Yet at the same time this review also indicates some of the potential pitfalls in the relationship. The unsettled and only partially reformed procedures in the UK and EU mean that there is a considerable possibility of friction as new limits are tested in practice and new approaches are proposed for incorporation. Differences about how to update systems of government in order to make them more responsive could re-ignite divisions.

In both systems there is an incentive to move towards a further formalization of arrangements—towards something that looks much more like a constitution for Europe in the case of Europe's Treaties, and towards some further consolidation and codification in the UK which could bring the UK itself closer to a written constitution. The incentive is particularly strong in the case of Europe in order to provide a sense of stability and clarity to the arrangements, both of which are lacking at the moment. Whether this 'constitutionalization' will actually happen over the next ten years is however unclear. 'Muddling along' is not just a British habit.

The hinge on which Europe's ability to 'muddle along' may turn is likely to be enlargement and the related argument about 'flexibility'. It is difficult to see a union of 25 operating in the same way as one of 15. Postponing enlargement is consistent with a 'muddling along' scenario. That may happen, but if so, it could damage the strategic rationale for the Union itself—providing the web and threads that tie democratic and market-based societies together in Europe as a whole.

What is evident is that the UK will need to be ready for further debate about European political union and the UK relationship, because it will be triggered both by the referendum over UK membership of Economic and Monetary Union and by moves either for the comprehensive review of institutions envisaged by the Amsterdam Treaty or for turning the Treaties into more obviously constitutional documents.

This prospect in turn begs the question as to what the UK will be bringing to the table from its own reforms in the further evolution of the EU. In looking to play a central role in the development of the EU, 'centrality' means two things: first, the ability to form winning coalitions with other Member States and secondly, the need to ensure that principles which are important to the UK are central to the debate. It does not mean being the median player. On many policy matters the UK is frequently a part of winning coalitions and active and successful in putting together the necessary majorities. It has been much less successful in playing this role on institutional and procedural matters. The hope must be that Britain's own constitutional renewal will make it a more confident and convincing advocate of institutional and procedural change in the Union, better able to help form the winning coalitions on matters of principle, and as a result, a more comfortable member of the Union.

5

Constitutionalism, Regulation and Review

PAUL CRAIG

This chapter examines certain legal doctrines which are of central importance for the nature of our constitutional ordering. There is a wealth of relevant material and limits of space have meant that choices have had to be made. The ensuing discussion focuses on three issues which are undoubtedly of significance to the book's overall enterprise: supremacy, rights, and review. Domestic law, European Community (EC) law and the law relating to the European Convention on Human Rights (ECHR) are considered within each section. The conclusions are based on the cumulative impact of the norms derived from these systems.

SUPREMACY AND CONSTITUTIONAL REVIEW

Any legal and political system has to make choices as to the nature of the constraints which are imposed on the majoritarian will as expressed through the legislature. A classic legal form which such constraints can assume is for the courts to have some power of constitutional review over acts of the legislature, including primary legislation itself.

It is important to recognize at the outset that these limits on the majoritarian will can take different forms. The classic form of constitutional review is one in which the courts have the power to invalidate primary legislation on the grounds that it violates, either procedurally or substantively, principles contained in a written constitution or Bill of Rights. There are, however, other variants on the power which the courts can wield in this regard. A court may have the power to engage in pre-enactment constitutional review, even though there is no such power once the relevant legislation has actually been enacted. The Conseil Constitutionnnel in France exercises a jurisdiction of this nature. It is also possible to structure constitutional review so that while the courts can strike down legislation for infringement of the constitution or a Bill of Rights, this can be overridden by the legislature through re-enactment of the provision with a special majority. Softer forms of constitutional review, such as that which exist in New Zealand and in the UK, do not allow the courts to strike down primary legislation. They may none the less provide for intensive judicial scrutiny with the object of reading legislation, in so far as is possible, to be in compliance with human rights, coupled with a reference back to the legislature should the judiciary not feel able to square the legislation with such rights. The picture can become more complex when it is realized that the relationship between the courts and the legislature may be affected by the very nature of the rights contained in the constitutional document. It is possible, for example, for there to be classic 'hard' constitutional review in relation to traditional civil and political rights, while at the same time having some 'softer' constitutional review in relation to social and economic interests which are contained in the framework constitution.

In the UK the concept of Parliamentary sovereignty has customarily been taken to mean that there can be no substantive legal limitations on the capacity of Parliament, and, on one view, that there can be no procedural constraints either. This view has most commonly been associated with the work of writers such as Dicey and Wade, and constitutes the constitutional orthodoxy. This is not the place for a detailed exegesis on the correctness of this reading of our constitutional heritage. Suffice it to say for the present that the empirical and normative assumptions which underlie this constitutional vision are questionable to say the very least.[1] This issue will be touched on in the course of the subsequent discussion. The immediate focus will, however, be on the ways in which this traditional concept of supremacy has been affected by constitutional changes which have occurred. Three such changes will be briefly considered here.

The first flows from our membership of the European Union (EU). The UK courts have consistently attempted to blunt the edge of any conflict with Community law by the use of strong principles of construction, the import of which was that UK law would, whenever possible, be read so as to be compatible with Community law requirements,[2] although they did not always feel able to do so.[3] *Factortame* is now the seminal case on sovereignty and the EU.[4] *Factortame (No.2)* contains dicta by their Lordships on the general issue of sovereignty, and the reasons why these dicta are contained in the decision are not hard to find. The final decision on the substance of the case involved a clash between certain norms of the EC Treaty itself, combined with EC rules on the common fisheries policy, and a *later* Act of the UK Parliament, the

---

[1] For general discussion of sovereignty, see Wade, H.W.R., 'The Basis of Legal Sovereignty' (1955) C.L.J. 172, 174; Jennings, I., *The Law and the Constitution*, 5th edition, (London: Hodder and Stoughton, 1959), ch. 4; Heuston, R.F.V., *Essays in Constitutional Law*, 2nd edition, (London: Stevens, 1964), ch. 1; Marshall, G., *Constitutional Theory* (Oxford: Clarendon Press, 1971), ch. 3; Craig, P.P., 'Parliamentary Sovereignty of the United Kingdom Parliament After *Factortame*' (1991) 11 Y.B.E.L. 221.

[2] *Lister* v. *Forth Dry Dock* [1989] 2 W.L.R. 634.

[3] *Duke* v. *GEC Reliance* [1988] 2 W.L.R. 359.

[4] *R.* v. *Secretary of State for Transport, ex p. Factortame Ltd.* [1990] 2 A.C. 85; *R.* v. *Secretary of State for Transport, ex p. Factortame Ltd (No.2)* [1991] 1 A.C. 603. See also, *R.* v. *Secretary of State for Employment, ex p. Equal Opportunities Commission* [1994] 1 All E.R. 910.

Merchant Shipping Act 1988, combined with regulations made thereunder. One aspect of the traditional idea of sovereignty in the UK has been that if there is a clash between a later statutory norm and an earlier legal provision the former takes precedence. The strict application of this idea in the context of the EC could obviously be problematic, since the European Court of Justice (ECJ) has repeatedly held that Community law must take precedence in the event of a clash with national law. The dicta of the House of Lords in *Factortame (No.2)* are therefore clearly of importance. Lord Bridge had this to say:[5]

Some public comments on the decision of the Court of Justice, affirming the jurisdiction of the courts of the member states to override national legislation if necessary to enable interim relief to be granted in protection of rights under Community law, have suggested that this was a novel and dangerous invasion by a Community institution of the sovereignty of the United Kingdom Parliament. But such comments are based on a misconception. If the supremacy within the European Community of Community law over the national law of member states was not always inherent in the European Economic Community Treaty it was certainly well established in the jurisprudence of the Court of Justice long before the United Kingdom joined the Community. Thus, whatever limitation of its sovereignty Parliament accepted when it enacted the European Communities Act 1972 was entirely voluntary. Under the terms of the 1972 Act it has always been clear that it was the duty of a United Kingdom court, when delivering final judgment, to override any rule of national law found to be in conflict with any directly enforceable rule of Community law. Similarly, when decisions of the Court of Justice have exposed areas of United Kingdom statute law which failed to implement Council directives, Parliament has always loyally accepted the obligation to make appropriate and prompt amendments. Thus there is nothing in any way novel in according supremacy to rules of Community law in areas to which they apply and to insist that, in the protection of rights under Community law, national courts must not be prohibited by rules of national law from granting interim relief in appropriate cases is no more than a logical recognition of that supremacy.

In strict doctrinal terms the decision means, at the very least, that the concept of *implied repeal or implied disapplication*, under which inconsistencies between later and earlier norms were resolved in favour of the former, will no longer apply to clashes concerning Community and national law. If Parliament does ever wish to derogate from particular Community obligations, whilst still remaining within the EC, then it will have to do so *expressly and unequivocally*. The reaction of our national courts to such an unlikely eventuality remains to be seen. In principle two options would be open to the national judiciary. Either they could choose to follow the latest will of Parliament, thereby preserving traditional orthodoxy on sovereignty. Or they could argue that it is not open to our legislature to pick and choose which obligations to subscribe to while still remaining within the Community. The

---

[5] [1991] 1 A.C. 603, 658–9.

reasoning of Lord Bridge, which utilizes both functional and contractarian arguments to sustain the conclusion that EC law must be accorded priority, could certainly provide the foundation for the second of these options. We will, however, have to await a concrete case before we can be certain how the judiciary would resolve the problem. In any event the second option is based on the assumption that the relevant substantive issue is one which does fall within the Community's competence. Where there are serious questions as to whether this is so, matters may become more complicated.

The second area where there have been changes which have some impact on supremacy is concerned with human rights, and in particular the Human Rights Act. The courts do not, as is well known, have the power under this Act to engage in 'hard' constitutional review: they are not able to strike down primary legislation which is inconsistent with the European Convention rights which are recognized by the Act. The Government has, rather, opted for a 'softer' form of constitutional review. Primary and secondary legislation must be read and given effect in a way which is compatible with the Convention rights. If the courts decide that a provision of primary legislation cannot be read in this way, then they are empowered to make a declaration of incompatibility. Such a declaration does not affect the validity or continuing operation of the primary legislation. It operates rather to send the issue back to the political forum. The relevant minister then has the power, but not the duty, to amend the offending legislation and can do so by an expedited form of procedure which allows the statute to be altered by the passage of delegated legislation. The expectation is that a judicial declaration of incompatibility will render it difficult for Parliament to resist modification of the offending provisions. Whether this proves to be the case remains to be seen. The Human Rights Act does at the very least provide the courts with a legitimate foundation for the interpretative exercise of reading primary legislation in a way which is compatible with Convention rights.

The final area which is of relevance for the discussion of constitutional review is, of course, devolution. On the traditional conception of sovereignty the power which has been devolved to the Scottish Parliament could be taken back by Westminster, although, as Chapter 3 argued, practical political reality renders this a very unlikely eventuality. The devolution of power to Scotland and Wales does, however, raise interesting and important issues of constitutional review which are rather different from those considered thus far. It is axiomatic that any system of devolved power will, of necessity, involve the drawing of boundary lines which serve to define the spheres of legislative competence of the Westminster Parliament in relation to other bodies which have legislative power. This has been recognized in, for example, the Scotland Bill. This is not the place for a detailed examination of the complex provisions in the Bill concerning judicial oversight. Suffice it to say for the present that the Bill has, in effect three different mechanisms by which boundary disputes can come before the courts:

1. There is a limited form of pre-enactment constitutional review. Section 28(1) of the Scotland Act states that an Act of the Scottish Parliament will not be law so far as any provision of the Act is outside the legislative competence of that Parliament. Section 28(2) then defines when such a provision is 'outside that competence' to mean: where it would form part of the law of a country or territory of a country other than Scotland; where its effect would be to modify any provision of the Scotland Act; where it relates to reserved matters; where it is incompatible with any of the Convention rights or Community law; or where it would remove the Lord Advocate from his position as head of the systems of criminal prosecution, etc., in Scotland. A member of the Scottish executive who is in charge of the Bill must make a statement to the effect that in his view the proposed Act is within the legislative competence of the Scottish Parliament.[6] The provisions concerning pre-enactment review are to be found in Section 32 of the Act. This provides that the Advocate General, the Lord Advocate or the Attorney General may refer the question of whether a Bill, or a provision thereof, would be within the legislative competence of the Scottish Parliament to the Judicial Committee of the Privy Council for decision.[7] The Judicial Committee does not have direct mandatory powers in the context of a referral. It cannot itself prevent the proposed measure becoming an Act of the Scottish Parliament, even where it has given an opinion that the matter lies outside the competence of that Parliament. What the Scotland Act provides is that there shall be standing orders which ensure that if the Judicial Committee decides that a Bill will not be within the legislative competence of the Scottish Parliament, the Presiding Officer must not submit the Bill in its unamended form for Royal Assent.[8] This is reinforced by standing orders which provide for an opportunity for the reconsideration of a Bill after its passage if the Judicial Committee decides that such a Bill will be outside the legislative competence of the Scottish Parliament.[9] It should, moreover, be remembered that Section 32 is framed in discretionary terms: the Advocate General, etc., 'may' refer a Bill to the Privy Council. It will be interesting to see whether the Privy Council proves to be the most appropriate forum for dealing with boundary disputes.

2. The discretionary nature of the pre-enactment scrutiny clearly raises the possibility of subsequent legal challenges to a Scottish Act, where someone believes that it was outside the powers of the Scottish Parliament. The

---

[6] Section 30.
[7] Such a reference can be made at any time during the period of four weeks beginning with the passing of the Bill, section 32(2).
[8] Section 31(5).
[9] Section 34(3).

peremptory wording of Section 28, which states that 'an Act of the Scottish Parliament is not law so far as any provision is outside the legislative competence of the Parliament', certainly provides the conceptual foundation for such a direct or collateral form of attack. The possibility of such challenges is expressly recognized by Section 93 of the Act which is concerned with the powers of any court or tribunal which decides that an Act of the Scottish Parliament is *ultra vires*.

3. Schedule 6 of the Scotland Act provides, moreover, for a legal officer such as the Attorney General to raise a matter before the courts as to whether an Act of the Scottish Parliament is properly within its powers. This same Schedule contains provisions for the possible referral of such matters from one court to another for final resolution.

It is unlikely that boundary disputes as to legislative competence will be a rarity. A glance at Schedule 5 of the legislation, which contains the list of reserved powers, will reveal the range of subject-matter dispute over which could give rise to legal challenge. Schedule 5 has general reserved powers, the list of which includes matters such as the constitution, foreign affairs, defence and the like. It also has an extensive list of specific reserved powers in areas as diverse as fiscal and monetary policy, misuse of drugs, elections, firearms, immigration and nationality, scientific procedures on animals, national security and lotteries, to name but a few. If a person is dissatisfied with the content of a Scottish Act of Parliament and minded to mount a legal challenge, then Schedule 5 will be one of the first areas considered as the possible foundation for such an action.

It should be recognized that the judicial mechanisms described above are asymmetrical in the sense that they do not allow, for example, for any referral to the Privy Council where it is argued that the Westminster Parliament has legislated on a topic which is meant to be within the remit of the Scottish Parliament. The rationale for this is the traditional conception of sovereignty itself. The relevant clauses are framed in terms of whether a Scottish Bill would be, or was, within the legislative competence of the Scottish Parliament. On the orthodox theory of sovereignty, talk of limits to the legislative competence of the Westminster Parliament is either meaningless or heresy, and thus a reference to a judicial organ framed in these terms would be at odds with this foundational constitutional doctrine. This would not, however, prevent the courts from interpreting legislation of the Westminster Parliament so as not to impinge upon those areas left to the Scottish Parliament.

Predicting change in constitutional doctrine is never easy. It is all the more difficult when the nature of such changes may be affected by legislative developments. None the less it is possible to suggest a minimalist and a maximalist position in this respect.

On the minimalist view the traditional Diceyan concept of sovereignty would continue to hold sway, subject to an ever-increasing range of 'practical political' limitations. The omnicompetence of the legislature would continue to be regarded as a cornerstone of the constitution, but it would become increasingly understood that the Westminster Parliament would not legislate in areas covered by Community law, in breach of the Human Rights Act, or in spheres over which the Scottish Parliament had legislative competence. It should be recognized that, even on this minimalist view, the force of these practical limitations on the sovereign legislative capacity of the Westminster Parliament would be of considerable significance. The modification of sovereignty doctrine in relation to the UK and the EC now means, at a minimum, that while the European Communities Act 1972 remains in force, the courts will consider nothing short of an express statement by Parliament that it intends to derogate from EC law as sufficient to preclude according superiority to Community law. The strong rules of construction built into the Human Rights Act, combined with the political pressure which would attach to a declaration of incompatibility, will mean that it is increasingly difficult for Parliament to act contrary to judicial dictates in these matters. The need to ensure that devolution is perceived as a workable form of constitutional ordering means that the Westminster Parliament will not lightly trespass on those areas which the Scottish Parliament or Welsh Assembly are intended to regulate.

On the maximalist view, the traditional idea of Parliamentary supremacy would itself be modified. It would no longer be accepted, even in theory, that the majoritarian will as expressed in the legislature would necessarily be without limits. It might well come to be acknowledged that there are indeed rights-based limitations on what the elected Government can attain, and that these should be monitored by the courts. It might come to be accepted that Parliament could not even expressly derogate from a norm of EC law, while still remaining a member of the Community. There might be further developments relating to the structure of the UK, taking us away from devolution, and more towards federalism, with the consequence that there would be constitutional review formally delimiting the legislative competence of both the Scottish and Westminster Parliaments. This is of course conjecture, but reasoned conjecture is, in part, what this enterprise is about. Lest anyone think that these notions are too fanciful it should not be forgotten that the foundations for what is taken to be the traditional notion of supremacy were part conceptual and part empirical, and that neither aspect is, in any sense, unalterable.[10] Nor should we forget that there are already extra-judicial utterances casting doubt on the traditional notions of sovereignty, at least in

---

[10] Craig, P., *Public Law and Democracy in the United Kingdom and the United States of America* (Oxford: Clarendon Press, 1990), ch. 2.

those contexts where the unconstrained exercise of the majoritarian will threatens individual rights, or upsets the fairness of the political process itself.[11]

RIGHTS AND JUDICIAL REVIEW

The preceding discussion of supremacy has already touched upon the Human Rights Act. It is, however, clear that the protection of rights requires analysis in and of itself. An individual who feels that his or her rights have been infringed now has a number of legal options at his or her disposal.

In terms of *domestic law* the most obvious focus for the individual will be on the Human Rights Act. Much of the public comment and debate has focused on Sections 3 and 4 of the legislation, which are concerned with challenges to primary and subordinate legislation, and the implications which such challenges will have for traditional conceptions of supremacy. It is, however, likely that much judicial time will be devoted to adjudicating claims based on Sections 6 and 7 of the Act. The reasons for this are not hard to divine. Actions will be based on Sections 3 and 4 where it really is the legislation itself which is felt to infringe the Convention rights. The remedy under this section is none the less limited. If the court is unable to read the legislation to be in conformity with the Convention rights then it can only make a declaration of incompatibility. It is of course the intent of the Act that Parliament will amend the offending provisions and this will be what the individual or interest group desires.

Where, however, the applicant's principal objective is to obtain a 'harder' remedy in the instant case then Sections 6 and 7 provide the more attractive option. Section 6(1) stipulates that it is unlawful for a public authority to act in a way which is incompatible with one or more Convention rights. It thereby provides a new statutory head of illegality. It is of course true that Section 6(2) qualifies this by making it clear that the peremptory force of Section 6(1) does not apply if the challenged act was either: the result of primary legislation and the public authority could not have acted differently; or where there were provisions of, or made under, primary legislation which could not be read so as to be compatible with the Convention rights. Section 6(2) is therefore designed to prevent Section 6(1) from being used as a backdoor route to contest primary legislation itself. If the applicant is really attempting to contest the compatibility of primary or subordinate legislation with the Convention rights then this must be done through Sections 3 and 4. It is, none the less, likely that many rights-based claims will be adjudicated pursuant to Section 6 for the following reason. The court is likely to read Section 6(2) in a restrictive

---

[11] Laws, J., 'Law and Democracy' (1995) *Public Law*, 72 and 'The Constitution: Morals and Rights' (1996) *Public Law* 622; Lord Woolf, 'Droit Public—English Style' (1995) *Public Law* 57.

manner, as is justified by its very wording. It is only where the authority 'could not have acted differently' because of the primary legislation, or where provisions made under primary legislation 'which cannot be read or given effect in a way which is compatible with the Convention rights', that Section 6(2) operates as an exception to Section 6(1). The courts have in the past made it clear that they will construe restrictively legislation which impinges on fundamental rights, so as to read the legislation in a manner most beneficial to the individual. The probable scenario in claims of this nature is therefore that the applicant will rely on Section 6(1), the public authority will seek to rely on Section 6(2), and the court will often deny the public authority's defence by rejecting the argument that the primary legislation meant that the public authority could not, for example, have acted differently.

There are many attractions for the applicant in utilizing Section 6(1). It provides a new statutory head of illegality which litigants can use offensively in judicial review proceedings or defensively in actions brought against them. It applies to a wide range of bodies. The definition of public authority in Section 6(3) includes a court, a tribunal exercising functions in relation to legal proceedings, and most expansively, 'any person certain of whose functions are functions of a public nature'. Moreover, the court does have a wide range of remedies at its disposal. It can grant such relief or remedy as it considers appropriate, provided that the relief lies within its jurisdiction. A damages remedy is also available, subject to certain conditions, under Sections 8(2)–(4).

The principal obstacle facing an applicant who seeks to use Section 6(1) is that the standing rules are defined narrowly for the purposes of this section. The Human Rights Act provides in Section 7(3) that where proceedings are brought on an application for judicial review the applicant will only be taken to have a sufficient interest if he is, or would be, the victim of the act. There has been considerable disquiet as to the restrictive effect of these rules. The courts could interpret Section 7(3) liberally, but there are limits to what could be achieved through such judicial construction if the courts are not to be accused of rewriting the Act.

This points to the interesting possibility of a residual role for the common law in rights-based claims, in particular for those applicants who would not be afforded standing to pursue a Section 6(1) claim. There is nothing in the Human Rights Act which expressly precludes reliance on the pre-existing common law, and it is very doubtful whether the courts would interpret the Act in this manner. The common-law courts had, even before the Human Rights Act, made significant strides in cases concerned with rights. In the *Spycatcher* case[12] Lord Goff, in delineating the ambit of the duty of confidentiality, and the exceptions thereto, stated that he saw no inconsistency between the position under the Convention, and that at common law. This was further emphasized

---

[12] *A.-G.* v. *Guardian Newspapers (No.2)* [1990] 1 A.C. 109, 283–4.

in *Derbyshire County Council* v. *Times Newspapers Ltd.*[13] Their Lordships held that, as a matter of principle, a local authority should not be able to maintain an action in its own name for defamation, since this would place an unwarranted and undesirable limitation upon freedom of speech. Lord Keith, giving judgment for the House, reached this conclusion on the basis of the common law itself and echoed Lord Goff's satisfaction that there was no difference in principle between the common law and the Convention. A similar trend is apparent in other cases where the affected interest is a fundamental right. Lord Templeman in *Brind*[14] reasoned in a manner directly analogous to proportionality. The court was not restricted, in cases involving human rights, to asking whether the governmental action was perverse or irrational. The judge must rather inquire whether a reasonable minister could reasonably conclude that the interference with the right in question was justifiable. Any such interference must be necessary and proportionate to the damage which the restriction was designed to prevent. Lord Bridge's reasoning was similar. While his Lordship denied that proportionality could advance the applicant's claim, he none the less made it clear that the real inquiry was as to whether the reasonable minister could reasonably reach the conclusion which was now being challenged. In answering this inquiry the court was entitled to start from the premise that any restriction of the right to freedom of expression must be justified and that nothing less than an important competing public interest will suffice in this respect. We can see evidence of the same approach in *Smith*[15] where there was a challenge to the policy of prohibiting gay men and women from serving in the armed forces. Sir Thomas Bingham MR, as he then was, followed the suggestion advanced by counsel for the applicants, David Pannick QC, and held that the more substantial the interference with human rights, the more the court would require by way of justification before it would accept that the decision was reasonable.[16] In formulating the test in this manner he drew explicitly upon the dictum of Lord Bridge in *Bugdaycay*[17] and that of Lord Templeman in *Brind*.[18] There are a number of other post-*Brind* cases which adopt the same test, *Leech*[19] and *McQuillan*[20] being among the most notable examples. An applicant who is unable to use Section 6(1) of the Human Rights Act may then seek to reach a similar result by reliance on this common law jurisprudence. It is true that the Act still provides a preferable route, in part at least because of the breadth of relief which the court can order. An action based

---

[13] [1993] 1 All E.R. 1011.

[14] *R.* v. *Secretary of State for the Home Department, ex p. Brind* [1991] 1 A.C. 696.

[15] *R.* v. *Ministry of Defence, ex p. Smith* [1996] 1 All ER 256.

[16] Ibid., 263.

[17] *Bugdaycay* v. *Secretary of State for the Home Department* [1987] AC 514, 531.

[18] *R.* v. *Secretary of State for the Home Department, ex p. Brind* [1991] 1 A.C. 696, 748–9.

[19] *R.* v. *Secretary of State for the Home Department, ex p. Leech* [1994] QB 198.

[20] *R.* v. *Secretary of State for the Home Department, ex p. McQuillan* [1995] 4 All ER 400.

on the common law will, however, be of real use for those who cannot avail themselves of the Act's provisions, more especially since the effect of this common-law jurisprudence is to render *ultra vires* action which cannot meet the standards of reasonableness adumbrated above.

A person who feels that his or her rights have been infringed without justification may also still use the machinery of the *European Convention* itself. The Human Rights Act brings most of the Convention rights into UK law. It is none the less clear that our courts are not formally bound by the jurisprudence of the European Court of Human Rights. Section 2 of the Human Rights Act states that a court, when determining a question concerning a Convention right, 'must take into account' a judgment of the European Court of Human Rights, as well as certain decisions and opinions of the Commission and the Committee of Ministers. Domestic courts will undoubtedly strive to ensure that their own interpretations of Convention rights do not deviate from those of the European Court of Human Rights. There is still the possibility that domestic interpretations of Convention rights will not be the same as those given by the European Court, and this may well be so even after our courts have 'taken into account' their rulings. This eventuality may be all the more likely in those instances where the judgments of the European Court of Human Rights are particularly controversial, and where there is a strong dissent within the European Court itself. This 'disharmony' may also occur where the Convention jurisprudence itself is unclear on a particular matter, so that the domestic courts have to interpret the Convention rights without the benefit of any direct precedent. In such circumstances an applicant may well feel that the domestic interpretation does not accord with that which would be given by the European Court of Human Rights itself. It will then be open for the applicant, in either of these types of case, to pursue their action before the European Court of Human Rights. If that Court should produce a ruling which is at odds with that provided by the domestic court there would then be a tension between an international obligation owed by the UK under the Convention, as enshrined in the ruling of the Strasbourg Court, and the domestic case law. It cannot be taken for granted that the Government or the domestic courts would necessarily feel compelled to modify their position.

Legal redress may also be sought by relying on *Community law*. The European Court of Justice (ECJ) has held that the fundamental rights doctrine, which was originally applied as a control over the legality of Community norms, can also apply to Member State action, in certain circumstances at least. These circumstances include those such as in the *Johnston* case[21] in which the ECJ interpreted EC norms based on protection for human rights in the light of the relevant principles of the ECHR. The ECJ has also made it clear that

---

[21] Case 222/84, *Johnston* v. *Chief Constable of the Royal Ulster Constabulary* [1986] ECR 1651, [1986] 3 CMLR 240.

Member States which are enforcing Community policies and interpreting Community rules will be bound by the principles concerning fundamental rights which it has developed.[22] It has been suggested that in these circumstances the Member States must act in conformity with the requirements of human rights because they are acting as agents or delegates of the Community in implementing its policies.[23] The ECJ has now gone beyond this and found that Member States which are seeking to derogate from EC law provisions will also be bound by the Community doctrine of fundamental rights. This was a development of some importance given the structure of the EC Treaty. The standard format of the Community provisions on free movement is for there to be an exception to such obligations allowing a Member State to derogate from this obligation for reasons of public policy, health, security and the like. The *ERT* case[24] firmly established that such derogations would themselves be subjected to scrutiny for compatibility with fundamental rights. It is true that the domestic applicability of Community fundamental rights is limited to areas which themselves fall within the scope of Community law. The breadth of the Community's competence has however expanded with every revision of the constituent Treaties. The ECJ has none the less made it clear that there are limits to the Community's competence in this respect and it has not allowed applicants to utilize the Community notions of fundamental rights in cases where the factual connection with the EC was contrived or incidental.[25]

The focus thus far has been on the extent to which individuals might derive assistance from Community conceptions of fundamental rights developed by the ECJ when challenging Member State action. It should not however be thought that this is the only way in which Community law might be of relevance in rights-based cases. The Community legislature might itself enact norms concerning rights. The political institutions have confirmed the Court's general approach to fundamental rights through a series of measures of increasing legal significance, including: a Joint Declaration of the three institutions in 1986, various Declarations and Resolutions on Racism and Xenophobia by the European Council,[26] a Declaration of Fundamental Rights

---

[22] Case 63/83, *R.* v. *Kent Kirk* [1984] ECR 2689, [1984] 3 CMLR 522; Case 5/88, *Wachauf* v. *Germany* [1989] ECR 2609, [1991] 1 CMLR 328.

[23] Temple Lang, J., 'The Sphere in Which Member States are Obliged to Comply with the General Principles of Law and Community Fundamental Rights Principles' (1991) LIEI 23.

[24] Case C–260/89, *Elliniki Radiophonia Tileorassi AE* v. *Dimotiki Etairia Pliroforissis* [1991] ECR I–2925, [1994] 4 CMLR 540; Case C-368/95 *Vereinigte Familiapress Zeitungsverlags- und vertriebs GmbH* v. *Heinrich Bauer Verlag*, ruling of 26 June 1997.

[25] Craig, P. and de Burca, G., *EU Law, Text, Cases and Materials*, 2nd edition (Oxford: Oxford University Press, 1998), ch. 7.

[26] See e.g. [1986] OJ C158/1, Bull. EC 5–1990, 1.2.247., Bull. EC 6–1991, I.45, and Bull. EC 12–1991, I.19.

and Freedoms by the European Parliament in 1989,[27] a Community Charter of Fundamental Social Rights, signed by 11 of the then 12 Member States in 1989,[28] as well as references in the preamble to the Single European Act to the ECHR, the European Social Charter and to 'equality and social justice'. These statements and resolutions were primarily symbolic, although in legal terms they did add weight to the ECJ's development of unwritten Community law, and could be drawn upon when 'harder' sources of EC law were being interpreted. The Treaty on European Union (TEU) then added to these developments by making reference to human rights and freedoms in a number of its provisions. Article F(2) of the TEU, which was not at that stage justiciable, provided that the Union would respect the fundamental rights guaranteed by the ECHR and by national constitutional traditions, and respect for human rights and fundamental freedoms was also mentioned in the two other 'pillars' of the TEU, in Article J.1(2), as being amongst the objectives of the common foreign and security policy and in Article K.2(1), in the context of justice and home affairs.[29] The major change introduced by the Amsterdam Treaty, however, is the amendment of Article F (now Article 6) of the TEU, and the addition of a new Article F.1 (now Article 7). Whereas the previous Article F stated that the Union would respect fundamental rights etc., the amended provision adds to this by declaring that the Union 'is founded on' the principles of liberty, democracy and respect for human rights and fundamental freedoms. The most legally significant feature of the changes is that this provision has now been rendered justiciable, so that the ECJ will have jurisdiction not only under the EC Treaty, but under any provision of the other two pillars over which it has been given jurisdiction (which is primarily pillar three), to review the conduct of the European institutions for compliance with these principles. The Amsterdam Treaty has also made respect for these fundamental principles a condition of application for membership of the European Union. It has moreover conferred on the Community a general legislative competence to combat discrimination in the new Article 6a (Article 13 as renumbered). This provides that the Community legislature may, within the limits of the Community's powers, take 'appropriate action to combat discrimination based on sex, racial or ethnic origin, religion or belief, disability, age or sexual orientation'. How far the Community has legislative power to take positive action in the field of human rights was also touched on by the ECJ in its Opinion on Accession of the Community to the ECHR.[30] The

---

[27] [1989] OJ C120/51.

[28] COM(89)471 Final. See Bull. EC 12–1989, 2.1.104.

[29] Following the changes made by the Treaty of Amsterdam to the third pillar, Article K(2)(1) no longer exists and the reference to the rights of non-Community nationals and the Geneva Convention on refugees now appears in the new title of the EC Treaty on the free movement of persons, as well as, alongside the ECHR, in the Protocol on asylum for EU nationals.

[30] *Opinion 2/94 on Accession by the Community to the ECHR* [1996] ECR I-1759.

ECJ ruled that the Community at present lacked competence under the Treaty to accede to the Convention, and gave some indication of the limits of human rights as a legislative foundation for Community action. Detailed discussion of the Opinion can be found elsewhere.[31] Suffice it to say for the present that, on one reading of the Opinion, the Community might still be regarded as having legislative competence under Article 235 (now Article 308) to adopt specific Community measures for the protection of human rights, so long as they do not amount to an amendment of the Treaty by going beyond the scope of the Community's defined aims and activities. What appeared to place accession to the ECHR beyond the scope of Community competence, in the ECJ's view, was not the fact that it would entail concluding an agreement for the protection of fundamental rights, but the fact that the agreement envisaged would bring with it fundamental institutional and constitutional changes which would actually require a Treaty amendment, with the associated national ratification processes, rather than merely a piece of Community legislation under Article 235 (308).

If we stand back from the details of the preceding material we can identify two points of general importance which are likely to influence rights-based claims over the next decade.

On the one hand, there is the very choice open to individuals of ways in which to pursue such claims. To be sure, most applicants will begin their campaign through the Human Rights Act, but if this does not prove to be successful they may well plead either EC law or rely on the Convention rights before the European Court of Human Rights itself. It should not be forgotten that EC law will continue to have a particular attraction in the areas to which it applies, since it can be used against primary legislation as well as norms of an administrative or executive nature. It is equally important to remember that legislation affecting human rights will, after the Treaty of Amsterdam, increasingly emanate from the Community.

On the other hand, there is but little doubt that the opportunities for presenting rights-based arguments will lead to an increasing juridification of relations between state and individual. The peremptory force of Section 6 of the Human Rights Act will be a powerful attraction for those seeking to pursue claims against a public body. If a claimant can characterize the action as one involving Convention rights then they will be able to present their case in harder-edged terms, relying on the statutory head of illegality created by Section 6, rather than being forced to fall back on traditional grounds of review. All public lawyers, indeed all lawyers, will have to become acquainted

---

[31] Craig, P. and de Burca, G., *EU Law, Text, Cases and Materials*, 2nd edition (Oxford: Oxford University Press, 1998); see also Arnull, A., M., Schermers, H. G., and Dashwood, A., A., *The Human Rights Opinion of the ECJ and its Constitutional Implications*, Cambridge University CELS, Occasional Paper No.1 (1996).

with the detail of the ECHR in much the same way that they did in relation to EC law when we joined the Community.

Rights-based challenges to governmental action are of real importance, but they should, none the less, be kept within perspective. The great majority of judicial review actions do not involve claims of this nature, and this will continue to be so even taking account of the Human Rights Act. A purely quantitative breakdown of the subject-matter of judicial review actions is, of course, a crude criterion for judging the importance of a class of claims. Many significant points of principle are, however, involved in judicial review cases even where no human right is involved. It is important therefore to address both the scope of review and the general principles which govern review and to make some estimation as to how they are likely to evolve over the next decade.

Scope of Review

The issue as to whether a body exercises public power so as to be amenable to judicial review can arise in a number of differing contexts. In the UK system the question has arisen most recently in judicial decisions as to whether an institution is sufficiently public to have the public law procedures which are contained in Section 31 of the Supreme Court Act 1981 applied to it. This issue has become more difficult and important in recent years because of changes in the pattern of governance: privatization, contracting-out, self-regulation and the like have all served to blur the traditional line between the public and the private sphere.

The courts have, not surprisingly, eschewed purely formalistic tests, based on the source of the authority's power, and have focused on a more open-textured criterion which requires them to consider the nature of the power wielded by the particular body. The formulation of this criterion has varied. Thus in the *Datafin* case[32] Lloyd LJ stated that if the source of the power was statutory then the body would be subject to judicial review, but would not if the source of power were contractual. However, in between these 'extremes' one would have to look at the nature of the power. Thus if the body was exercising public law functions, or such functions had public law consequences then Section 31 would be applicable. This formulation appears to beg the question, as do such statements that if a duty is a public duty then the body is subject to public law. The uncertainty which this approach generates is to be expected. It is the price

[32] *R v. Panel on Takeovers and Mergers ex parte Datafin Plc and others* [1987] Q.B. 815, 846–69.

to be paid for moving away from a purely formalistic test based upon the source of the power. Statements that a body must have a sufficiently 'public element' or must be exercising a public duty cannot function as anything other than conclusory labels for whatever we choose to pour into them. They cannot guide our reasoning in advance.

In *Datafin* itself the court was influenced by a number of such factors including: the undoubted power wielded by the Panel, the statutory cognizance given to its existence, the penalties, direct and indirect, which could follow from non-compliance with its rules, and the absence of any other redress available to the applicants. The courts have generally brought within the ambit of public law those bodies which represent the 'privatization of the business of government': regulatory bodies which are private, but which have been integrated, directly or indirectly, into a system of statutory regulation. They have, however, drawn the line in relation to regulatory bodies which, although they have control over a particular industry, are not directly or indirectly part of a schema of statutory regulation.[33] A number of factors have influenced the courts in drawing the line at this point. It is clear that the courts do not regard all power as being public power; that they are concerned about the suitability of public law controls for these types of bodies; and that they are worried about the possibility of drawing any line at all should bodies of this nature be held to fall within public law.

Time will tell whether the courts continue to draw the line which delineates the scope of review in the above manner. The concentration on the institutional dimension should not, however, cause us to lose sight of the consequences of ascribing the label 'public' to a particular body. We should not feel compelled to conclude that the possession of public power by a particular institution must lead inexorably to the application of all public law principles. The more broad ranging is our definition of public power, the more we require a nuanced approach in order to determine which of the public law principles should be held to apply in these instances. We should recognize that legal systems have in the past tackled questions of this kind. They have, for example, demanded that some private bodies which wielded *de jure* or *de facto* monopoly power as a result of governmental grant, or flowing from the nature of the activity in question, did not have the normal contractual freedom over pricing policy. The courts, reasoning from first principle, imposed an obligation to charge no more than reasonable prices for the services or goods which were being provided. We should recognize also that private law itself has been modified both by the courts and by Parliament, with the consequence that the divide between the principles which apply in the public law and private law context is not as great as it might once have been.

---

[33] *R.* v. *Disciplinary Committee of the Jockey Club, ex p. Aga Khan* [1993] 2 All E.R. 853.

The Principles of Judicial Review

It is well-known that the courts have made great strides in the development of the principles of judicial review since the 'low point' of the inter-war years. Principles of procedural justice have been much expanded. Substantive review has now been freed from the shackles of the unworkable dichotomy of jurisdictional and non-jurisdictional error. The courts have made it clear that they will control broad discretionary power which has been accorded to the executive, and that they will be impatient with executive claims that such discretion is unreviewable. Judicial review applications have increased markedly. Parliament has made its own contributions. Legislation on matters such as freedom of information is important both in and of itself, and also because it will have an impact on other doctrines of administrative law, such as the duty to give reasons, and public interest immunity.

It would none the less be mistaken to be complacent. There are real challenges to be faced by the need to accommodate EC law, and there is still much debate about the proper intensity of domestic judicial review. These issues will be considered in turn.

It is increasingly recognized that much regulatory activity stems from the Community. The EC will either undertake the regulatory activity itself, or it will place constraints on the ability of Member States to regulate for themselves. This shift in power from the national to the Community level has meant that many legal actions arise from challenges to Community regulations or their implementation by national authorities. It has also led to an increase in challenges where the substance of the claim has been that the Member State's own regulatory competence was constrained by Community law. In cases which have a Community law component our national courts are under a duty to apply the relevant norms of EC law. In other cases there is no obligation as such, but our national courts may, none the less, draw inspiration from the ECJ's jurisprudence. EC law may well, therefore, have a direct impact and also a spillover impact on domestic administrative law doctrine. There are certain aspects of Community administrative law which do not differ markedly from domestic jurisprudence. Thus, for example, EC doctrine will lead to the annulment of the exercise of discretionary power where that power has been used for improper purposes. The Community heads of substantive review which may have the most influence upon domestic administrative law are proportionality, legitimate expectations/legal certainty, fundamental rights and damages claims. It is in relation to these doctrines that EC law is more developed than domestic doctrine, and it is therefore these doctrinal principles which applicants are most likely to seek to draw upon when challenging governmental action at national level.

The strides which have been made by our courts in domestic administrative law should not serve to conceal the real differences of view which continue to exist as to the proper limits of judicial review. Two examples will suffice in this regard.

In relation to substantive review, all agree that it is not the role of the courts to substitute judgment for that of the executive over the merits of a particular policy choice. The political arm of government has assigned such matters to the executive or to an agency and it is not for the courts to intervene on the ground that they would have made a different decision had they been the primary decision-makers. There is, however, no similar agreement as to the appropriate reach of judicial review. The traditional view has been that the courts should only intervene in relation to discretionary choices where the contested decision was so unreasonable that no reasonable minister or agency could have made it. This view has been challenged by those who argue that this criterion is too minimalist. The courts should, it is argued, use proportionality as the criterion. This would provide a more structured form of inquiry, and also a more demanding standard of review, while still falling significantly short of substitution of judgment. The present stance of the courts is that proportionality is not an independent head of review, although it may be taken into account when deciding whether the challenged action is unreasonable in the sense articulated above. It is difficult to predict whether the judicial attitude on this matter will shift over the next decade. The very fact that our courts have to apply proportionality in cases which have a Community law dimension will, at the very least, make them more accustomed to the concept. It should, moreover, be pointed out that while the courts remain formally wedded to the unreasonableness criterion they are not averse to modifying it when it is felt proper to do so. This has already occurred in cases concerning fundamental rights where the courts have made it clear that the criterion will be applied more intensively than in other cases. The desire to remain within the legitimating umbrella of unreasonableness has been further undermined by the very fact that this test has been used to strike down agency action which could not plausibly be regarded as so unreasonable that no reasonable agency could have taken the challenged action.

In relation to procedural review, there is debate as to how far the courts should enhance participation rights through judicial review. The traditional stance has been that the rules of natural justice do not apply to norms of a legislative nature. This has effectively precluded the development of any general right to participate in rule-making activity. There have been some developments through the application of the doctrine of legitimate expectations, but these have not markedly affected the matter. It remains to be seen how far the courts or the legislature will see fit to enhance the limited rights which presently exist.

CONCLUSION

Predicting change within any sphere of life is always difficult. It is especially so in relation to constitutional doctrine. The nature and direction of legal change will be affected by a range of factors the incidence of which cannot be readily foreseen. Primary legislation will have the most immediate impact on the pre-existing constitutional order, as exemplified by the range of measures introduced by the new Government. Whether these measures will be supplemented by other important constitutional legislation is less certain. The reaction of the courts to such legislation is another important variable, and commentators may well reasonably differ in their views on this matter. The attitude of the judiciary to judicial review is a further factor of importance which will shape the constitutional and administrative landscape as it has done in the past. These caveats are of importance when venturing any thoughts on our constitutional future. They should not, however, serve to stifle reasoned analysis of the possible direction of constitutional and administrative law over the forthcoming years. By standing back from the detail we can, at the very least, make plausible conjectures as to the maximum and minimum changes which might occur within a particular area. This enterprise will itself enable us to appreciate the range of options which are at our disposal. What is none the less certain is that the legislation on human rights, devolution and the like means that the courts will be one of the principal players in shaping constitutional development for the foreseeable future. Moreover, if experience from overseas is any guide, judicial decisions may shape relations between Westminster and other parts of the UK in a manner not wholly intended by the framers of the original legislation.[34]

---

[34] Zines, L., 'Federal and Supra-National Features', pp 75–112 in Zines, L., *Consitutional Change in the Commonwealth,* (Cambridge: Cambridge University Press, 1990).

6

Fragmentation in the Party and Political Systems

JEREMY MITCHELL AND BEN SEYD

In few areas will the Government's constitutional programme have as significant an impact as on the UK's party and political systems. Political parties are essential institutions in any democratic machine. At the most obvious level, they provide the link between voters' preferences and the forming of governments. The nature of that link is largely determined by the political system, including the electoral formula. This chapter examines what changes we can expect in the party and political systems, and what the implications of these will be. The changes are sometimes the direct result of government actions (e.g. the likely stricter legal regime governing the funding of the parties), and sometimes a more indirect product of constitutional measures (e.g. the possible fragmentation of the Westminster parties following devolution). There is also a close relationship between the party and political systems, most evident in this Chapter in the discussion of electoral reform, which highlights the link between the nature of the voting system and that of the party system.

An initial clarification regarding geography is needed. Being precise, there is no such thing as the 'UK party system'. The only party which fields candidates and contests elections throughout the UK is the Conservative and Unionist Party; the other major parties—Labour and the Liberal Democrats—do not put up candidates in elections in Northern Ireland. So most of the following analysis relates to changes in the party system in Great Britain, since Northern Ireland has a distinct party system, based on specific social and cultural factors, as well as a different electoral system.[1]

A second clarification concerns terminology. This chapter refers to the parties whose candidate base is limited to one part of Britain only (e.g. the Scottish Nationalist Party (SNP) in Scotland, and Plaid Cymru in Wales) as 'regional' parties. The Scottish Nationalist and Plaid Cymru are seen by their supporters, and many of their political foes, as 'national' parties. While

---

[1] The Single Transferable Vote (STV) is used in Northern Ireland for local government, Northern Ireland Assembly and European Parliament elections, but is used nowhere else in the UK.

respecting this distinction, the 'regional' description is used to avoid confusion with the pan-British parties, which we refer to as 'Westminster' parties.

THE CURRENT PARTY SYSTEM IN GREAT BRITAIN

The UK used to be described as a good example of a strong two-party system.[2] Between 1945 and 1966, voters in half of all seats at general elections had a choice of candidates from the two main parties (Conservative and Labour) only. From the mid-1970s, the two parties' hold on the political system began to wane. From 1974, all seats at general elections were contested by three or more parties. While from 1945 to 1966 Parliament contained an average of six parties, this number increased to ten over the period 1970 to 1992.

The changes can best be shown in the declining share of the vote attracted by the two main Westminster parties, down from almost 90 per cent in 1966 to just over 75 per cent in 1997. And at the local level, the hold of the two parties has diminished even more rapidly: the number of hung councils has increased significantly, and the third Westminster party, the Liberal Democrats, has seen its number of councillors increase from 1,000 in 1979 (as the Liberal Party) to 4,300 by 1993. Thus, the current party system in Britain[3] might best be characterized as a 'declining two party system'.[4]

Yet a duopoly still exists, largely as a result of the disproportional electoral system: the two main parties retain control of almost nine out of every ten seats at general elections (although this figure is also falling slowly), with one party usually securing an overall majority of seats and able to form a government.[5] Minor parties outside Northern Ireland still struggle to gain parliamentary representation: with the exception of the Liberal Democrats, the only other parties holding seats in the House of Commons are the two nationalist parties, Plaid Cymru and the Scottish National Party. Single issue parties (such as the Greens) perform far worse in UK elections than their counterparts in much of the rest of Europe.[6]

The current UK party system can be broadly characterized as being:

---

[2] This section draws on the discussion in Norris, P., *Electoral Change Since 1945* (Oxford: Blackwell, 1997).

[3] Although less so in Scotland and Wales, in both of which Labour is currently dominant at national elections, gaining over three quarters of Westminster seats at the 1997 election.

[4] Norris, P., *Electoral Change Since 1945* (Oxford: Blackwell, 1997).

[5] In spite of the fact that no party has won an absolute majority of votes since 1935.

[6] In general elections held in 1994, for example, Green parties gained parliamentary seats in Austria, Germany, Luxembourg, the Netherlands and Sweden.

- centralized: the existence of a single legislative body (the Westminster parliament) ensures that the two main Westminster parties are hierarchical bodies, with their regional arms enjoying limited autonomy ;
- cohesive/restrictive: the electoral system (first past the post) creates high entry barriers, and thus deters the creation of new parties;
- biased in favour of large parties: the electoral system means that even parties with significant national support (e.g., the Liberal Democrats) as well as those with regional following (e.g., the SNP) fail to gain proportionate reward in terms of seats won at general elections.

This chapter explores how these features of the party system might alter as a result of the Government's constitutional reform measures. The two reforms of particular relevance to the political and party system are devolution and electoral reform. In addition, the impact of possible further European integration is also considered.

The possible effects of these changes are shown in Figure 6.1 (overleaf). In some cases, the effects represent a 'maximum' rather than a 'minimum' scenario. This is deliberate, in order to show the potential for change that the constitutional reforms have.

It can be seen that the reforms do not always act in distinct ways; some of the more significant likely changes to the party system occur as a result of their interaction. For example, the establishment of new regional parties depends, among other things, both on the establishment of devolved assemblies and on changes to the electoral system, in the absence of which small parties would be unlikely to gain many seats. Electoral reform will also encourage groups disaffected with their party's response to possible further European Union integration to split and form separate parties.

In exploring what impact the constitutional changes will have on the UK's party system, this chapter will also address the consequences for the nature and quality of democracy in the UK: broadly, will the changes usher in a more participatory and democratic culture?

DEVOLUTION AND THE PARTY SYSTEM

While remaining a 'union' state, devolution to Scotland, Wales, Northern Ireland and London, and possibly to the English regions, will significantly alter the UK's political framework (see Chapter 3). The establishment of legislatures in the regions will allow the development of distinct policy agendas at the various levels of government, and will also create new political bases outside Westminster. The impact will be to boost the position of the regional parties and to encourage fragmentation among the Westminster parties, as both seek to respond to the new policy agendas.

Figure 6.1. Constitutional drivers of change in the party system			
Factors of change in the party system	**Devolution**	**Electoral reform**	**Further integration of EU**
Control	More autonomy for regional arms of Westminster parties	Centralization of candidate selection	Creation of pan-European political parties
Cohesion	Breakaway regional splits in the Westminster parties	Breakaway ideological splits in the Westminster parties	Splits in Westminster parties between supporters and opponents of further EU integration
Regional diversification	Strengthening of existing regional parties	Strengthening of existing regional parties	Strengthening of existing regional parties (based on a stronger appeal to 'Europe')
Party diversification	Creation of new regional parties	Creation of new parties (national, regional and single issue)	
Territory	Creation of alternative political power base to Westminster	Increased likelihood of governments being formed from different parties at the national and regional levels	Strengthening of existing alternative political power base to Westminster
Political reward		End of two-party duopoly	
Governance		Coalition or minority governments	

Strengthening Regional Parties

In population terms, Scotland and Wales are dwarfed by England. As a result, the regional parties (the SNP and Plaid Cymru) never gain more than a small share of the seats in the national legislature, the House of Commons. The establishment of regional legislatures and, crucially, the introduction of a more proportional voting system for elections to these bodies, offers new opportunities to these parties.

By focusing attention on regional needs and policy issues, the devolved legislatures will play to the SNP's and Plaid Cymru's agenda. This may well be reflected in more complex voting patterns, where a substantial section of the electorate in Scotland and Wales support regional parties in elections to the devolved assemblies, while voting for Westminster parties at general elections. Such behaviour has been found in a recent survey,[7] which shows the regional parties to be the main beneficiaries of differential voting behaviour.[8] While these results arise from a snapshot survey, evidence from other countries suggests that we should expect this pattern to continue in the longer term. In Spain, for example, the regional elections in Catalonia have been dominated for over a decade by the main regional party grouping (Convergence and Union: CiU), while in general elections, the CiU has always been pushed into second or third place by national parties.[9]

The relatively well developed powers of the Scottish Parliament will encourage a distinctively regional agenda in Scotland; the likely initial beneficiary will be the SNP, although the powerful 'regional dynamic' will also spawn new parties to challenge the existing parties in Scotland (at the time of writing a possible new party is the Highlands Party). It is less likely that devolution will give a similar boost to regional parties in Wales. The Welsh Assembly will wield more limited powers than the Scottish parliament; there will thus be fewer opportunities for the Assembly to develop a distinctive agenda which might favour regional parties and encourage splintering within the Westminster parties. Over time, as the Assembly takes on greater responsibilities, this might change. In the short term, however, Plaid Cymru is predicted to fare less well in regional elections than the SNP in Scotland, and the party system in Wales is likely to be less fragmented as a result.[10]

The more proportional electoral systems for the new legislatures will provide an instant boost to the regional parties, enabling them to win more seats than under first past the post. By lowering the threshold for representation, the systems will also make it easier for factions to establish themselves as separate parties (Labour might be seen as particularly prone to splits, especially on issues that involve defining its relationship with the SNP, such as coalition formation, or a referendum on independence).

---

[7] Dunleavy, P., Margetts, H., and Weir, S., *Devolution Votes—PR Elections in Scotland and Wales*, Democratic Audit paper No. 12 (University of Essex), September, 1997.

[8] A more recent poll (June 1998) by ICM for *The Scotsman* newspaper shows the SNP gaining the support of 39 per cent of voters when asked how they will vote for the Scottish Parliament elections, but only 29 per cent for Westminster elections; Labour's position is the opposite, with its support running at 35 per cent for the Scottish Parliament and 44 per cent for Westminster.

[9] Ross, C., 'Nationalism and Party Competition in the Basque Country and Catalonia', *West European Politics*, Vol 19 No 3 (1996).

[10] Dunleavy, Margetts, and Weir, *Devolution Votes* (n.7 above).

Although indirectly elected regional Chambers, or even directly elected Assemblies, may be established in some or all of the English regions over the next ten years, these will have less of an impact on the party system than their counterparts in Scotland and Wales. The English regional institutions will probably have fewer powers, offering only weak incentives for the creation of regional parties. There is also less of a cultural and political identity in the English regions with which to nurture regional parties.

Impact on the Westminster Parties

Devolution and the development of distinctive policy agendas in the regions will intensify the pressures on the Westminster parties to give greater autonomy to their regional arms. The latter will also need to emphasize their distinctiveness in order to counter the threat of the regional parties. This process has already been initiated; for example, with the Scottish Labour Party's plea for greater autonomy from the central party organization to meet the threat of the SNP.

Over the longer term, we might expect to see the Westminster parties responding along the lines of their equivalents in Spain. There, the minimum strategy of the national parties has been to run campaigns in particular provinces under a regional party label to reinforce their appeal to voters. More radically, the parties have responded to regional pressure in Catalonia by granting far greater autonomy to their regional arms: the Catalan Socialist Party is formally linked to its national Party (the PSOE) through a Protocol, but it has full sovereignty of action, has merged with the separate Catalan socialist group (PSC), and now campaigns under a distinct 'PSC-PSOE' banner. The centre-right national party (UCD) has not granted this degree of autonomy to its Catalan arm, although it, too, has given it a more regional identity by changing its name to 'Centristes de Catalonia'.

The three main Westminster parties in the UK already have regional structures. Yet, with the exception of the Liberal Democrats, which is a federal organization, these regional arms wield little power. The Scottish arms of the parties tend to be more powerful than the Welsh arms; for example, the Scottish Labour Party has more autonomy over policy making than its Welsh counterpart.[11] Yet, while devolution will increase the pressure for the Westminster parties to give greater autonomy to their regional arms—in relation to policy making, campaigning and the selection of candidates—it is questionable whether this will lead to separatism within the parties. A major constraining factor is the weakness of the regional arms themselves, since their (or more precisely, the constituencies') membership levels are low and they are

---

[11] Deacon, R., 'Trimming the borders: A study on the Wales Labour party's policy process', PSA conference 1997, in *Contemporary Political Studies*, Vol. 1, 1997.

financially dependent on the central party bodies, limiting the degree to which they can employ specialist staff and operate independently.[12]

A model of intra-party relations following devolution might distinguish between the following structures:

- integrated: control over decision making on policy issues, candidate selection, etc., rests with the centre
- confederal: decision making on some areas (e.g., identified policy issues and/or candidate selection) devolved to the regional arm
- autonomous: regional party with full control over its affairs, and only bound to the Westminster party through an electoral agreement.

In the short to medium term at least, it is unlikely that any of the Westminster parties will move to a fully autonomous structure (the relationship in Germany between the federal CDU and its 'sister' party, the Bavarian CSU, would be an example of such a model); the regional arms lack the capacity to 'go it alone', and the centre will wish to retain a large degree of control over the regions' activities. The parties might, however, adopt 'confederal' relations with their Scottish arms, reflecting the relative power of the Scottish Parliament and the distinctive policy agenda to which this gives rise. Such a relationship may be a tense one, however, should the regional arms wish to develop separate policies to fit the mood of Scottish voters. Tension may also occur when a party is in opposition either at Westminster or in the Parliament, and where this produces an attempt by the party out of office to radically revise its policies to appeal to voters.

The more limited range of powers available to the Welsh Assembly suggests that the policy agenda will be less distinct than in Scotland. While relations within the parties may therefore be closer, a degree of flexibility will be required to allow for the development of a Welsh dimension to primary legislation set at Westminster (see Chapter 3). Should there be a levelling up of powers in Wales towards those held by the Scottish Parliament and Northern Ireland Assembly, this will increase the differentiation between the central and regional arms of the Westminster parties. We might thus characterize the central parties' relations with their Welsh arms as falling somewhere between the 'integrated' and 'confederal' models, but in the expectation that the shift over time will be in the direction of the latter.

We should also expect to see different responses by each of the Westminster parties; already, for example, the parties have adopted different methods for selecting their candidates for the devolved legislatures, with varying degrees of central involvement.

---

[12] Lynch, P., *New Labour in Scotland: Hegemony, Autonomy, Ideology* (EPOP conference, September 1996).

Territorial Fragmentation in the Party System

A key element of the current UK party system is its centralization; competition between the parties is based primarily on ideological, rather than territorial, disputes. While there is evidence of regional polarization in support for the parties,[13] manifestos and policy programmes remain primarily national in scope, with relatively little attention paid to territorial variations. How far will devolution shift the dynamics of party competition, with left-right party competition giving way to core–periphery contests?

We have seen that the party system may become more territorially fragmented, as devolution boosts the fortunes of the regional parties and the Westminster parties become less centralized in response. But it is unlikely that the Westminster parties will contract fully into distinct regional blocs; they will remain national in scope, and general elections will remain dominated by national policy issues.

Between these 'minimal' and 'maximal' models, however, we might see a more subtle shift towards regional differentiation in the party system. The Labour Party will expect to perform well in elections to the Scottish Parliament and Welsh Assembly. While the new voting system for these elections will enable the Conservative Party to gain a number of seats in both legislatures, it is unlikely in the short term to be in a position to be included in coalition administrations. The party might thus be tempted to focus more clearly on its core constituency and recast itself as a representative body for England, counterpoising itself to Labour, which is likely to retain the majority of Westminster seats in Scotland and Wales (although the number of seats in Scotland is to be examined in the next Boundary Commission review, and will fall in order to make its 'voter:seat' ratio equivalent to that for England).[14]

While the Labour Party might try to retain a centralized organization and structure, in order that it appeals to voters in England, Scotland and Wales (it does not contest elections in Northern Ireland), this scenario suggests that the Conservative Party might be willing to grant more autonomy to its Scottish and Welsh arms, with the Westminster party concentrating on issues particularly relevant to England.

Should regional government be introduced into England (see Chapter 3), further concentration by the parties could take place, with the Conservatives dominating the southern, eastern and midlands regions, the Liberal Democrats appealing particularly in the south west and Labour doing likewise in the north. However, it is unlikely that regional government in England will enjoy the

---

[13] Johnston, R. J., Pattie, C. J., and Allsopp, J. G., *A Nation Dividing? The Electoral Map of Great Britain, 1979–87* (1988); and Field, W., *The Basis of Electoral Support in Britain* (1997).

[14] See Ch. 3.

powers accorded to the legislatures in Scotland, Wales and Northern Ireland and, as such, it poses less of a fragmentary potential to the party system.

The internal structures of the parties in England are more likely to be affected by events such as the new arrangements for selecting candidates for the European Parliament elections. While both the Labour and Conservative parties have allowed a degree of regional input to the selection procedure for the 1999 contest, it is likely that pressure will increase for the role of party members to be strengthened prior to the next elections, in 2004.

A final, more general, point is to highlight the importance of devolution in creating alternative centres of political and administrative power outside Westminster and Whitehall. Thus, the new legislatures, and the strengthened regional arms of the Westminster parties, will provide important new vehicles for political career building well away from London. Britain will thus increasingly mirror the model of other European countries, such as Spain and Germany, where careers at the national level are often forged in regional institutions and party structures.

The Parties' Role in Integrating the Regions

In a territorially more fragmented political system, what role can the Westminster parties play in acting as a unifying force between the regions; how far can they act as the binding 'glue'? One means of achieving this would be through party representatives holding multiple mandates. Members of the Scottish Parliament, the Welsh Assembly and the Northern Ireland Assembly will be allowed to hold simultaneous mandates, as Westminster MPs, members of the European Parliament and local councillors. In the short term, however, it is unlikely that there will be sufficient numbers holding such multiple mandates to act as a strong mediating link between the different levels of government.[15]

In the short term, it is likely that relations between the regional legislatures and Westminster will be strained (see Chapter 9). In this environment, the parties may well have a role in binding the layers together through, for example, reconciling disputes within their internal structures and developing flexibility in their policies to allow them to be tailored to meet regional needs. Should the relations become more strained, however, the parties may be incapable of providing such a link. Tensions between the core and periphery in Canada were initially dealt with through the national party system, but as these tensions intensified, the integrative role of the parties became inadequate for the task, and had to give way to formal mediation institutions, such as ministerial conferences and federal-provincial executive meetings. One

---

[15] With the exception of Northern Ireland—where a few MPs also hold positions as MEPs—the UK is unaccustomed to politicians with multiple mandates. Compare this with France, where multiple mandates are more prevalent, and provide a far stronger link between the central, regional and local layers of government.

commentator has noted that 'the impulses of national party competition were largely irrelevant to the politics of federal-provincial diplomacy'.[16] Territoriality is unlikely to impinge as strongly in the UK as in Canada; none the less, the Westminster parties will need to be sensitive to the regions, and develop some flexibility in their structures, if they are to respond to regional needs and concerns.

THE IMPACT OF EUROPEAN UNION REFORMS

A European Party System?

Further reform of the EU will bring pressures to change the party systems at both the European and national levels.

At present, the dominant units within the European party system are the national parties. Yet further EU political and economic integration will highlight the weak popular legitimacy of the EU institutions (see Chapter 4). This will focus attention on the European Parliament, and the role within it of the pan-European party groups. How far will EU integration lead to a more powerful European Parliament, composed of strong EU-wide parties which will supplant the distinct national party systems with which we are currently familiar?

The main building blocks for such trans-national parties already exist, in the form of the European party groups, established in the early 1970s. The main groups are the European People's Party (EPP), the European Socialist Party (PES) and the Liberal, Democratic and Reformist Group (LDR). Currently, however, these groups are far weaker than their constituent national parties. The development of a European party system that draws support *across* EU member states depends on at least two interconnecting factors:

- a growth in the powers of the European Parliament, both in relation to national parliaments and to the other EU institutions, notably the Commission and Council
- the evolution of a distinctively European political culture and a growing sense of European citizenship for a substantial segment of the European electorate.

The powers of the European Parliament are likely to increase, in an attempt to strengthen the accountability of the EU's executive institutions. In particular, the European Parliament might gain greater powers of scrutiny and legislative

---

[16] Carty, R. K., 'Three Canadian Party Systems' in Carty, R. K. (ed.), *The Canadian Political Party System: A Reader* (Peterborough, Ont: Broadview Press, 1992).

competence. However, pressures towards subsidiarity will remain, encouraging decision making at the national and/or regional level where appropriate. The Westminster parliament will continue to scrutinize EU legislation and debate its implementation in the UK; as such, it will continue to see itself as providing legitimacy at a national level for the EU's institutions and policy–making functions.

At the European level, executive responsibility will remain located primarily in the Commission and Council, where actors are aligned on national, rather than party, lines. The legislative arm will remain weak in relation to the executive bodies.[17] Even assuming that the Parliament gains greater powers, this may not translate into a more effective European party system, but may rather loosen the already weak levels of co-operation within the party groups.[18]

The organizational structure of the European party groups militates against their role as strong transnational bodies. As corporate institutions, they exhibit little centralization of policy making and enforcement. At a wider level, the party groups play a weaker role than the national parties in relation to office seeking.[19]

Thus, national parties are unlikely to be superseded by European ones. Concerns over the democratic legitimacy of EU institutions are as likely to be addressed through national legislatures as through the European Parliament. And many of the key short to medium term issues on the EU's agenda (e.g., enlargement, the size and nature of the budget) will relate more closely to national and territorial sensibilities than to socio-economic ones; this may well hinder the further development of transnational party groups. The evidence is that, 'given the present institutional arrangements in the EC, the formation of genuine 'Euro-parties' is thus rather unlikely'.[20]

This is not to say that the development of the EU will have no effect on Great Britain's party system; the impact is likely to be significant, and felt at both the national and regional levels.

EU Integration and Party Unity

At the national level, further EU integration (particularly the UK's decision over whether to join economic and monetary union) will sharpen the division between supporters and opponents of a federal Europe. What is currently a fault line as much within, as between, parties could become a far more significant cause of intra-party fragmentation. The crucial interaction will be with any

---

[17] Hix, S., and Lord, C., *Political Parties in the EU* (Basingstoke: Macmillan, 1997).

[18] Bardi, L., 'Transnational Party Federations, European Parliamentary Party Groups and the Building of Europarties', in Katz, R. and Mair, P. (eds.), *How Parties Organize: Change and Adaptation in Party Organizations in Western Democracies* (London: Sage, 1994).

[19] Hix, and Lord, *Political Parties in the EU* (n. 17 above).

[20] Bardi, 'Transnational Party Federations (n. 18 above).

move to a proportional voting system for the House of Commons, since this will increase small parties' chances of gaining representation, in turn providing an incentive for groups disaffected by their party's stance on EU integration to split and form their own parties. While this will be of particular concern to the Conservative Party in the short term, it may also provide an opportunity for anti-EU figures on the left wing of the Labour Party too.

The Regions and Europe

Many of the UK's regions have already developed close bilateral relations with the EU, based on issues such as industrial and regeneration funding, and the devolved legislatures will wish to strengthen these incipient links. While even the most powerful of these new bodies, the Scottish parliament, will have to cede to Westminster ultimate authority in relations with the EU, this will not prevent the regions forging far closer relations with EU institutions (e.g., over financial aid, environmental policies, etc.). These institutions will provide alternative political arenas for regional parties, such as the SNP and Plaid Cymru, for whom the developing EU institutions will become forums for differentiating themselves from the national political system (by emphasizing their position as 'Euro-parties', potentially involving alliances with regional parties in other EU Member States). In other words, the EU offers the regions the means of partially bypassing Westminster on some policy issues, an opportunity that the regional parties will use to their own advantage.

ELECTORAL REFORM

Devolution and, to a lesser extent, further European integration will play an important role in recasting the nature and shape of the UK's political and party system. The most significant contribution to these changes may come, however, from reform of the voting system.

A number of forthcoming elections in the UK are to be held under new voting systems (Figure 6.2).[21] As discussed above, the introduction of a more proportional system for elections to the devolved legislatures in Scotland and Wales will provide a boost for the regional parties (and may help to restore the position of the Conservative Party, which lost all its seats in both areas at the 1997 general election). In the European Parliament elections,[22] minor groups, such as the Green Party, may also gain representation.[23] But the most far

[21] The first elections to the new Northern Ireland Assembly have already been held (June 1998), under a proportional voting system.

[22] The European Parliamentary Elections Bill is likely to be reintroduced in 1998–9. Without co-operation from the Lords, who objected to the choice of closed lists, it may not take effect until 2004.

[23] These parties will need to clear a nominal threshold in each region to gain one seat; the thresholds range from 8.3 per cent of the vote in the South East, to 20 per cent in the North East.

reaching impact on the political system would come through any change to the voting system for the House of Commons. The most likely change is to the 'AV Top-up' system, although this will be put to a referendum whose outcome is uncertain.[24]

Figure 6.2. Forthcoming elections under alternative voting systems		
Election	**Voting system**	**Date**
Scottish Parliament & Welsh Assembly	Additional Member System	May 1999
European Parliament	Regional lists	June 1999, but see above
London Mayor London Assembly	Supplementary Vote Additional Member System	likely in spring 2000

Electoral systems can be classified as in Figure 6.3 overleaf.

In considering the impact of proportional electoral systems, we might distinguish between the effects on the party system and those on the wider political system.

Impact on the party system:

- increase in the number of parties;
- representation of small parties;
- fragmentation of existing parties.

Impact on the political system:

- increased likelihood of coalition government;
- end to one party domination in the legislature.

Impact on the Party System

The interaction between the electoral and party systems depends on a variety of factors, a key one being what kind of electoral system is used. The UK's current

---

[24] It is not clear whether voters will support a change to the electoral system in a referendum. A recent opinion poll (NOP, 1998) suggested that 65 per cent of voters supported a change to the current voting system, with 30 per cent wanting to retain it. However, the results of opinion polls on electoral reform are particularly sensitive to the question asked (Dunleavy, P. and Margetts, H., 'The Electoral System', *Parliamentary Affairs,* vol. 50, No. 4 (1997); Curtice, J. and Jowell, R., *Is There Really a Demand for Constitutional Reform?* CREST paper number 65, (Feburary 1998). Curtice and Jowell (1998) also find little evidence of a long term shift in favour of PR, and conclude 'there are not any signs of a growing majority for electoral reform; indeed, there must be doubts about whether there is a majority at all'.

party system—a declining two-party model (see above)—is partly facilitated by the current plurality voting system that skews political rewards in favour of the two main parties. All other things being equal, we can say that the further the UK's electoral system moves from the disproportional first past the post model to a proportional model, the greater the impact on the party system.[25]

Figure 6.3. Features of the main electoral systems
Plurality systems (such as first past the post):   • single seat constituencies   • voters have only one vote (categoric)   • winner must receive only the largest (plurality) share of the vote, not necessarily an absolute majority   Majoritarian Systems (such as alternative or supplementary vote):   • single seat constituencies   • voters list candidates in order of preference (ordinal)   • the aim is for the winner to receive an absolute majority of the votes; this is achieved by reallocating between the candidates voters' second (and third, fourth etc. if need be) preferences   Mixed Systems (such as the AV Top-up additional member systems):   • a proportion of candidates elected from single member constituencies with 'top up' elected from larger unit   • both constituency and top up members can be elected either categorically or ordinally   • seats allocated in proportion to votes received by the parties   Proportional Systems (such as STV or list systems):   • multimember constituencies   • ordinal (can be categoric under certain types of list)   • seats allocated in proportion to votes received by candidates or parties

A move to a proportional electoral system would shake up the parties' representation in Parliament. By lowering the threshold needed to gain one seat, a proportional electoral system would increase the rewards to those parties which currently fail to win seats commensurate with their vote share (largely due to their geographically dispersed support: the Liberal Democrats, the Scottish Nationalists and the Greens, at present), and lower the entry barriers for new parties.

A proportional electoral system may thus change the underlying dimensions of Britain's party system. Single-issue parties may gain the representation that

---

[25] The recommendation by the Independent Commission on the Voting System for 'Additional Vote Top-up involves only a limited element of proportionality. Under this system, we might expect the impact on the party system to be relatively limited, involving minor fragmentation.

has so far eluded them, creating the potential for a more pluralistic party system, more weakly based on the left–right ideological split. Such a change can be illustrated by reference to the example of New Zealand which, in 1993, decided to change the electoral system for its single-chamber parliament from first past the post to the Mixed, or Additional, Member system (see Figure 6.4).

Figure 6.4. Case study of electoral reform and the party system in New Zealand

The Mixed Member Proportional (MMP) system replaced first past the post following a national referendum in 1993. Between 1993 and the first MMP election, in 1996, major fragmentation in the New Zealand party system took place, although this was due mainly to a reduction in the number of constituency seats (from 99 to 65), rather than the introduction of a proportional voting system per se.[26] Four new parties were created within parliament (although one was subsequently absorbed into another) so that, by the end of the 1993 parliament, there were seven parties represented in parliament. In addition, eleven new parties were also created outside parliament. The fifteen new parties established prior to the first MMP election represented both the traditional social-economic divisions in New Zealand society, but also single issues and other social cleavages, such as ethnic, animal welfare and natural law groups (Boston 1998).

The 1996 general election was contested by 22 registered parties and 28 independent candidates. However, this initial fragmentation did not survive the election. Taken together, 14 of the 21 parties, and all the 28 independent candidates, gained only 3.2 per cent of the vote. Of this total, the independent candidates gained only 0.8 per cent; Proportional Representation (PR) did little to boost their position, since their share of the vote in the 1993 election had been only slightly lower, at 0.4 per cent.

Of all the parties formed after the 1993 election, only one gained more than the 5 per cent of the party vote needed to gain seats. Six parties were represented in the 1996 parliament, against four in the 1993 parliament. The new electoral system brought only a minor reduction in the two main parties' vote share (at 63.4 per cent, their combined total was not far short of the 70 per cent gained in 1993). Rather, it loosened their hold over political representation, with their combined share of seats in parliament falling from 96 per cent in 1993 to 67.5 per cent in 1996.

The introduction of PR has weakened the two main parties' grip on government, without upsetting the political balance in New Zealand. As one commentator summarizes the political situation post-1996: 'MMP has made possible the emergence of viable new parties which have successfully tapped into niche markets, but at the same time, many of the traditional cleavages still appear to be present.'[27]

---

[26] Roberts, N., 'The Introduction of a New Electoral System in New Zealand', in Elklit, J., *Electoral Systems for Emerging Democracies—Experiences and Suggestions* (Copenhagen: Danish Ministry of Foreign Affairs,1997).

[27] McRobie, A., 'Raw Statistics and Raw Facts', in Boston, J., Levine, S., McLeay, E. and Roberts, N., *From Campaign to Coalition—The 1996 MMP election* (Palmerston North, Dunmore Press, 1997).

The New Zealand case study highlights the likely initial fragmentation of the party system, but also indicates how unlikely it is that this fragmentation will extend into the legislature. Research suggests that a move from a plurality system (e.g., first past the post) to a more proportional one (e.g., the Additional Member System (AMS) with a limited number of 'top up' seats) will increase the number of parties with sizable parliamentary representation (or 'effective number of parties') from an average of 3.1 to an average of 3.9, with a move to a fully proportional system (e.g., lists or AMS with 50:50 constituency to top up seats) increasing the number of parties to 4.0.[28]

While the Westminster parties may continue to hold dominant positions under proportional electoral systems, the New Zealand case study shows that they will not be immune to fragmentation themselves. Under the current electoral system, there is little incentive for disenchanted factions (e.g., the Europhiles in the Conservative Party, and the left wing within the Labour party) to splinter from their parties. Proportional voting systems will create such incentives, and may well be the catalyst for new parties to be established at the margins of the Westminster ones. This possibility might, in turn, have implications for management within the Westminster parties, which will need to placate and respond to such factions if they do not wish to see them secede (see *Funding and Regulation of Party Competition*, below).

Impact on the Political System

The AV Top-up system recommended as the replacement for first past the post by the Jenkins Commission, would reduce the likelihood of a party forming a majority government on a minority of votes (as has happened in the UK for the last 60 years, with the exception of the February 1974 election). This system would thus significantly reduce the degree to which any one party could dominate the legislature and executive (this outcome might help to strengthen the scrutiny function of the House of Commons; see Chapter 7). Majority governments would be formed only as the result of coalitions between two or more parties; one-party administrations would enjoy only minority status.

One implication of this would be to alter the significance of elections themselves. Under first past the post, elections constitute the sole factor in determining the shape of the government. This is not always so under proportional systems, where the principal role of elections is in determining the size of the parties' parliamentary representation; the formation of government usually constitutes a second stage, once the size of these groups is known. A graphic example of the relationship between the election and the formation of a government under different voting systems is to examine the period that elapses between the two. In the UK, under plurality rule, the period is usually 24 hours

---

[28] Norris, P., 'Choosing Electoral Systems', *International Political Science Review*, Vol 18, No 3 (1997).

or less; the switch to a proportional voting system in New Zealand in 1996 resulted in post-election inter-party bargaining and a time lag of 59 days before a government was formed. After this delay, the Government that emerged was not that expected by many voters at the time of the poll, thus reducing even further the significance of the election itself.[29]

Parties can, of course, announce their intentions to enter into coalitions prior to an election, in which case the election retains its role as the key event in the formation of a government. Should parties leave open their options, however, elections lose their conclusive nature, since the exact shape of the government remains to be determined by negotiations between the parties.

Another way of analysing the relationship between the electoral system and the nature of government is to examine the longevity of the executive under different systems. Using data from 44 countries between 1946 and 1985, Katz[30] shows that single-party cabinet governments last longer than multi-party ones.[31] Moreover, the creation and termination of cabinets under plurality rule depend largely on the electoral process, whereas under proportional voting systems, their lifespan is often the result of events in parliament (e.g., the resignation from the coalition of one partner, or the passing of a vote of no confidence). The increased tendency, under proportional voting systems, for the fate of governments to be decided in parliament, rather than only at election time, might have an important side effect in helping to compensate for the shifting of political attention from Westminster, brought about by devolution and further EU integration.

Coalition government also affects the accountability of the executive, since responsibility for policies is not located in a single party, but is split between two or more parties. With one-party executive government—the norm under plurality rule in the UK—it is relatively clear to voters who is responsible for particular programmes. How far this would change under PR depends on the type of coalition formed. If the constituent parties in the executive share the responsibility for each government department (as in New Zealand following the 1996 election, where National and New Zealand First jointly decide policy through a cabinet system), it becomes difficult to tell which party is responsible for which policy programme. Under the alternative model, parties would divide the government departments between them, so that it is clear which party is responsible for which policies (as happens in Germany, where the Free

---

[29] Boston, J., Levine, S., McLeay, E. and Roberts, N., *The 1996 General Election in New Zealand—Proportional Representation and Political Change* (1996) at:
http://www.vuw.ac.nz/pols/nzpcp/australian_quarterly.html.

[30] Katz, R., *Democracy and Elections,* (New York, NY: Oxford University Press, 1997).

[31] Although this finding has far from law-like status. Farrell, D., *Comparing Electoral Systems* (London, New York: Prentice Hall/Harvester Wheatsheaf, 1997) quotes evidence to show that, of all the European countries, Luxembourg, the Netherlands and Austria—each of which uses a proportional voting system—boasted the highest cabinet longevity figures between 1945–92.

Democrats, for example, have historically controlled foreign affairs and can thus be praised or blamed by voters for the government's foreign policies).

Electoral Reform and Party Campaigns

As mentioned above, there is good evidence that the electoral support for each of the Westminster parties is becoming more regionally polarized. This is due primarily to broad social and economic change, rather than the current electoral system.[32] None the less, the properties of plurality rule exacerbate this regional cleavage, and often result in the parties concentrating their resources on a few marginal seats. One of the reasons why Plaid Cymru has a lower 'vote share:seat' ratio than the Scottish National Party,[33] and why the Liberal Democrats fared better at the 1997 election than at previous elections,[34] is that the concentration of their vote was higher. In other words, the current electoral system builds in incentives for both the Westminster and regional parties to concentrate their support, rather than spread it across a large number of seats.

A proportional electoral system will not be sufficient to end the regional cleavage in voting patterns. But, by more closely matching votes with seats, it will offer greater incentives for parties to campaign in areas where their support is low. The need, under a proportional electoral system, for parties to campaign across a wider territorial area is already being recognized by the parties in Scotland and Wales; should the voting system for the House of Commons be changed in favour of a largely proportional one, these incentives will apply across the UK.

The parties will no longer be able to concentrate on a small number of key 'target' seats as they do at present. Instead, campaigns will be stretched across a larger number of seats which, among other things, will place a strain on the parties' financial and human resources. The parties' response may be to try and increase the level of grassroots activity across a larger number of constituencies. On the other hand, it may encourage them to move even further in the direction of national campaign strategies, drawing particularly on media and poster advertising, rather than grassroots approaches. The Neill Committee on Standards in Public Life has already recommended the introduction of spending caps for national election campaigns, and the pressures arising from the introduction of proportional electoral systems may encourage further regulation of party campaigns. The rules governing campaign spending will

[32] Johnston, R. J., Pattie, C. J., and Allsopp, J. G., *A Nation Dividing? The Electoral Map of Great Britain, 1979–87* (London: Longman, 1988); and Field, W., *Regional Dynamics: The Basis of Electoral Support in Britain* (Portland, Or: Frank Cass, 1997).

[33] At the 1997 general election, Plaid Cymru gained 4 seats (10 per cent of the total) on 9.9 per cent of the vote in Wales, while the SNP gained only 6 seats (8.3 per cent of the total) on more than double PC's vote share, at 22 per cent of the Scottish vote.

[34] At the 1997 general election, the Liberal Democrats gained 46 seats on 17.2 per cent of the vote, while at the 1992 election, they gained only 20 seats on 18.3 per cent of the vote.

need to be changed anyway, as the UK introduces electoral contests that are based on large electoral units, rather than constituencies.

The Electoral Cycle

The establishment of directly elected legislatures in Scotland, Wales, Northern Ireland and London (and, possibly, in the English regions) will increase the number of elections faced by voters. The possible implications of this are:

- voter confusion, should they be faced simultaneously with different electoral systems for different legislatures;
- voter fatigue, as the increased frequency of elections leads to virtual permanent campaigning by the parties;
- the possibility of aligning elections, so that they fall on the same day, thus maximizing turnout and minimizing administrative costs.

The electoral cycle between 1999 and 2007 is set out in Figure 6.5 overleaf. In Scotland and Wales, regional and local elections will be held simultaneously[35] and voters will need to adapt to using different electoral systems when casting their ballot. The Government and the parties will need to consider how best they can educate the public in these regions to cast two different ballots. Should directly elected regional assemblies be established in some or all of the English regions, voters there might also face the same difficulties.

The main impact of the electoral cycle, however, will be on the parties, rather than on voters. Elections to local government are already held in at least one part of the UK each year, and the Government is proposing that all areas elect a certain percentage of councillors on an annual basis. Devolution will increase the number of elections; taking an electoral cycle of five years, in only two years will there be no elections to a regional legislature. Regional contests are likely to be higher profile than local government elections, and will therefore demand more resources from the parties.

One solution to the problem of party 'overstretch' and voter fatigue would be to hold elections to different tiers of government simultaneously. This will be the case with the Scottish Parliament and Welsh Assembly, but it is difficult to see how this solution could be extended more widely. An option would be for the elections for the Greater London Authority to be moved over time to fit with the London borough contests, although this would risk blurring the distinctive role played by the different 'layers'. In any case, a decision on changing the electoral cycle so that more elections were held at the same time would

---

[35] This will be the case in the 1999 elections at least. After this, the Secretaries of State for Scotland and Wales will retain the power to alter the date of local elections where these fall on the same day as the regional elections.

probably have to be deferred until after the referendum on voting reform for the House of Commons, since this debate will raise the issue of whether that chamber should move to fixed terms, as with the devolved legislatures.

Figure 6.5. The electoral cycle: 1999–2007[36]		
	National	Regional	Local
May 1999		Scottish Parliament Welsh Assembly	Scotland Wales Met/non-met districts and unitaries (Eng)
June 1999	European Parliament		
Mar/Apr 2000		*Greater London Authority*	
May/Jun 2000			Met/non-met districts and unitaries (Eng)
May/Jun 2001			Non-met counties (Eng) Districts (N Ireland)
May/Jun 2002	Last date for general election		London boroughs Met/non-met districts (Eng)
Jan/Feb 2003		*NI Assembly*	
May/Jun 2003		Scottish Parliament Welsh Assembly	Scotland Wales Met/non-met districts and unitaries (Eng)
Mar/Apr 2004		*Greater London Authority*	
May/Jun 2004	European Parliament		Met/non-met districts (Eng)
May/Jun 2005			Non-met counties (Eng) Districts (N Ireland)
May/Jun 2006			London boroughs Met/non-met districts (Eng)
Jan/Feb 2007		*NI Assembly*	
May/Jun 2007	Last date for general election	Scottish Parliament Welsh Assembly	Scotland Wales Non-met districts and unitaries (Eng)

[36] Elections to unitary authorities (UAs) in England are only shown when they are being held in 50 per cent or more of the 47 UAs in any one year. Elections to all the UAs are held at the same time in Scotland and Wales. *italics indicate where the exact date of elections have yet to be confirmed.*

FUNDING AND REGULATION OF PARTY COMPETITION

So far, we have examined what impact the constitutional changes might have on the strategies and activities of the UK parties. Yet major changes are on their way that will also affect their internal structure and operations.

Until recently, political parties were deemed to be voluntary bodies, and were not subject to statutory regulation. This has changed under recently introduced legislation, which places the parties on a formal legal footing and requires them to register both their name and logo. This is a relatively minor measure, however. In the longer term, will legal regulation play a more decisive role in shaping party competition, and what will the implications of this be?

The main pressure to move in the direction of greater regulation arises from the funding of the parties. The report from the Neill Committee recommended the introduction of legal regulations governing the disclosure by the parties of donations above £5,000 and the publication of their annual accounts, although the Committee rejected the case for a more formal system of state funding for the parties. New proportional electoral systems will encourage parties to campaign in seats hitherto neglected as 'unwinnable'. We have suggested that this will encourage the parties to focus even more on national campaign strategies, rather than on local campaigning. While limits on national election campaigns were also among the Neill Committee's recommendations, this may not end the calls for stricter regulations in this area.

The likely growth in the regulations affecting the parties may well shift the balance of power within these bodies. As parties are forced to become more open in accounting for resources received and spent (particularly if a greater share of their revenues derives directly from the state), this will encourage the centre to take closer control of the party's operations, in order to ensure compliance with its legal obligations.[37] Greater central control of party activities may also be created by the new electoral systems, particularly in relation to the selection of candidates. By selecting candidates in a block (e.g., regional candidates under AMS or list systems), rather than on an individual constituency basis, the new arrangements make it easier for the centre to help determine who will stand as a party candidate. Finally, any significant increase in the level of state funding for the parties will raise the issue of which part of the party organization it should be channelled through: the party leader's office or the party's executive body—which would strengthen the centre's position— or through a designated arm of the party (e.g., the research department), which would do little to increase the powers of the centre.

---

[37] Such legal obligations already exist at the constituency level, where each party's Electoral Officer, or Agent, must ensure compliance with the rules governing elections (e.g., on spending).

As the discussion on devolution (see *Impact on the Westminster Parties* above) and electoral reform (see *Impact on the Party System* above) suggested, the pressures on the parties will be centrifugal as well as centripetal. Devolution will create incentives for the parties to give greater autonomy to their regional arms; a move to a proportional voting system will give disaffected factions an incentive to split from their parties, encouraging a more consensual style of party management to avoid such fragmentation. These forces will pull in the opposite direction to the likely centripetal forces arising from stronger legal regulation. The parties will adopt different strategies in response to these pressures; what is clear is that the demands placed on them are going to become increasingly sharp.

ADMINISTERING ELECTIONS AND PARTIES

The increase in the number of elections, the different systems under which these will be held and the likely increase in the regulations applying to the political parties are just three of the pressures that increase the likelihood of reforms to the administration of elections and electoral matters. Drawing on the experience of bodies in Australia, Canada and New Zealand, among others, there are already proposals for an Electoral Commission for the UK.[38] This would assume the electoral functions of the Home Office (electoral law, voter education), the Boundary Commission (redistribution of seats) and local authorities (voting administration and counting).

REFERENDUMS

One function of any UK Electoral Commission would be to oversee future referendums. Recently, we have seen a flurry of referendums, principally on constitutional issues, and more are in prospect (see Figure 6.6.)

In spite of the recent flush of referendums, they are not set to become a central feature of the UK's political system. The Government's programme of constitutional reform has been seen to require the underpinning of direct popular consent. It is unlikely that further constitutional reforms will be sufficiently radical to merit similar recourse to a referendum (the possible exception being proposals to radically reform the House of Lords). In other words, the use of referendums is an integral part of the current constitutional reform programme, but one that we might expect *not* to continue in the future.

---

[38] Institute for Public Policy Research, *A Written Constitution for the United Kingdom* (1991); and Butler, D., *The Case for an Electoral Commission—Keeping Election Law up to Date*, King-Hall paper No. 5, Hansard Society (1998).

Figure 6.6. Recent and forthcoming referendums in the UK			
Recent referendums	**Date**	**Future referendums**	**Likely date**
Greater London Authority	May 1998	Voting system for House of Commons	not known
Northern Ireland Assembly	May 1998	Entry into EMU	2002
Welsh Assembly	Sept 1997	English regional assemblies	2002–7
Scottish Parliament	Sept 1997		

More likely is the use of referendums by local and regional tiers of government. The Government is currently considering the merits of referendums at a local level, enabling greater participartion by voters in local policy decisions. Local authorities will be given the power, under proposed legislation, to hold more frequent referendums on controversial local issues, such as spending increases, planning applications and environmental measures. People in metropolitan areas might also be able to initiate a referendum on whether to move to a directly elected mayor; if a local authority decided to move itself towards such a model, it will have to consult local voters through a referendum.[39]

The use of referendums might also become a popular tool for the devolved legislatures in Scotland, Wales and Northern Ireland. Under the devolution legislation, these will be able to call referendums on issues not reserved to Westminster. As new institutions, they may wish to put non-manifesto proposals on controversial policy issues (e.g., health or education) directly to the population, to underpin the legitimacy of their actions. Referendums may also be used to bolster the positions of the devolved legislatures in disputes with Westminster. As Chapter 9 shows, it is unlikely that the *de jure* division of powers between the centre and the regions will neatly reflect the policy-making reality. Instead, we can expect disputes between the centre and the regions where there is overlap in policy making, and where the priorities of the devolved legislature differ from those at Westminster. An example might be a region's status as a nuclear-free zone; environmental protection is devolved to the Scottish parliament, yet defence policy remains the responsibility of Westminster.

The likely use of referendums as a tool of government by the devolved legislatures will increase the pressure on Westminster to provide a defined legislative framework for regulating the holding and conduct of referendums. Calls for such a framework are already being made, in anticipation of closely

---

[39] Department of the Environment, Transport and the Regions, *Modern Local Government—In Touch with the People* (July 1998).

fought contests on electoral reform for the House of Commons, and entry into the European single currency.

CONCLUSION

Forecasting the likely future shape of the UK's party and political system is extremely difficult, since one of its vital determinants—the electoral system for Westminster—remains uncertain. The constraint of space has meant that this chapter has also not been able to take into account possible drivers of change to the party system that arise from factors outside the Government's constitutional programme. Examples whose impact might be significant include:

- the increasing use of focus groups and other citizen consultation mechanisms as a means of informing policy decisions: these methods bypass the normal party-based channels for policy making;
- the use of new technology: for instance in developing new methods of voting ('electronic democracy'), potentially increasing voter turnout.

But even if we assume that the voting system for Westminster remains unchanged, other constitutional changes will bring significant new features to our political landscape. Devolution will produce centrifugal pressures within the Westminster parties, and we will see more differentiation of policy within the parties in response to the particular needs of the regions. The new legislatures will also represent alternative centres of power to that in Westminster. Distinct policy agendas will be followed and political careers fashioned well away from the House of Commons.

It is less easy to assess the Government's constitutional reform programme in relation to the enhancement of democracy in Britain. Over the next ten years, voters in Scotland, Wales, Northern Ireland and London (and possibly some or all of the English regions) will be able to vote for new assemblies wielding varying degrees of power. New parties are likely in Scotland and Wales, and this will give voters a greater choice in expressing their preferences on the ballot paper. To the extent that decision making is brought closer to voters, allowing them to make a clearer input to policy making and for government programmes more accurately to reflect people's views, the devolution programme probably enhances democracy in those areas.

A major determinant of the nature of democracy across Britain rests, however, with the shape of the voting system. Should the Government decide to move to a proportional system, this has the potential to increase the number of parties from which voters can choose, and to create new forms of government, based on coalitions between parties and greater consensus of decision making. However, we should also not expect wholesale changes in the form of government to arise automatically from the introduction of a proportional voting system: the ability of the governing parties in New Zealand to retain the essential elements of plurality rule, even after the country had shifted to a more proportional system,[40] shows the need for institutional reform to be matched by cultural reform among the parties.

How far the changes explored in this chapter—devolution, electoral reform, an increase in the frequency of elections, a possible rise in the use of referendums by government—strengthen or weaken democracy in Britain must remain a normative judgment. What has been shown in our brief analysis, however, is that the nature of democracy in Britain will undergo fundamental change in the coming decade

[40] Boston, J., Levine, S., McLeay, E. and Roberts, N., 'Enthusiasm and Entropy: New Zealand's Experience with Proportional Representation', *Representation*, Vol. 85, No. 1 (1998).

7

Westminster: Squeezed From Above and Below

ROBERT HAZELL

Even with the creation of regional assemblies and Parliaments, Westminster is likely to remain the main focus of political activity and, in the time frame we are concerned with, its core functions will not disappear. At a rhetorical level, the doctrine of parliamentary sovereignty will almost certainly endure. It has already survived 25 years of European Community (EC) membership, and was strongly reasserted by the Government in the Scottish and Human Rights White Papers.[1] But at a practical level political power will continue to leach upwards to Europe as the European Union (EU) further extends its competence; and downward to the Scottish Parliament and devolved assemblies. This will throw into ever sharper relief the gap between the rhetoric of parliamentary sovereignty and the reality of a more pluralist system in which political power is shared between different levels of government, with Parliament being squeezed from above and below.

As far as the public perception of Parliament is concerned, national parties and politicians will almost certainly continue to dominate national television and press coverage. This will only be countered somewhat by the indigenous media in Scotland, Northern Ireland, and to a lesser extent Wales, which will focus on the new assemblies. The impact of Europe on domestic politics will continue to increase, particularly if we join the single currency; but media coverage will remain focused on Europe as it relates to the UK, rather than on the EU as a supra-national body.

This chapter takes each of the main constitutional reforms in turn and considers the changes they will induce in Westminster, starting with those measures which will have the biggest impact: proportional representation (PR), reform of the House of Lords, and devolution. It then discusses recent proposals for parliamentary reform, the impact of the EU, the Human Rights Act and freedom of information.

---

[1] *Scotland's Parliament* (Cm 3658) para 4.2; *Rights Brought Home* (Cm 3782) para 2.13.

IMPACT OF PR ON THE HOUSE OF COMMONS

The Independent Commission on the Voting System chaired by Lord Jenkins reported in autumn 1998. The Government is committed to holding a referendum on the alternative system to be proposed by the Commission during this Parliament;[2] but it is unlikely that any change involving a major boundary review could be implemented in time for the next general election in 2001/2.[3] If the electorate vote for change, the first general election to be held under the new system is likely to be the following election in 2005/7.

The Jenkins Commission was required by its terms of reference to observe four principal conditions: 'broad proportionality' in any scheme proposed; 'the need for stable government'; 'an extension of voter choice'; and 'the maintenance of a link between MPs and geographical constituencies'.[4] Given these criteria, it was no surprise that the Commission recommended a form of the Additional Member System ('AV Top-up') to be put to referendum, because that retains single-member constituencies. The relatively small number of additional members will not be sufficient to provide full proportionality; but the basic idea of constituency and additional members is consonant with the electoral systems for the new Scottish Parliament and Welsh Assembly.

The scheme may be rejected by the electorate. The attitude of the parties will be important, but not necessarily determinative of the outcome. In New Zealand both major parties and big business favoured retention of first past the post but the electorate in 1993 nevertheless voted for change.[5] If there is a change to PR, New Zealand illustrates some of the likely effects on the workings of Parliament and the party systems. These are more fully explored in Chapter 6.

The main consequence of PR is that coalitions could become the norm instead of the familiar British pattern of single-party governments commanding a majority in the House of Commons. Chapter 6 has shown how the stranglehold of the two-party system is begining to break up anyway, increasing the likelihood of coalition government. In these circumstances governments would be formed and business carried through as a result of negotiation between different parties with much greater consultation, for example, about legislation. The coalition would need to agree the contents of the legislative programme; the power of veto in minority partners would be as important as

---

[2] The commitment on timing is not in the manifesto, but in the report of the Joint Consultative Committee with the Liberal Democrats on Constitutional Reform (March 1997). Para. 5.6 said: 'Both parties believe that a referendum on the system for elections to the House of Commons should be held within the first term of a new Parliament.' Jack Straw repeated the commitment in a parliamentary debate on 2 June 1998 (Hansard, HC Deb col 190).

[3] Constitution Unit briefing, *Changing the Electoral System* (March 1997).

[4] Home Office News Release, 1 December 1997.

[5] Constitution Unit briefing, *Electoral Reform in New Zealand* (July 1998).

the power of proposal. Overall there might be less legislation, and moving at a slower pace, than with single-party governments. Consideration of bills in Standing Committees would have to operate on a different basis, seeking cross-party agreement rather than relying on automatic party majority. The nearest the UK has come to this in recent times was the last Labour Government of the 1970s, which had constantly to juggle to maintain its majority, was highly vulnerable to pressure from sectional and constituency interests, and in its final year became a minority government governing with Liberal support.

Contrary to popular belief, coalition governments in Europe have often been surprisingly stable. From the voters' point of view the difficulty may be whether a government can be changed at all. Stability of coalition rule has been experienced in Germany, the Netherlands, Norway, Belgium and Austria; and in Switzerland, where a four-party coalition has ruled now for about 40 years. Parties in most European countries make their coalition preferences known in advance of elections, though this is not binding and does not mean that the process of negotiating a coalition is necessarily shortened. In many countries the formation of a new government can take several weeks; in New Zealand the negotiations after the 1996 election took two months. Another feature of coalition government in Europe (but one which might not cross the Channel) is that there is less institutionalized official opposition in the form of a party which presents itself, and has recognized public status, as the alternative government.

The other issue to watch is whether AV Top-up would lead to two classes of MP: constituency MPs who remained proud of their constituency links, and additional members who were not weighed down by the responsibilities of constituency case work and so might be regarded by other members as free riders, or as carpet-baggers seeking to poach constituencies from the sitting Member. In New Zealand the additional members engage in constituency work: it will be interesting to see whether they do so in Scotland and Wales. In Germany no distinction is drawn between constituency and additional members; but the constituency case work is performed by members of the regional Länder Parliaments and by local councillors. It might not be a bad thing if constituency case work found its proper level in the UK as well: it is absorbing more and more of MPs' time, and makes it harder for them to develop a strategic or effective scrutiny role.

REFORM OF THE HOUSE OF LORDS

Even if the reason for embarking on Lords reform is the simple desire to remove the hereditary peers, the process set in train is likely to entail a wide-ranging review of the Lords' role, powers and composition. The Government will find it difficult to confine the focus solely to compositional issues. This is because it is impossible to decide a satisfactory system for Lords' membership without first deciding what interests peers are there to represent. It will be difficult to avoid addressing the question of what the role of the Lords should be in our political system, its relationship with the Commons and other levels of government and the functions and powers it needs. Only then will it be possible to determine the composition required to carry out those functions, exercise those powers and fulfil that role.[6]

A further reason why it will be difficult to avoid this fundamental analysis lies in the demands arising from other items in the Government's constitutional reform programme. The whole of the UK's constitutional architecture is changing, and the role of the Lords is likely to change with it. In particular, any consideration of the role of the Lords must take account of:

- devolution, with the emergence of national and regional assemblies within the UK;
- the growing influence of the EU, and the increasing demands on national parliaments to scrutinize European legislation;
- incorporation of the European Convention on Human Rights (ECHR), and possible roles for the Lords as a human rights and constitutional watchdog;
- the growth of constitutional litigation, and the future of the Lords as the UK's highest court;
- possible changes to the electoral system for the Commons.

Each of these points will be briefly considered in turn.

Devolution

The function most often proposed for a fully reformed Lords would be to represent the nations and regions of the UK. It is the classic function of second chambers in federal systems, where the lower house represents the people, and the upper house typically represents the states. In so doing it helps to bind the federation together, by giving the states and provinces a strong stake in the institutions at the centre. But the method of representation can vary:

- Direct election. In the USA and Australia, directly elected senators represent the people of the different states. However, as senators may have few links to the state government, this model does little to cement federal/state relations.

---

[6] These points were originally made in The Constitution Unit, *Reform of the House of Lords* (April 1996) and *Reforming the Lords: A Step by Step Guide* (January 1998). They are reflected in the September 1998 Initial Report of the Constitutional Commission to consider options for a new Second Chamber, established by William Hague and chaired by Lord Mackay of Clashfern.

- Indirect election, as with the German Bundesrat. In Germany it is the state governments themselves which are represented in the Bundesrat; an alternative is to elect representatives of the state parliaments, as in India.
- Appointment, as with the Canadian Senate. The UK's rolling programme of devolution might require that representatives be appointed from those regions which do not initially have devolved assemblies.

European Union

The Lords has a Select Committee on the European Communities which does most of its work through six sub-committees, and is widely respected for the quality of its work. It conducts in-depth inquiries which complement the work of the equivalent Commons committees. One possibility would be for a reformed House of Lords to take more of this burden from the Commons; and perhaps involve the UK's MEPs in some of its European scrutiny work.

European Convention on Human Rights

Parliament will need to develop an enhanced capacity to scrutinize legislation to ensure compliance with the ECHR. The Lords have considerable expertise here, and could contribute to the scrutiny exercise. The Human Rights White Paper (Cm 3782) suggested that Parliament establish a Joint Committee of both Houses, or separate committees for each House, partly for this purpose.

The Law Lords

ECHR, devolution and other constitutional changes will bring more political issues before the courts and may lead to increased questioning of the presence of the law lords in the legislature. Lords reform will need to examine the case for a constitutional or supreme court separate from the Appellate Committee of the Lords.

Electoral Reform

The role of the Lords must be complementary to that of the Commons, and if both chambers are elected, it must be on a different basis. It makes little sense to decide on the franchise for an elected Lords until it has been decided whether the electoral system for the Commons is to change.

Powers of the Second Chamber

Some of these changes in function might be introduced without any increase in the Lords' formal powers. The Commons is unlikely to agree to any significant increase in the Lords' powers, but it will also need to take account of any indirect effects caused by changes to the Lords' composition. Reforms that boost the democratic legitimacy of peers may reduce their inhibition in using existing powers to revise primary legislation and veto secondary legislation (the latter power has been used only once, in 1968).

Any increase in the legitimacy and strength of the second chamber increases the risk of deadlock between the two Houses. There will need to be more formal procedures of the kind found in other Parliaments to conciliate and resolve such disputes.

Impact of Lords Reform on the Commons

One effect of Lords reform is that the Commons will have to pay more attention to 'the other place'. An illegitimate and ineffective House of Lords can conveniently be ignored, and the occasional government defeat is generally reversed when a bill returns to the Commons. MPs have very little to do with the House of Lords and the support services (clerks, libraries, catering) operate quite separately, with little transfer between them.

As a result of Lords reform there might be more cross-over between the two Houses. Some politicians might leave the House of Commons earlier to go into the Lords, rather than transferring late in life and at the end of their Commons careers. The profile of the Lords front bench might improve, with more Cabinet Ministers coming from Lords. If the Lords became more democratic and representative it might no longer be axiomatic that senior Ministers had to be in the Commons. For example, if the House of Lords became a chamber which represented the nations and regions, it might make sense for a Secretary of State for Territorial Relations (the successor to the Secretaries of State for Scotland, Wales, etc.) to sit in the Lords and not in the Commons.

There might also be more cross-over through Joint Committees, which are currently relatively few; and through Ministers appearing to introduce measures or answer questions in the House other than the one in which they sit. This already occurs sometimes in Committee, such as the appearances by the Lord Chancellor before the Commons Home Affairs and Public Administration Committees. That is not uncommon in other bicameral parliaments. And there could be a more systematic division of functions between the two chambers, with each chamber playing to its own strengths. If, for example, the House of Commons did strengthen its scrutiny procedures, with publication of bills in draft, pre-legislative scrutiny, etc. (see below), there might be less need for revision of legislation by the second chamber; and more time for scrutiny of European legislation, and for specialist enquiries which play to the Lords' current strengths (science and technology, ethics, human rights) or future interests (regional and local government).

DEVOLUTION

One of the long-standing arguments for devolution has been that our over-centralized system of government overloads the central government machine.

In their Memorandum of Dissent to the Kilbrandon Report[7] Norman Crowther-Hunt and Professor Alan Peacock argued that Whitehall is overloaded, so that Ministers have insufficient time for strategic and policy planning; there is a lack of co-ordination between different parts of the over-large Whitehall machine; and the lack of close contact between Whitehall and the regions leads to failures of policy planning and policy implementation. And they perceived similar failings at Westminster. Despite sitting longer than most comparable legislatures, Parliament gave inadequate scrutiny to legislation; failed to call Ministers effectively to account; and had become a rubber stamp for the executive.

Much of that critique still echoes today; but it is questionable to what extent devolution to Scotland and Wales alone will significantly lighten the load on central government in London. That will only come if Scotland, Wales and Northern Ireland are merely the first step in a wider process of devolution which does lead to a significant shift of power away from London to the regions as well as the nations of the UK. And the co-ordination problems around Whitehall will be replaced by quite different problems of co-ordination between the different devolved bodies. It is also questionable whether Crowther-Hunt identified the right targets. The fact that Ministers have no time to think owes as much to the pressures of the modern media as to the over-centralization of government. And the fact that Parliament has become a rubber stamp for the executive owes more to the gradual emergence of disciplined mass political parties and the power of the Whips.

Size of the House of Commons and Number of Ministers

Nevertheless devolution will have an impact. In Parliament the most obvious immediate change will be a significant reduction in the number of Scottish Office, Welsh Office and Northern Ireland Office Ministers. At present there are seven Ministers in the Scottish Office (the Secretary of State, two Ministers of State and four Parliamentary Under-Secretaries), five in the Northern Ireland Office (the Secretary of State, two Ministers of State and two Parliamentary Under-Secretaries) and three in the Welsh Office (the Secretary of State and two Parliamentary Under-Secretaries). The number of Ministers is certain to be cut, probably just to the three Secretaries of State; although in the longer term even they may cease to retain separate seats in the Cabinet.

There is also likely to be a reduction in the number of Scottish and Welsh MPs. At present Scotland has 72 MPs and Wales has 40. The Scotland Act 1998 (Section 81) repeals Scotland's protected minimum of 71 seats, and provides that at the next Parliamentary Boundary Commission review due to be completed in around 2005 Scotland should adopt the electoral quota for England. This will mean a reduction to around 57 seats.

[7] Report of the Royal Commission on the Constitution, Cmnd 5460-I (1973).

Welsh representation should similarly be reviewed, although the Welsh White Paper said that the number of Welsh MPs would remain unchanged.[8] Wales too is over-represented at Westminster: if Wales were represented in proportion to the English quota she would have 33 seats. There is no need for a reduction for Northern Ireland: with 18 MPs at Westminster Northern Ireland is not over-represented. If both Scottish and Welsh representation were reduced in this way there would be a reduction of around 20 seats at Westminster. This is not as big a reduction as reformers like George Walden or Peter Riddell would like, or the Liberal Democrats—who have argued for a reduction to around 500 MPs[9]—but it is moving in the right direction.

Impact on Westminster Legislation and Procedure

In general, less Scottish, Welsh and Northern Irish business will come before Westminster in the form of debates, motions, questions, etc.; but these will not be removed altogether. The Secretaries of State will still have to appear at the despatch box to answer questions; but they may do so less frequently, and this is likely to cover a much narrower range of subjects.

There will also continue to be legislation passed by Westminster affecting Scotland and Wales. This will clearly be the case in areas where legislative competence is reserved to Westminster, such as (in relation to Scotland) certain aspects of criminal law (drugs and firearms), regulation of the financial services industry, or health and safety. But less obviously, it will also occasionally include legislation by consent on matters devolved to Edinburgh. The Scotland Act confirms (Sections 28 and 29) that Westminster remains the sovereign parliament. This means that Westminster will be able to legislate even on devolved matters. Generally it will do so by consent, because both parliaments may be required to legislate on the same subject, for example to comply with an international obligation. The officials preparing the legislation in Whitehall will ask their opposite numbers in Scotland whether they would like their legislation to extend to Scotland, and the Scots might well say yes, because they would be saved the trouble of having to legislate in similar terms.

But consent may occasionally be forced or more reluctant. Writing about the history of the Stormont Parliament, Professor Harry Calvert said:

There have been cases where Westminster legislation within the sphere of transferred matters has been extended to Northern Ireland, but it has always been with the consent of the Northern Ireland government, sometimes willingly, sometimes without great enthusiasm on their part. There have also been occasions when interference was threatened failing the taking of legislative action on the part of Northern Ireland by its

---

[8] *A Voice for Wales*, (Cm 3718), July 1998, para. 3.37.
[9] Liberal Democrats' Policy Review Commission report on Constitutional Affairs (June 1998).

Parliament, and legislative action has consequently been taken, even with great reluctance.[10]

(The examples cited by Calvert are all from the field of finance: an education levy, rating revaluation, capital gains tax and corporation tax).

Westminster will also continue to pass all primary legislation for Wales, because the Welsh Assembly will have powers of secondary legislation only. The Welsh White Paper says:

Parliament will continue to be the principal law maker for Wales. The Assembly will need to establish a close partnership with Members of Parliament representing Welsh constituencies. They will continue to be involved in considering new legislation that applies to Wales ... The Government will consider, in drafting each Bill that it introduces into Parliament which of the new powers it contains should be exercised in Wales by the Assembly ... The Government expects bills that confer new powers and relate to the Assembly's functions, such as education, health and housing, will provide for the powers to be exercised separately and differently in Wales; and to be exercised by the Assembly. (para 3.7–9).

As a result devolution to Wales will have a significant impact on the drafting of statute law at Westminster: an impact greater than that of devolution in Scotland.

Influence on Statute Law

The Welsh Assembly's powers will be largely dependent on the amount of discretion offered by the laws passed at Westminster. The Assembly is likely to demand greater room for manoeuvre within a broader statutory framework. The extremely detailed, complex statutes in which the parliamentary draftsman seeks to cover every eventuality may no longer meet the case. The pressure from the Assembly will add to the voices of those who call for clarity, simplicity and brevity in drafting, with statutes laying down general principles rather than dealing with problems in detail. But there may be counter-pressures in England; and criticism from lawyers, parliamentarians and the general public if bills confer too much discretion on Ministers to develop the policy in secondary legislation rather than simply fill in the details.

The difficulty is that in our system there is no clear dividing line between primary and secondary legislation. Most statutes continue to be extremely detailed; but others are very broad, and some are bare of everything except a framework of ministerial powers, with all the substance being left to ministerial regulations. An example was the Student Loans Act 1990. A lot of concern was expressed about this to the Hansard Society Commission on the Legislative Process, which nevertheless concluded:

[10] Calvert, H., *Constitutional Law in Northern Ireland* (London: Stevens, 1968), 88–9.

On balance, we believe that the main advantages of making greater use of delegated legislation outweigh the very real disadvantages ... We recommend that the main provisions of statute law should be set out in Acts of Parliament, but that most detail should be left to delegated legislation, provided that much more satisfactory procedures are adopted by Parliament for scrutiny of delegated legislation.[11]

The key therefore lies in the development of better scrutiny of delegated legislation. This ought to be forthcoming in the Welsh Assembly. How good will it be at Westminster? Since the Hansard Society Commission reported in 1992 there have been interesting developments, through the new procedures adopted by the Deregulation Committee in the Commons, which consults extensively with interested parties likely to be affected by proposed Deregulation Orders; and also from the tighter scrutiny into the propriety of conferring upon ministers order-making powers which is now exercised by the House of Lords Delegated Powers Scrutiny Committee. Scrutiny of delegated legislation is also on the agenda of the new Modernisation Committee of the House of Commons; but it is an item which in 1997–8 had not yet been reached.

Rules of Debate: Scottish and Welsh Matters

The Speaker will need to develop a new set of rules defining those devolved matters on which debate will no longer be allowed at Westminster. Here too the best precedent is to be found in the history of the Stormont Parliament described by Calvert as follows:

The first attempt to limit discussion of Northern Ireland affairs was made before the Northern Ireland Parliament had actually come into existence. Immediately after its establishment, the prevailing attitude seems to have been that it was in order to ask the Westminster government to make representations to the Northern Ireland government; and members were allowed to ask for information in the hands of Ministers at Westminster. In this early phase, lengthy discussion of transferred matters sometimes took place, though there was considerable uncertainty as to the proper bounds...

This uncertainty prevailed until 1923 when the first definitive ruling was given in the following terms:

'...the fact that Northern Ireland sends Members to this House does not affect the question. With regard to those subjects which have been delegated to the Government of Northern Ireland, questions must be asked of Ministers in Northern Ireland, and not in this House. In the case of those subjects which were reserved to this Parliament, questions can be addressed here to the appropriate Ministers—for instance the President of the Board of Trade, the Postmaster-General etc. The policy of voting money

---

[11] Hansard Society, *Making the Law* (November 1992), para 267.

here in aid of Irish services may be discussed here, but ... this right does not cover matters of administration for which a Minister in Northern Ireland is responsible.'[12]

This seemingly clear-cut ruling on occasion proved difficult to apply in practice, because the Northern Ireland Government operated within a framework laid down by the Westminster Parliament; and ingenious MPs were often able to show that some failing in the framework had led to the difficulty which they wished to raise. The dividing line sometimes proved as elusive as the equally notorious dividing line between responsibility for policy and responsibility for administration. Increasingly in the post-war years the House authorities seemed to develop the practice of allowing questions, but leaving it to the Ministers to whom they were addressed to determine the bounds of their responsibilities in their answers.[13]

Rules of Debate: English Matters

Then there is the reverse question, of whether there will need to be new rules governing the debate of English issues. This is one aspect of the West Lothian question, which need not be fully discussed here: it has been analysed in previous Constitution Unit reports and by others,[14] and no one has come up with a satisfactory answer. 'In and out' would not work, and devolution all round or federalism do not meet the political reality of an asymmetrical, rolling programme in which some parts of the kingdom are likely to enjoy significantly more devolution than others.

At bottom the West Lothian question is about fairness. It is partially met by reducing the number of Scottish and Welsh MPs; but there still remains the issue of whether those Scottish and Welsh MPs should be allowed to intervene in English debates. One possible way forward would be the development of a self-denying ordinance whereby they did not seek to do so. Another which would be less drastic than a separate English Parliament, and more in keeping with recent developments, would be an English Grand Committee.[15] This could fulfil the same function as a legally separate English Parliament in providing a forum where domestic English matters would be dealt with solely by Members representing English constituencies. The Grand Committee approach would, for example, avoid the need for the creation of a separate body with its own powers, staff, etc., and could be set up under Standing Orders and make use of existing Westminster facilities and resources. However, it would probably

---

[12] Calvert, H., *Constitutional Law in Northern Ireland* (London: Stevens, 1968), 95–6.

[13] Ibid., 99.

[14] House of Commons Research Paper 98/3: *The Scotland Bill—Some Constitutional and Representational Aspects.* Constitution Unit, *Scotland's Parliament* (1996) ch. 7, *An Assembly for Wales* (1996) ch.7.

[15] Ibid., 37-8. *Financial Times,* 18 May 1998, 'English MPs only to sit in revived regional committee'.

demand more powers than have hitherto been ceded to the Scottish, Welsh or Northern Irish Grand Committees.

A Standing Committee on Regional Affairs already exists under Standing Order No. 117. It consists of all members for English constituencies, with up to five others. It last met on 26 July 1978. The history and background of this Committee is described by Griffith and Ryle as follows:

> The procedure for a Standing Committee on Regional Affairs was adopted in 1975, and for two years significant use was made of it. This enabled attention to be paid to the problems of various regions (in 1975–76, for example, there were debates on East Anglia, the North West, the South East, and Yorkshire and Humberside economic planning) and gave Members from those parts outlets for expression of their concern without taking up time on the floor of the House or requiring the attendance, in case of a division, of Members from all other parts of the United Kingdom. Again there were sometimes divisions within the Committee which, although largely meaningless, could be embarrassing for the Government. As any English Member could attend, the task of the Whips on either side was not easy. It may be that this was one of the reasons that these debates, although they appear to have been popular with the back-bench Members who took part, did not flourish. A debate on plans for the South East in 1977–78 was the last use of the procedure, although Standing Order No. 100[16] is still available.[17]

Recent changes to the procedure of the Scottish and Welsh Grand Committees suggest that such a Committee could be granted some Chamber-like features, such as questions and adjournment debates. Due to its size—it would have 529 Members from English constituencies—it might also need to meet in the Commons Chamber, although the symbolism of this could be problematic and a different venue might need to be found. Depending on its organization, this could help ease pressure in the Chamber. An example could be taken from the House of Lords' capacity to create a 'Committee of the whole House off the floor', which meets concurrently with the House itself, allowing peers to attend either session according to choice. For such a Committee to succeed it would need a defined role: a focus on regional policy in England, like that adopted by the Standing Committee on Regional Affairs in the 1970s, might be a good starting point.

As much of the detailed scrutiny at Westminster takes place in Committee and not in the Chamber, the English question might be dealt with instead through changes to committee procedure. Committees such as health and education are already almost *de facto* English Committees, since in Scotland and Wales these matters fall within the remit of the Welsh Office and Scottish Office. With minor modifications—for example the Education and Employment Committee has UK responsibilities for the New Deal—this arrangement could be formalized, with 'English' Standing Committees and

[16] Now Standing Order No. 117.

[17] Griffith, A.G., and Ryle, M., *Parliament* (London: Sweet & Maxwell, 1989), 361.

Select Committees to deal with exclusively English matters. This, perhaps coupled with specific 'English' ministries, with their own question times, might make the omnibus scrutiny provided by an English Grand Committee superfluous.

Future of the Scottish, Welsh and Northern Ireland Committees

Long before any English Grand Committee appears at Westminster, some of the Scottish and Welsh Committees are likely to disappear. First, a word of explanation about the three kinds of committee. These are the Scottish and Welsh *Grand Committees*, consisting of all the MPs for Scotland and Wales respectively, which hold general debates; the Scottish and Welsh Affairs *Select Committees*, which scrutinize the policy, expenditure and administration of the Scottish Office and the Welsh Office; and *Standing Committees*, established *ad hoc* for the Committee stage of Scottish and Welsh bills.

It seems likely that two out of the three Scottish committees will probably go. There will be very little for the Scottish Grand Committee to discuss, because in future the main action will be in Edinburgh. There will be little or no Scottish legislation, so no role for Scottish Standing Committees. Similarly the Welsh Grand Committee will probably go, because it has long been criticized as no more than a talking shop. However, we may still need a Welsh Standing Committee, because there will be occasional primary legislation exclusively for Wales; and indeed this may become more frequent post-devolution, because the Welsh Assembly will press for more changes to the law in Wales.

The Select Committees are more likely to be retained. Despite the powers devolved to the Scottish Parliament and Welsh Assembly, there may remain a need for committees which monitor the spending of central government funds by these bodies. Such committees could also retain a role in scrutinizing the work of the Secretary of State and would provide a forum for Scottish and Welsh MPs at Westminster looking for a role. These changes may require adoption of new standing orders for the committees, which would probably want new powers to call members of the assemblies as witnesses.

The fate of the Northern Ireland Committees is in theory more certain, at least in the short term, because both are guaranteed a continued existence in the Belfast Agreement of April 1998. Strand One of the Agreement provides:

the Westminster Parliament (whose power to make legislation for Northern Ireland would remain unaffected) will

(a) legislate for non-devolved issues, other than where the Assembly legislates with the approval of the Secretary of State and subject to the control of Parliament;

(b) legislate as necessary to ensure the United Kingdom's international obligations are met in respect of Northern Ireland;

(c) scrutinise, including through the Northern Ireland Grand and Select Committees, the responsibilities of the Secretary of State (Para 33).

In the long term there might be changes to the Northern Ireland arrangements, mirroring those for Scotland and Wales. However, these would require a revision of the agreement and will therefore be slow to emerge.

An alternative might be to sweep up the Scottish, Welsh, and Northern Ireland Select Committees into a wider Select Committee on Devolution, which would be set up to monitor the devolution settlement generally, and to call to account those responsible in Whitehall for making the devolution settlement work. This is unlikely in the short term, because the Scottish, Welsh, and Northern Irish MPs may not feel they have a sufficient common interest. But it might emerge in the long term, especially if the individual Secretaries of State wither away. A possible parallel might be the 1995–6 Select Committee on Central/Local Government Relations established by the House of Lords and chaired by Lord Hunt of Tanworth. One of the recommendations in the Committee's report was that there should be a permanent committee on central/local government relations;[18] a devolution Select Committee could be seen as an extension of that. If in time there is a single department in Whitehall responsible for intergovernmental relations (see Chapters 8 and 9) the task would fall to the Select Committee monitoring that department.

PARLIAMENTARY REFORM

It may seem perverse to mention parliamentary reform halfway through this chapter: but on current showing it is unlikely to be as significant a force for changing the way Parliament works as the reforms already discussed. A new Select Committee on Modernising the House of Commons was announced early in the life of the new government, on 4 June 1997. Its remit is to improve the quality of legislation by allowing more effective consultation and scrutiny; reviewing the structure of the parliamentary year; overhauling the process for scrutinizing European law; and strengthening the ability of MPs to call Ministers to account.

The Select Committee published its first report on 29 July 1997, on the Legislative Process (HC190). It recommended:

- a more open and formal approach to timetabling;
- increased consultation on draft bills;
- more pre-legislative scrutiny, including by Select Committees;
- more effective use of Standing Committees;
- carry over of bills from one session to the next.

[18] HL Paper 97, July 1996.

The report was debated in November 1997. This debate brought out the cautious nature of the Committee's report, which emphasized the need for the House to make more flexible use of existing procedures, and to conduct more experiments. But although expressed in tentative terms, the Committee's proposals are potentially far reaching. How big a change they represent in legislative procedures will depend on how bold the new government is in making use of them. This is not simply a matter for Margaret Beckett as Leader of the House, but also for her ministerial colleagues in using the power to experiment; and for the Whips' Office (now headed by Ann Taylor, who began the reforms) in not blocking them. It is also a matter for the Opposition, because the government side has been very anxious to proceed with all-party support on parliamentary reform. So far the Opposition have shown themselves to be relatively conservative in procedural matters.[19]

Changing Commons procedures is a notoriously slow process, and it will take several years for the changes proposed by the Committee to work their way through the system. The most important single change proposed is the timetabling of all legislation. This should give adequate time for consultation and scrutiny whilst allowing the Government the knowledge that it will get its legislation through the House in a predictable time frame. The main difference will be to remove the power of delay as the main weapon of opposition and to make reasoned opposition more attractive. Other changes which might gradually become accepted parts of parliamentary procedure over the next five to ten years could include:

- the publication and parliamentary consideration of draft bills;
- the examination of Green and White Papers by departmental Select Committees;
- the increased use of pre-legislative scrutiny, and of the Special Standing Committee procedure, including its use for more controversial matters than has been the practice in the past;
- more regular post-legislative reviews of legislation by appropriate committees;
- more debate and scrutiny of public expenditure plans and of quangos;
- more time for constructive debate of Select Committee reports;
- improved scrutiny of secondary and European legislation;

[19] William Hague highlighted the need for parliamentary reform in his first speech on the constitution to the Centre for Policy Studies, 24 February 1998. But the Opposition business managers have been conservative, blocking the Government's proposal to refer the Government of Wales Bill to Standing Committee in February 1998, where it would have received more detailed scrutiny.

- changes to Parliament's pattern of work and the structure of the parliamentary year to ensure a better spread of business and a better balance between constituency and parliamentary commitments.[20]

The other source of pressure for procedural reform might be the alternative blueprints provided by devolved assemblies, which are likely to develop their own distinctive *modus operandi*. For example, Bernard Crick and David Millar's proposals for how a Scottish Parliament should work deliberately reject 'the tradition-bound procedures of the Westminster Parliament and its excessively confrontational nature'.[21] If successful, it is possible that such innovations will, in turn, influence practice and procedures at the Westminster Parliament.

Procedural changes will, however, only go so far. A fundamental shift in the culture of the House will be necessary if the acceptance on merit of criticism and amendments from the Opposition is to be seen as a strength rather than a major defeat. This can only be achieved through political will and through Ministers setting a new example. It will also require a change in the attitudes of parliamentarians towards their own roles, but this could break either way. The arguments of Peter Riddell and others to enhance the standing of back-bench and Committee work by reducing the government payroll and paying Committee Chairmen an additional salary might encourage MPs to consider the scrutiny role as prestigious and satisfying as a job in the government.[22] Or if it went the other way, in a continuation of the current vicious circle, MPs would remain tightly whipped, show perfunctory interest in the residual legislative programme remaining at Westminster and concentrate more on constituency case work and lobbying, as more and more legislation came from Europe, and in future from the devolved assemblies.

THE IMPACT OF EUROPE

Scrutiny of EU Business

For Westminster, the most significant consequence of accession to the EU is that its approval is no longer required to give legislation domestic legal effect. Power rests with the Executive rather than with national parliaments. In Lord Nolan's words:

---

[20] For a useful summary of proposals for parliamentary reform, see Power, G., *Reinventing Parliament* (London: Charter 88, 1997).

[21] Crick, B., and Millar, D., *To Make the Parliament of Scotland a Model of Democracy* (John Wheatley Centre, 1995).

[22] Riddell, P., *Parliament under Pressure* (London: Gollancz, 1998).

Ministers still have the power of veto over Brussels decisions, except where qualified majority voting has been conceded, but Parliament has not. It can only draw Ministers' attention to aspects of draft Directives. It cannot block them, or force Ministers to block them.[23]

Moreover, legislation made by the European institutions can trump domestic legislation where there is an inconsistency. In short, where legislation is concerned, the assent of Westminster is neither necessary nor absolute. The impact of membership is also apparent in the changing scope of the domestic legislative programme. The Department of Trade and Industry has estimated that over one third of existing UK legislation and 70 per cent of UK business legislation derives from Brussels.[24] A recent Demos report put the total even higher, at 80 per cent of economic and social legislation and 50 per cent of all legislation across Europe.[25]

The same report went on to say 'British MPs are rarely either interested in Europe or able to hold Ministers to account, and British governments often agree behind closed doors to decisions in Brussels, and later treat them as alien intrusions when they are discussed on the floor of the House.' It is true that in the UK comparatively little parliamentary time is devoted to activity that might influence European decision making, whether relating to legislation or other matters. The main arenas for such debate are:

- the House of Commons Select Committee on European Legislation (ELC)
- two House of Commons Standing Committees on EC legislation
- the House of Lords Select Committee on the European Communities (ECC)
- to a lesser extent, the House of Commons Foreign Affairs and Home Affairs Committees (on Second and Third Pillar matters).

Debate about how to influence or control Ministers negotiating in Brussels has been at the heart of all parliamentary consideration of procedures for dealing with EU matters ever since the subject was first considered by the Foster Committee in 1973. That Committee insisted that the Government must accept that 'it will not cause or permit the law of the UK to be changed contrary to a resolution of the House.'[26] Such an undertaking was given voluntarily by the Government, and subsequently was given in the form of a declaratory resolution of the House of Commons (now embodied in the House of Commons' Scrutiny Reserve Resolution of October 1990). But the practical

---

[23] Lord Nolan, Radcliffe Lecture (1996) in *The Making and Remaking of the British Constitution* (London: Blackstone Press, 1997), p.6.

[24] DTI, *Review of the Implementation and Enforcement of EC Law in the UK* (1993).

[25] Leonard, M., *Politics without Frontiers* (London: Demos, August 1997).

[26] Second Report from the Select Committee on European Community Secondary Legislation, 1972–3, HC 463.

arrangements have never proved to be entirely satisfactory—recurring areas of concern expressed by both Commons and Lords Select Committees include the timing of debates (arranged too near the final stage of negotiations); the increasing number of instruments that are adopted before reaching the Commons for scrutiny; and failures by Ministers and departments to follow the requirements imposed by the scrutiny reserve procedure; in particular, failure to provide timely information, mostly as a result of administrative inefficiency rather than wilful disregard.

These failings have been criticized in successive reports: in the Commons Select Committee's 1996 reports on The Role of National Parliaments in the European Union, and on The Scrutiny of European Business,[27] and in the 1998 report of the Modernisation Committee on The Scrutiny of European Business.[28] That report recommended that:

- the number of Commons standing committees charged with debating proposed EU laws and questioning Ministers about them be expanded from two to five (the Lords now has six European Sub-Committees);
- Parliament should establish an office in Brussels, as do the Danish and Finnish Parliaments, to act as a forward observation post and give early warning to the various European Committees at Westminster;
- scrutiny should continue up to and beyond meetings of the Council of Ministers, where the final decisions are made.

The next ten years may see a strengthening of the control elements of the domestic scrutiny process, whether as a result of greater resistance to the 'Europe project' or as a result of close ties raising the perceived importance of European business through, for example, a single currency (see Chapter 4). This reassertion of parliamentary authority could take two forms: increasing the range of issues considered by the UK Parliament (and by devolved assemblies), and a more rigorous insistence on a link between Parliamentary assent and Executive decision.

In the past MPs and peers have been unmoved by, or ignorant of, the exhortations of their colleagues towards more and better scrutiny arrangements. Ministers and Whitehall departments have failed time and again to provide information and documents in time, under this government as under its predecessor. Improvements will require much greater interest on the part of MPs, in attending European standing committees (which every MP can do);[29] and in insisting on more debates of European matters on the floor. And on the

---

[27] HC-xxviii and HC-xxvii, 18 July 1996.

[28] HC 791, 9 June 1998.

[29] In the last Parliament the average number of 'non-members' who attended meetings of the Commons EC Standing Committees varied between three and four.

government's side it requires a willingness to provide timely information, and to continue keeping Parliament informed in the run up to meetings of the Council of Ministers: and for Ministers to exercise their negotiating powers and, where necessary, their veto to reflect the views of the UK Parliament.

National Parliaments and the European Parliament

George Brock points to recent opinion surveys which, in his view 'suggest that the 'permissive consensus' which allowed political elites to pursue integration without accounting to their electorates in detail may have evaporated after the Single European Act.'[30] One impact of that Act was to enhance the role of the European Parliament in decision making. The European Parliament, the fount of democratic legitimacy within the EU, has suffered from being something of an afterthought, and the turnout levels in national European Parliament elections reflect the lack of connection that voters feel with the Parliament. In turn, this has led to proposals for more effective links between national Parliaments and the European Parliament, and specifically in the UK between MPs and MEPs, both through their respective parties and through formal parliamentary channels. (See Chapter 4 for discussion of the interplay between constitutional change in the EU and the UK).

The Select Committee on European Legislation has suggested, for example, that: 'If the Member States wished to give their National Parliaments an influential role in the European Union of the future, then the fact must be faced squarely: the most direct way of doing so would be through a Second Chamber.'[31] This idea has been supported in the past by Sir Leon Brittan and Michael Heseltine, and more recently has been raised by Robin Cook. Alternatives mooted by others include:

- the holding of periodic assizes—meetings of MPs and MEPs (perhaps as a conference of Parliaments). One such meeting took place on the initiative of the European Parliament before the 1997 Intergovernmental Conference. More regular meetings have faced opposition on the grounds that any proclivity towards consensus resolutions would require considerable time, at odds with the accelerated legislative process agreed in the Single European Act and at Maastricht;
- committees of national MPs and MEPs;
- formalizing the relationship between the European Parliament and the Council of Ministers as a bicameral system, making the European Parliament the legislature and the Council of Ministers a second chamber. In other words, federalism.

---

[30] Brock, G., 'Britain in Europe', in Halpern et al. (eds.), *Options for Britain* (1996).
[31] *The Role of National Parliaments in the EU*, HC 51-xxviii, para. 23.

It already seems likely that developments in giving Parliaments a collective role will build on the existing activities of COSAC (the Conference of European Affairs Committees). COSAC was first established by the French Presidency in 1989 and meets every six months. It consists of delegations of up to six members from the European Affairs Committees of each national Parliament and the European Parliament. At a meeting in Dublin in October 1996 unanimous agreement was reached on developing its future role, including support for treaty amendment to improve the flow of information to national Parliaments and other proposals which would allow COSAC to act as a collective voice of national Parliaments contributing to decision making processes.[32]

At present, it seems highly unlikely that pressure for change in the relationship between Westminster and European institutions and processes will come—except at the crudest political level—from the public at large. But some commentators believe that the next few years will mark a shift in public opinion: 'As the European Union moves towards economic and monetary union and closer political union, and the powers of the European Parliament remain too limited for it to monitor these areas adequately, national Parliaments will increasingly be called upon to develop, adapt and sharpen their scrutiny procedures. Public opinion will demand no less.'[33] Equally, the creation of new devolved assemblies, with new rules and procedures, will provide new models of co-operation and influence; and increase the pressure on national governments to accelerate the flows of EU information.

Nevertheless, bearing in mind the slow pace of procedural reform in both Westminster and in Europe, and the capacity for muddling through described in Chapter 4, the hallmarks of the arrangements we might anticipate over the next ten years are probably already visible in contemporary debate. This suggests a range of potential directions for the future: improvements in audit arrangements (including, but not limited to, the changes proposed by the Court of Auditors); greater involvement of national Parliaments in ratification procedures; the extension of freedom of information using information technology (both raw information and monitoring data); more frequent conferences of national Parliaments; an initiating and pre-legislative role for national Parliaments; links with wider national interests; and the extension of scrutiny reserve procedures.

---

[32] See Leicester, G., *Westminster and Europe—Proposals for Change* (London: Hansard Society King-Hall Paper No. 4, April 1997).

[33] Millar, D., 'The Way Forward?' in Giddings, P., and Drewry, G., (eds.), *Westminster and Europe* (Basingstoke: Macmillan, 1996).

HUMAN RIGHTS LEGISLATION

The Human Rights Act 1998 and the accompanying White Paper *Rights Brought Home* (Cm 3782, October 1997) will impact on the working of Parliament in three respects:

- to make transparent the human rights implications of all government legislation
- introduction of a fast-track legislative procedure to remedy legislation found in breach
- a new Human Rights Committee.

On the first, the White Paper proposes that the sponsoring Minister of a Bill should be required to provide a statement to Parliament that the legislation is compatible with the ECHR. This statement will be included alongside the Explanatory and Financial Memorandum which accompanies a Bill when it is introduced into each House of Parliament. In cases where the government is taking a risk, or the human rights issues are not clear cut, the Minister will be expected to explain the position during the normal course of the procedures on the Bill. This could either be during the normal Committee stage in Standing Committee or for pre-legislative scrutiny before a special Standing Committee, or the issue could be referred to the new Human Rights Committee. The Institute for Public Policy Research has proposed that where the Minister signals that a bill might not comply with ECHR standards, there should be a delay of one month before Second Reading to permit the Human Rights Committee to investigate.[34] Routine scrutiny might best be done by the House of Lords Delegated Powers and Deregulation Committee, which has an established reputation and track record for scrutinizing draft legislation for compliance with a body of constitutional principles.

The fast-track legislative procedure is a significant new departure. The Human Rights Act provides for a fast-track procedure for changing legislation in response either to a declaration of incompatibility by the courts in the UK or to a finding of a violation of the Convention in Strasbourg. The appropriate Minister will be able to amend the legislation by Order so as to make it compatible with the Convention. The Order will be subject to approval by both Houses of Parliament before taking effect, except where the need to amend the legislation is particularly urgent, when the Order will take effect immediately but will expire after a short period if not approved by Parliament.

---

[34] Bynoe, I. and Cooper, J., *Human Rights in Whitehall and Westminster* (London: Institute for Public Policy Research, forthcoming).

Scrutiny of the government's draft Order should be by the Human Rights Committee, which is the body best equipped to assess whether the government's legislative remedy is sufficient. In terms of procedure, it could follow the procedures of the Deregulation Committee, which can hear evidence from parties affected by proposed Deregulation Orders before approving the Order to amend the primary legislation. The procedure can be very thorough (more thorough, departments complain, than putting through ordinary primary legislation): so it could be suitable for debating and hearing evidence on how a finding of incompatibility can best be remedied. In cases involving clashes of human rights there is seldom a single right answer.

The new Parliamentary Committee on Human Rights could be a Joint Committee of both Houses, or each House could have its own Committee. The White Paper suggests that the Committee might:

- conduct inquiries on a range of human rights issues relating to the ECHR;
- examine issues relating to other human rights treaties to which the UK is signatory;
- conduct an inquiry into whether a new Human Rights Commission is needed and how it should operate.

The IPPR has suggested that the most appropriate avenue would be a Joint Committee of both Houses, to reflect the constitutional significance of the Committee and its work; and to combine the experience and interes: currently found in the Lords with the political weight and influence of MPs from the Commons.[35] In terms of functions it suggests that the Committee should be consulted as part of the process of human rights treaty ratifications, and contribute to the formal process of monitoring of UK compliance with the human rights treaties by the UN, the Council of Europe and other international bodies to which the UK is a party.

How wide the parliamentary committee spreads its wings will depend critically upon whether or not there is also a Human Rights Commission. But they are not alternatives. A parliamentary committee cannot perform many of the tasks which would fall to a Commission (public education, advising individuals and organizations, test case litigation); it can only conduct inquiries and scrutinize the activities of government.[36]

---

[35] Ibid.

[36] Spencer, S. and Bynoe, I., *A Human Rights Commission: The Options for Britain and Northern Ireland* (London: Institute for Public Policy Research, 1998)

FREEDOM OF INFORMATION

Freedom of Information (FOI) will not initially make much difference to the way Parliament operates. Experience from Australia and Canada where freedom of information laws were introduced in 1982 shows that in the early years MPs and the Opposition made very little use of the new legislation.[37] They were creatures of habit, and continued to seek information from the government by writing to Ministers or putting down Parliamentary Questions. But in Australia Opposition MPs began to make more systematic use of the legislation after three years or so; and in Canada Opposition spokespeople now routinely make FOI requests in their areas of responsibility.

The extent to which the right to freedom of information is used in the Westminster Parliament depends primarily on the determination of MPs. It requires a dogged tenacity, of the kind displayed by MPs like Tam Dalyell and Richard Shepherd, to make targeted FOI requests, pursue complaints and take cases to appeal. Such MPs are rare, and many may be deterred if asked to pay charges: MPs are used to getting their information for free. But the Opposition may start to use FOI when it delivers its first Ministerial scalps, as it has done in Canada and in Australia: in the former case over ministerial expenses on an overseas trip, in the latter over a government building contract. FOI will not enable Parliament to get involved in policy making, but it provides an extra line of accountability, along with auditors and ombudsmen. It offers Parliament a further small means of checking on the efficiency, fairness and integrity of government.

CONCLUSIONS

Westminster will be subject to a lot of conflicting pressures over the next ten years. It will remain the central focus of political activity, and some of the constitutional changes (Lords reform, ECHR, PR) could strengthen it as an institution; but Europe and devolution will weaken it, as parliamentary sovereignty is squeezed from above and below. How Westminster copes with these pressures, and in particular how it reorganizes in response to devolution and to EMU, will determine whether it occupies a central place in the new constitutional settlement, or whether it remains dominated by the executive and becomes further marginalized.

The signs are not particularly encouraging. In the past Westminster has shown itself slow to adapt, and governments tend to be reluctant to force the pace of parliamentary reform and enable better scrutiny of their own activities.

[37] Hazell, R., 'Freedom of Information in Australia, Canada and New Zealand', *Public Administration*, Vol. 67, No. 2 (Summer 1989), 203.

The conflicting pressures which emerge under the different headings in this chapter can be summarized as follows:

Proportional Representation

- if approved by referendum, will not be implemented before 2005
- coalition government could become the norm, with less legislation, and more policy stagnation, requiring a new culture of co-operation in order to be effective
- could lead to two classes of MP, with constituency and additional members.

Lords Reform

- should significantly reduce the size of the House of Lords
- will entail a wider review of the Lords' role, functions and powers
- could give the Lords a role in integrating Westminster upwards (with Europe) and downwards (with the nations and regions of the UK)
- could also involve the Lords as a human rights and constitutional watchdog
- should lead to more joint working and cross-over between Lords and Commons.

Devolution

- will reduce the size of government by ten Ministers, and of Parliament by 20 MPs
- might require a new Devolution Select Committee or English Grand Committee
- will require new approaches to debate on Scottish, Welsh and English matters
- Welsh devolution may require a new approach to statutory drafting by Westminster
- devolution to Scotland and Wales alone will not significantly lighten the load on central government.

Parliamentary Reform

- will work its way through slowly, proceeding with all party support
- will produce more flexible approach to legislation, with new procedures for
  —pre-legislative scrutiny
  —European legislation
  —subordinate legislation
  —fast-track remedial legislation (human rights, deregulation).

Europe

- already one third of UK legislation and 70 per cent of business legislation derives from Brussels

- few MPs are currently interested in Europe or involved in Westminster scrutiny of the EU
- scrutiny should extend to Second and Third Pillar matters, and non-legislative documents
- scrutiny is heavily reliant on effective flows of information
- more effective scrutiny may lie through conferences of national Parliaments, rather than the European Parliament.

Human Rights Legislation

- requires Ministers to state the human rights implications of all new legislation
- fast-track legislative procedure to remedy legislation found in breach
- new Parliamentary Human Rights Committee, probably a Joint Committee of both Houses.

Freedom of Information

- will not make much difference to Westminster.

8

Machinery of Government: Whitehall

ROBERT HAZELL AND BOB MORRIS

THE NEW CHALLENGES FOR WHITEHALL

So far the political energy and focus of the new Labour Government has gone into designing new institutions, and in particular the new assemblies in Scotland, Wales and Northern Ireland. But as the devolution settlement beds down, and other parts of the constitutional reform programme fall into place, the focus will shift back to the centre, and how the centre needs to be re-engineered to underpin the new arrangements. This chapter examines the restructuring which will be required in Whitehall.

The main features of the reform programme which Whitehall will have to come to terms with include:

Devolution

- three devolved assemblies, with different degrees of legislative power, established in a rolling programme of asymmetrical devolution
- new regional institutions in England, starting with Regional Development Agencies and Regional Chambers
- a patchwork of directly elected Regional Assemblies and directly elected mayors, emerging in response to local demand tested in referendums
- new machinery as part of the devolution framework, such as the Joint Ministerial Committee on Devolution, and the Council of the Isles which includes the Irish Government, the Channel Islands and the Isle of Man.

New Rights Culture

- a more challenging rights culture as a result of the incorporation of the European Convention on Human Rights (ECHR)
- more open government under a Freedom of Information Act.

New Electoral Systems

- electoral systems introducing proportionality and more frequent coalition government not only in the devolved assemblies but also possibly in the UK Parliament.

Parliamentary Reform

- a more effective second chamber, following reform of the House of Lords, and more effective procedures (pre-legislative scrutiny, etc.) in the first chamber.

What follows examines in each case the likely impact of these innovations for Whitehall, and Whitehall's possible response.

DEVOLUTION

Devolution represents the largest, the most significant and the least certain of the changes to the machinery of government. It is one thing for Whitehall to relate to the Scottish and Welsh Office as parts of the same administration, and quite another for it to conduct business with devolved legislatures and governments. It is difficult to predict the many changes this will bring in train, but they are likely to include the following:

End of the Territorial Secretaries of State

Although their present transitional roles are indispensable, it is difficult to see that the posts of the present Scottish, Welsh and Northern Ireland Secretaries can remain individually viable when devolution is up and running. The Scottish Secretary is likely to be the first to go. The Northern Ireland Secretary may remain so long as the security situation and North–South relations warrant it; and the Welsh Secretary may remain so long as the Assembly requires a godfather figure to promote primary legislation for Wales at Westminster. But these must be transitional arrangements; if either situation endures devolution will have failed.

That is the logic of devolution; but the politics may dictate otherwise. The Secretaries of State may remain in being for symbolic reasons, or political balance, or patronage for some time after there has ceased to be a real job to do; and the titles may remain long after that, rather like the Chancellor of the Duchy of Lancaster (who still has vestigial responsibilities in Lancashire). But over time the individual Secretaries of State are likely to be replaced in Whitehall with a single Minister responsible for the generality of territorial affairs, i.e., continuing rather than residual business. This Minister's principal role will be to manage intergovernmental relations, the annual block grant negotiations, etc. The Minister is likely to be a senior member of the Government. He or she could have a small central department, but could equally well be based within a reformed Cabinet Office. That is where the Canadian Minister for Intergovernmental Affairs is located, within the Privy

Council Office which services the Canadian Prime Minister and Cabinet (see Figure 9.3 in Chapter 9).

With the loss of the territorial departments there will be a reduction in the number of Whitehall departments, and a reduction in the number of UK Government Ministers. In 1998 the Scottish Office had six Ministers, the Welsh Office had three, and the Northern Ireland Office had five. This will be a small but significant loss in prime-ministerial patronage; overtime the government payroll will shrink from 96 Ministers and Whips to around 84.

End of the Unified Civil Service

The Government proposes that there will continue to be a unified Civil Service. The guidance issued to civil servants in Wales says:

Constitutionally, the position of the Civil Service will be unchanged by devolution. While the ultimate loyalty of civil servants will remain to the Crown, in practice, the loyalty of individual civil servants will be to whichever administration they are serving. Individual civil servants will continue to take their instructions from the Assembly as a whole, or from its Committees or Assembly Secretaries, to the extent that the Assembly has delegated power to them. [1]

This is obviously intended to be reassuring, and there is an understandable wish to preserve a common basis of employment and professional behaviour. But this is unlikely to be proof against the new loyalties and alternative (and sometimes opposing) centres of power that are to be established. Even where the controlling political parties are the same in Westminster and a devolved assembly, it cannot be assumed that there will be any automatic unity of purpose, for example, if there is a 'New Labour' government in Westminster but 'Old Labour' regimes in Edinburgh or Cardiff.

There will be pressure from the Scottish Parliament and Welsh Assembly to have their own civil service, like the Northern Ireland Civil Service. This may arise because of some triggering event or scandal; or simply because of a wish to control the recruitment and career development of their own officials. It cannot long be acceptable in Edinburgh and Cardiff for the professional head of their civil service to be the Cabinet Secretary in London. For how long will their political leaders be willing to consult him about the promotions and postings of their senior officials?

Concordats and Intergovernmental Relations

The next chapter on intergovernmental relations illustrates the new structures and networks which will be required to underpin the devolution settlement, by analogy with the machinery in Australia, Canada and Germany. These will range from high level summits of political leaders and bodies like the Council

---

[1] Welsh Office guidance, para. 14, February 1998.

of the Isles down to day-to-day working groups of officials negotiating about technical issues. The European Community (EC) also illustrates the range of intergovernmental meetings that will be required. Some of these meetings will simply be existing inter-departmental bodies transformed into inter-governmental ones; but others will be new, a number will be more adversarial, and all will be more formal. They will create a significant extra burden on the Whitehall machine.

The Government proposes that these relations will need to be governed by written understandings or 'concordats' individually negotiated between Whitehall departments and the new devolved administrations. While not necessarily having legal force, these agreements will bear a considerable weight of expectation. The current list of 'likely common topics' includes consultation arrangements, exchange of information, access to research, liaison between chief professional officers, consultation about appointments to and the direction of UK/GB public bodies, and dispute resolution over the concordats themselves.[2] These illustrate current perceptions of future tender points: whereas pre-devolution Whitehall could rely on mutual (though private) transparency between departments in negotiation, resort to concordats recognizes that, post-devolution, that kind of automatic co-operation will come to an end.

The Joint Ministerial Committee and the British-Irish Council

The Joint Ministerial Committee is likely to be the main forum for negotiating intra-UK devolution issues. It did not feature in the devolution White Papers, but was announced during the Committee stage debates on the Scotland Bill in the House of Lords:

The Government intend that there should be standing arrangements for the devolved administrations to be involved by the UK Government at ministerial level ... It is envisaged that this would be achieved through the establishment of a joint ministerial committee of which the UK Government and the devolved administrations would be members. The joint ministerial committee would be an entirely consultative body, supported by a committee of officials and a joint secretariat.[3]

The Joint Ministerial Committee is to be the mechanism for the devolved governments to negotiate with the UK Government about reserved matters which impinge on their functions, and to discuss devolved matters in the different parts of the UK. It may develop into a body similar to the Council of Australian Governments (see Figure 9.1 in Chapter 9), and will be serviced by the Constitution Secretariat in the Cabinet Office. The British-Irish Council

---

[2] Reply to Question from Rosemary McKenna MP, Scottish Office News Release, 27 February 1998.

[3] HL deb, 28 July 1998, col 1487.

(or 'Council of the Isles') will not be so important in the devolution context, and is likely only to discuss devolution issues which have an Irish dimension, or which are of interest to the other members of the Council (the Channel Islands and the Isle of Man). It emerged as a by-product of the Belfast Agreement, and it may be difficult to find substantive issues for it to discuss which have not already been debated in the other intergovernmental fora which underpin the Agreement (the North-South Ministerial Council and the British-Irish Intergovernmental Conference).[4]

Devolution Units within Individual Departments

Managing these processes will reinforce an already observable tendency for a number of Whitehall Departments to set up devolution units. At present shadowing and contemplating the devolution legislation, these will develop into permanent functions simultaneously looking outward to the devolved governments and inward to the central co-ordinating mechanism in Whitehall itself.

Representation of the Devolved Governments in London

Conversely, the Scottish, Welsh, and Northern Irish Governments will themselves need to establish missions in London. Most of their officials will be based in Edinburgh, Cardiff and Belfast; but they will need a base from which to operate when in London, and their Ministers will need prestige London offices in which to hold meetings and give receptions. It would be a handsome gesture by the British Government to give Dover House (home of the Scottish Office in Whitehall) to the new Scottish Government, and Gwydyr House (London home of the Welsh Office) to the new Welsh Assembly.

Representation to the EC

Simultaneously, it can be expected that the devolved governments will set up units for managing their relationships with the EC. The Scottish Office has already, with Foreign and Commonwealth Office (FCO) agreement, established a small team of two Scottish Office officials in the UK Delegation in Brussels. The Welsh and Northern Irish will no doubt wish to follow suit, and all three aspire to establish freestanding offices to represent their interests to all the EC institutions without relying on the UK's Foreign Service to act as intermediary. These will be listening and lobbying posts; formally, representation to the EC will continue to be through UK ministers and UKREP, the UK's permanent representation in Brussels.

---

[4] Belfast Agreement (Cm 3883) Strand Three. See also The Constitution Unit, *The Nordic Council: Lessons for the Council of the Isles*, (November 1998).

THE ENGLISH REGIONS

Chapter 3 describes how early in the life of the new Government it was decided to legislate for Regional Development Agencies (RDAs) but not for Regional Chambers. The RDAs will be appointed by Ministers and accountable through Ministers to Parliament; their budgets will come from Whitehall, and even though their members will be chosen from the region, the RDAs will be agencies of central government. They will work alongside the Government Offices for the Regions, from whom they will take responsibility for distributing the Single Regeneration Budget. But they will also have a line of accountability to non-statutory Regional Chambers. These are bodies composed mainly of the local authorities, but with business and other partners.

As Chapter 3 describes, there are forces at work which may yet lead to the development of more powerful Regional Chambers, or to directly elected Regional Assemblies. The question is how the machinery of central government will need to respond to these changes.

The underlying issue for Whitehall is whether the integration of government services on a regional basis can be achieved without change to continuing separate ministerial responsibilities. The solution in Scotland, Wales and Northern Ireland has been, even pre-devolution, to assemble all the regional responsibilities under regional ministers. In England, however, the division between ministerial responsibilities remains functional, not territorial.

It has to be remembered that the Government Offices for the Regions are of very recent creation—1994—and still struggle to resolve in themselves the different cultures of the four departments brought together (Environment, Transport, Trade and Industry, and Employment). The Regional Directors remain answerable to the four sponsoring Ministers and are still essentially out-stationed headquarters officers of the civil service: their primary function is to improve the effectiveness of central government activity in the regions.[5] They cannot develop a stronger role as a voice *for* their regions, because the Regional Directors are not political figures, and they lack political legitimacy and democratic accountability within the region. Regional Directors can enter into regional partnerships and can give an account to the Regional Chamber and other partners of the policies and programmes of central government, but they cannot be called to account; their priorities and resources will be ultimately determined by Whitehall and by Ministers, and not by any of the local actors.

How might these regional institutions evolve? Three different scenarios are possible:

[5] The new government has implicitly confirmed this in the terms of reference of the review to be conducted by the new Innovation and Performance Unit in the Cabinet Office, which is to conduct a study 'of the government's presence in the Cities and the Regions', HL deb, 28 July 1998, WA 186.

Mini. There is no development beyond the introduction of the RDAs, which continue to operate as national quangos appointed by Ministers and led by businessmen, with the Regional Chambers as optional appendages, left to wither on the vine.

Midi. Regional Chambers come to be accepted as necessary partners, and are given statutory recognition and statutory powers. These are mainly of a coordinating and strategic kind, but include the power to appoint and control the RDAs, but no other significant central government functions.

Maxi. The emergence of one or more directly elected Regional Assemblies, probably starting in the North of England, with the transfer to them of significant central government functions from the Government Offices for the Regions.

For Whitehall the mini and midi scenarios would involve relatively little change. Regional Directors would need to work closely with the Regional Chambers, and would be important partners in the development of economic and other regional strategies. The lines of accountability to the sponsoring Secretaries of State would still creak, but it could be made to work. Where it becomes more problematic is with the emergence of the Regional Assemblies. This would introduce asymmetry as between the regions of England, which is a step change from the asymmetry between the nations of Scotland, Wales and Northern Ireland. Asymmetry between the four nations of the UK already exists, and will roll forward post-devolution; but asymmetry between the English regions would be something new, and could be difficult to handle politically and administratively.

The second difficulty is that directly elected Regional Assemblies would expect to have transferred to them some or all of the functions of the Government Offices for the Regions. There would be no advantage to a Regional Chamber in progressing to a Regional Assembly unless it acquired significant new powers and functions as a result, and these powers would largely come from central government. Whitehall might find it difficult to handle the mix of functional and territorial responsibilities which would result; asymmetry is theoretically feasible for the spokes of regional devolution, but may be more difficult to accommodate in the hub. But in ten years' time the hub will have a lot more experience of managing relations with autonomous regimes, and more confidence perhaps in coping with political and administrative diversity.

THE NEW RIGHTS CULTURE

Ministerial and Departmental Lead

The immediate goals of the ECHR incorporation project are clear enough, but the long term implications less so. Whitehall's experience of the Strasbourg jurisdiction is limited to a relatively small number of government departments (the FCO, which handles all Strasbourg litigation; the Home Office, for cases involving the police, prison service and immigration; the Ministry of Defence, for cases involving service personnel; etc). The administrative arrangements reflect the reactive approach of previous governments to the development of human rights. A government intending to introduce a new rights culture across all departments and public authorities will need to have in place more rigorous co-ordination arrangements; and a strong ministerial and departmental lead.

In Whitehall the domestic policy lead lies with the Home Office. In many countries, responsibility for promoting and protecting human rights would fall more naturally to a Ministry of Justice. A department along these lines—bringing together parts of the Lord Chancellor's Department, the Law Officers, Home Office and FCO—has been proposed by the Liberal Democrats, and in the past by the Labour Party; although the Lord Chancellor does not favour the idea. An alternative would be to continue the Cabinet Sub-Committee, CRP (EC) which has supervised introduction of the Human Rights Act, supported by the official committee responsible for departmental co-ordination.

In parallel, the respective roles of the FCO and domestic departments will need clarification to eliminate the problems arising from division of responsibility; and a clear motor needs to be created in one of the central departments—Home Office, Cabinet Office, Lord Chancellor's Department or FCO—to drive the enforcement culture. This unit might operate in a similar way to the Efficiency Unit, Next Steps Project Team or Social Exclusion Unit in the Cabinet Office in promoting a cultural change within Whitehall; it would co-ordinate training, offer advice to departments and possibly provide clearance for government involvement in litigation (in ECHR cases at Strasbourg currently the responsibility of the FCO). Key to the success of such units is the commitment of a senior Cabinet Minister, who can provide support when other departments drag their feet. At present that role falls to the Home Secretary, but it could equally be the Lord Chancellor.

Pre-legislative Scrutiny: 'Human Rights Proofing'

Over the last decade, pre-legislative scrutiny of bills within Whitehall has become more systematic and has focused particularly on confirming compliance with the ECHR: a process known as 'Strasbourg proofing'. By its nature it involves making difficult legal judgments, and the decision on

whether to press ahead with legislation will be based only in part on the legal
assessment. But in future the legal assessment will loom much larger: see the
account of the impact in Canada in Figure 8.1 below.

Figure 8.1. Administrative impact of the Canadian Bill of Rights

Canada introduced a Bill of Rights in 1982, entitled the Canadian Charter of Rights
and Freedoms. A great effort was made by the federal Department of Justice to review
existing legislation and bring it into line with the Charter. Between 1982 and 1985 an
omnibus Bill was introduced each year designed to make pre-1982 legislation Charter-
proof. With new legislation, the Attorney General must report to Parliament before the
Second Reading of any Bill on its compliance with the Charter.

The Charter has had a far-reaching impact on the way policy is made and legislation is
prepared. A few expensive landmark cases had a seismic effect on the Government.[6]
Many interest groups now frame economic and social policy claims against the
Government in terms of Charter rights and freedoms. This has forced Canadian law-
makers and administrators routinely to consider Charter implications when drafting
legislation and regulations. It has led one commentator to conclude:

'Self-regulation has probably been a more important source of rights protection in the
long run in Canada than judicial outcomes, although the latter clearly reinforces the
inclination to engage in the former.'[7]

The Canadian Supreme Court has applied a large and liberal interpretation to the
Charter. As a result of adverse judgements the Canadian Government and its
provincial counterparts began to require that policy proposals were scrutinized with
the Charter in mind at much earlier stages of the policy process, and not when the
department's memorandum was being prepared for submission to Cabinet. A survey
of senior officials concluded that these new ways of policy making inevitably make a
difference to the outcomes:

'Many governments have instituted new procedures or bureaucratic structures
designed explicitly to ensure that the Charter is taken into account at the earliest stage
of the policy process ... The senior officials participating in this study believe that
'Charter values' have now been deeply and permanently integrated into the attitudes
of government decision makers across the country.'[8]

---

[6] Cases such as *Singh* v. *Minister of Employment and Immigration* [1985] 1 SCR 177, *R* v.
Askov [1990] 2 SCR 1199, and *R* v. *Schachter* [1992] 2 SCR 679 are said to have cost the
government unbudgeted outlays of hundreds of millions of dollars.

[7] Bayefsky, A., 'Mechanisms for Entrenchment and Protection of a Bill of Rights: the Canadian
Experience', *European Human Rights Law Review* (1997), Issue 5, 496–500, p.499.

[8] Monahan, P. and Finkelstein, M., 'The Charter of Rights and Public Policy in Canada',
Osgoode Hall Law Journal 1992, Vol. 30, No. 3, 501 at p.504.

They also argue that the Charter has altered the balance of power within Government, increasing the status and the role of Attorneys-General and their legal advisers as they were involved at an early stage in the policy-making process:

'In many governments the Attorney General has been constituted as a new central agency with a range of power and influence rivalling only that of the Finance Department.'[9]

In the UK much will depend on how seriously Ministers take their new obligations under the Human Rights Act; and on early decisions of the courts, which may help to concentrate minds in Whitehall. If the Canadian experience is replayed here, there will be a need to tighten up the procedural side of the policy-making process, and to make human rights assessment long before Cabinet consideration of legislative proposals. The Cabinet Office is to issue a new circular on *Policy Appraisal for Human Rights*, and the kind of mental discipline this will impose on administrators is illustrated in the extract from the New Zealand Cabinet Office Manual at Figure 8.2.

Suggestions have been made that Parliamentary Counsel could be asked to certify that all reasonable steps have been taken to ensure compliance. This has few attractions.[10] If certification is desired, responsibility might more appropriately fall to the Attorney-General. That would represent a major change in his role, and also his status: the Attorney is not normally a member of the Cabinet. It would also centralize a process which properly belongs in departments. What the Canadian experience shows is that the process of checking for compliance with human rights should not start when the legislation is being drafted but should be an integral part of the earlier stages of determining policy aims and objectives. Moreover, any central scrutiny for compliance should not absolve government departments of their primary responsibility, and their need to develop internal expertise and understanding.

This will require greater involvement of legally qualified staff in the policy process itself as opposed to retrospectively; with concomitant effects on the organization of government legal services, and the professional formation of administrative civil servants. The policy process itself will have to be a more rule-based exercise (see Figure 8.2). This will make it both more deliberate and more protracted. Officials, where they are not legally trained, will need to acquire a deeper knowledge of legal requirements and procedure. The gap that has in this respect existed between continental and UK civil services will narrow.

[9] Ibid, p.508.
[10] See The Constitution Unit, *Human Rights Legislation* (1996), para. 168.

Figure 8.2. Extract from the New Zealand Cabinet Office Manual

**Format for Submissions to Legislation Committee
on Draft Bills Ready for Introduction**

This form indicates the headings to be used. Each heading must appear in the submission. Write 'not applicable' if the heading is not relevant to the Bill.

OFFICE OF THE MINISTER [XX]
TITLE [Give the full title of the draft bill]
...

3. Compliance

Indicate whether the Bill complies with each of the following, with reasons if the Bill does not comply (list each sub-heading):

a. The principles of the Treaty of Waitangi.

b. New Zealand Bill of Rights Act 1990.

c. The principles and guidelines set out in the Privacy Act 1993. (If the Bill raises privacy issues, indicate whether the Privacy Commissioner agrees that it complies with all the relevant principles.)

d. Relevant international standards and obligations.

e. Guidelines in the Legislation Advisory Committee report, Legislative Change: Guidelines on Process and Content (r·vised edition, 1991).

4. Consultation

Summarise the consultation that has taken place under the following categories, as well as the results of that consultation:

a. Relevant Government departments or other public bodies.

b. Relevant private sector organisations and public consultation processes.

c. Government caucus(es) and other parties represented in Parliament.

5. Creating New Agencies or Amending Law Relating to Existing Agencies

a. If the legislation will create a new agency, will the Ombudsman Act 1975 and the Official Information Act 1982 apply? If not, why not? (The Office of the Ombudsman should be consulted on this issue and its views summarized.) ...

6. Allocation of Decision-Making Powers

a. Does the draft legislation involve the allocating of decision-making powers between the executive, the courts and tribunals?

b. Have the criteria relating to the qualifications and responsibilities of decision-makers and the procedures they follow (set out in paragraphs 85–84 of Legislation Advisory Committee, *Legislative change: Guidelines on Process and Content* (revised edition, 1991)) been applied?

c. If not, state departures from the criteria and reasons for these ...

OPEN GOVERNMENT

The new Government took early steps to seize the initiative on freedom of information (FOI). The Queen's Speech one week after the Election promised a White Paper and this was published on 11 December 1997 as 'Your Right to Know'.[11] It was hailed at the time as heralding one of the most progressive FOI regimes in the world. A draft Bill was promised for the spring of 1998, but failed to appear. In July 1998 David Clark, the Cabinet Office Minister in charge of preparing the Bill, was sacked in Tony Blair's first reshuffle, and responsibility for FOI was transferred to Jack Straw at the Home Office. Most of the Freedom of Information Unit in the Cabinet Office have not transferred, so preparation of the draft Bill will be significantly delayed. A new team of Home Office Ministers and officials need to get to grips with the issues, and even if a draft FOI Bill is published in 1998–9, it is unlikely to be introduced before 1999–2000.

Press comment at the time of the reshuffle questioned whether this indicated a weakening of the Government's resolve. It is likely that the draft Bill will modify some of the White Paper's proposals, but given transfer of responsibility that should cause no surprise. As the Constitution Unit commented at the time, the White Paper was too good to be true;[12] it made no mention of the resource implications for Government, and commanded less than whole-hearted support from other Government ministers. The challenge for the new Home Office team is to come forward with a set of proposals which command general ministerial support.

Overseas experience shows that the lead given by Ministers matters just as much as the detailed provisions of the new Freedom of Information Act. Civil servants will take their cue from Ministers; and FOI will need some strong Ministerial champions to change the culture. Legislation alone is not enough. Even after the introduction of FOI the Government continues to hold most of the cards; it can sit on information or delay its release, and even though the proposed Information Commissioner will have power to order disclosure, a reluctant Minister or department can spin things out for 6–12 months.[13]

At the policy level little will change. Departments will be required to publish all their internal manuals and staff instructions (their 'secret law'); but this requirement has already existed for five years under the Open Government Code of Practice. There will be a general statutory right to reasons for

---

[11] Cm 3818.

[12] Constitution Unit, *Commentary on the Government's Freedom of Information White Paper,* January, 1998.

[13] The White Paper proposed an Information Commissioner with power to order disclosure. Subsequent press reports suggested Ministers might want to superimpose an appeals tribunal, which could further delay enforced disclosure. See Maurice Frankel, *The Guardian,* 18 August 1998.

administrative decisions. The White Paper proposes that the policy-making process be protected by a simple harm test (a higher level of protection than for other exempt material), so that few if any policy papers will be released until after decisions have been made. Overseas experience suggests that FOI will not lead to increased public participation in policy making.[14] It may lead to the release of more policy papers after the event, but only upon request; and few such requests are likely to be made. Overseas experience also offers comfort to those who fear that policy making may suffer because officials will be reluctant to commit advice to paper: that fear, although widespread, has not been borne out in other countries which have introduced FOI.[15]

So what will change as a result of FOI? The impact is likely to fall mainly on the big caseworking departments. In Australia and Canada 80 to 90 per cent of requests are for personal files. If that pattern is repeated here, the departments in the front line will be the Department of Social Security, Benefits Agency, Child Support Agency, Department of Health, Immigration Department, Prison Service and Ministry of Defence. These client-oriented departments will also bear the brunt of requests for reasons for decisions; as will big caseworking operations like the National Lottery Charities Board, and the Department of Trade and Industry and Ministry of Agriculture, Fisheries and Food in operating grant and subsidy regimes. As for access to general government information, the main users will be business, the big law firms and the media rather than individuals or pressure groups; and they are as likely to be seeking information about government contracts, successful tenders or background details of the Private Finance Initiative as information of general public interest.

Most requesters will be pursuing a private interest rather than a public interest; few will make requests out of idle curiosity. A number will do so in pursuit of a grievance. For those contemplating litigation, FOI will enable the aggrieved party to make a better informed decision on whether to sue; it will marginally increase the incidence of litigation against the Government, and marginally increase litigants' chances of success.

To sum up, most FOI requests will be relatively low level; and FOI will not be the great panacea which its proponents sometimes suppose. When a request does carry a political charge, it is Ministers who have more to fear; in other countries FOI disclosures have led to Ministerial resignations. For civil servants the main concern will be the impact on resources, at a time of continuing cutbacks on staffing and tight expenditure constraints. If Ministers betray nervousness about FOI the impact will be keenly felt in the senior levels of the civil service, who will be expected to keep a close eye on all disclosures.

---

[14] Hazell, R., 'Freedom of Information in Australia, Canada and New Zealand' *Public Administration,* vol. 67, No. 2, summer, 1989.

[15] Ibid.

It will be one more extra task, leading to further reduction in Whitehall's already reduced policy-making capacity.

The Data Protection Act 1998 will provide an important part of the regime for access to personal files. The interplay between the Data Protection Act and the Freedom of Information Act will continue to cause difficulty, as it has overseas; although there should be some improvement following the ending of the longstanding separation of departmental responsibility between the Cabinet Office (which until July 1998 was responsible for FOI and open government) and the Home Office (which leads on data protection and access to personal files). The White Paper suggested there would also be a separate Information Commissioner and Data Protection Commissioner as the guardians of the rival values of openness and privacy. In time Whitehall may come to see the need for a more comprehensive policy on the collection, handling and release of all government information; especially as more and more information will be stored, processed and disclosed electronically. (The fact that 31 per cent of the replies to the Government's White Paper were by email indicates the extent to which the facility of electronic communication will itself influence the rate of flow, and the level of expectation about the material that should be available from government). An integrated approach would be greatly facilitated by a single Minister being made responsible for Government information policy. At present this is divided departmentally between the Home Office (freedom of information and data protection), Cabinet Office (integration of government records, ease of access for the citizen) and the Lord Chancellor's Department (archives and the Public Record Office). In this respect transfer of freedom of information to the Home Office was a retrograde step: it would have made more sense functionally for data protection to have moved to the Cabinet Office. It might also make sense to have a combined Information and Privacy Commissioner, as is found in some other jurisdictions.[16]

NEW ELECTORAL SYSTEMS

For Whitehall the electoral system which matters is the one at Westminster. If the report of the Jenkins Commission on the Voting System leads to a referendum which supports a move to a proportional voting system for Westminster the effects would be dramatic. Coalition governments which have been the exception in UK politics could become the norm. This century, with the exception of Lloyd George's coalition after the First World War and the National Government in 1931, they have occurred only in time of war when— most—political hostilities have been suspended.

---

[16] British Columbia and Ontario.

Coalition governments would bring a range of consequences for the civil service, in terms of both the written and unwritten rules of behaviour. New protocols would need to be developed on the formation of a new government; sharing out of portfolios; deciding on the contents of the legislative programme; and formal and informal consultation on other policies. The Civil Service Code of Conduct might also need to be adapted to cover the pressures which civil servants might face when serving Ministers from different political parties. Here Whitehall may have something to learn from local government, which has considerable recent experience of working for authorities with no overall political control.

Much depends on whether there is a formal coalition, or whether there is a minority government dependent upon other parties' support. The last experience of minority government was during the Lib/Lab pact of the 1970s, when the Liberals were consulted on the legislative programme and on other policy proposals. Formal coalitions could learn from the experience of coalition governments in the devolved assemblies, and from overseas. In Ireland the political parties negotiate agreed programmes of government, either before or after the election. In New Zealand, after their first Proportional Representation (PR) election, protracted negotiations were conducted which resulted in the Coalition Agreement of December 1996 between the National Party and New Zealand First, which adopts a formal, legalistic style. The collapse of the coalition in summer 1998 shows the difficulties two-party systems have in adjusting to the realities of PR, and the kind of upheaval for which civil servants will need to be prepared following its introduction here.

Whitehall may have to develop rules for caretaker administrations after elections, while negotiations are conducted between the parties. In Europe as in New Zealand it can often take several weeks before a government can be formed. And the negotiations do not end then. In Ireland programme managers are appointed to resolve any subsequent differences: emollient individuals who are good at fixing party disagreements. They are politicians appointed by each party; but in Sweden senior civil servants are appointed to act as go-betweens and to negotiate with the minor coalition parties.

The UK would be more likely to follow the Irish model; but civil servants will inevitably be drawn in, just as civil servants from the Cabinet Office currently service the joint Cabinet Committee between Labour and the Liberal Democrats. Some rewriting of the Whitehall rules will be required, which may need to be reflected in revisions to the Civil Service Code.

PARLIAMENTARY REFORM

Parliamentary reform may have little impact on Whitehall. As described in Chapter 7, the Modernisation Committee in the House of Commons has made a modest but useful start, in recommending increased publication of bills in draft, pre-legislative scrutiny, and greater use of timetabling. It remains to be seen how bold departmental Ministers are in making more flexible use of the legislative procedures open to them.

If the Government embraces those reforms new skills will be required amongst civil servants responsible for preparing legislation and piloting it through Parliament: skills of presentation, persuasion and negotiation, as the drafting of legislation becomes less of an internal dialectic within Whitehall and more of an open, consultative process involving outsiders. Similar skills are required of senior civil servants as they appear more frequently in front of Select Committees. They are becoming public figures, and they will increasingly be judged by their public performance. In this respect there is a creeping 'politicization' of the civil service: not in a political sense, but in the sense that Ministers are more likely to appoint civil servants who will represent them well in public fora, and who will be good at presenting and explaining government policy. For departments which already engage a lot with Parliament and the public, like the Department of Health, this should cause no difficulty; but for departments like the Foreign Office and Defence which have relatively little legislation (because they operate mainly under prerogative powers) the culture shock may be greater, as some of the disclosures in the Scott enquiry perhaps demonstrated.

As for Lords reform, the main consequence of a more effective or legitimate House of Lords is that Whitehall would be obliged to take it more seriously. Some departments have no Ministers in the Lords, but rely on Lords and Baronesses in Waiting to give departmental replies to questions and to represent them in debates; and they in turn rely on the courtesies in the Lords to get away with reading departmental briefs of which they sometimes have little understanding. A more effective House of Lords would not put up with this. Either each department will have to have a Lords Minister; or Ministers from the Commons should be able to appear before the Lords to represent their department.

IMPLICATIONS FOR THE CENTRE

The implications for the centre itself are potentially very significant. In 1998 the Prime Minister asked the new Cabinet Secretary, Sir Richard Wilson, to review the central machinery of policy making and delivery—'the hole in the centre of government'. Sir Richard's review identified a number of areas that needed improvement: the handling of cross-departmental issues; better strategic capacity to look ahead to future opportunities and threats; more systematic review of outcomes and the achievement of government objectives. The Cabinet Office is to be reshaped and given a new focus as the corporate headquarters of the Civil Service, with more emphasis on meeting the corporate objectives of the Government as a whole, rather than just the objectives of individual departments. Jack Cunningham was appointed as the new Minister for the Cabinet Office, with his deputy Lord Falconer having a seat on all the key Cabinet committees. The Office of Public Service is to be merged with the rest of the Cabinet Office, and two new units are to be created: an Innovation and Performance Unit, with an emphasis on the better co-ordination and practical delivery of policy and services which involve more than one department or public sector body; and a new Centre for Management and Policy Studies, incorporating the Civil Service College.[17]

At first blush these do not seem momentous changes; but further details were promised for the autumn. The Prime Minister's announcement of his conclusions on Sir Richard Wilson's review was interesting as much for what it left out as for the modest changes that it promised. In particular there was no mention of the impact of constitutional change; and no awareness that there may need to be more radical reconfiguration of the centre as it adjusts to its new role at the centre of a quasi-federal, more rights-based, more transparent system of government. (It is difficult to believe such thoughts have not crossed minds at the centre: the announcement of the new Joint Ministerial Committee on Devolution, which will need to be serviced by the Cabinet Office, was made on the same day as the announcement of the conclusions of Sir Richard Wilson's review).

A number of additional responsibilities are likely to fall on the Cabinet Office. The earlier sections of this chapter have identified the Cabinet Office as the probable or possible locus for:

- the conduct of intergovernmental relations, and the residual functions left with the territorial Secretaries of State (or successor)
- the conduct of negotiations with coalition partners
- ECHR policy, litigation and enforcement of the new rights culture
- co-ordination of EU policy.

The Cabinet Office will no longer lead in preparing the legislation on freedom of information; but (as with the ECHR) it may need to lead on implementation. Ensuring that there is a coherent approach to information technology is one of the key functions of the new corporate headquarters, and this will require the Cabinet Office to be responsible for information policy across government as a whole.

In addition the Cabinet Office will be the sponsoring department for a growing number of constitutional watchdogs. It is already the sponsoring department for the Parliamentary Ombudsman, the Civil Service Commission,

---

[17] Hansard HL deb, 28 July 1998, WA 186.

the Committee on Standards in Public Life, the Commissioner for Public Appointments, and the Political Honours Scrutiny Committee (and provides a home for the last three bodies). If it takes the lead on information policy generally, and becomes responsible for the implementation of FOI and data protection, it could become the sponsor of the Information and Data Protection Commissioners. It would also be the obvious home for any more systematic and transparent appointments machinery established to process nominations for the House of Lords.

More generally the Cabinet Office could become the department responsible for the constitution. That may seem an odd prediction when responsibility for constitutional issues is so dispersed. At present the Cabinet Office is home only to the Constitution Secretariat, which co-ordinates the constitutional reform programme; and which now provides the policy lead on Lords reform. The policy lead on all other constitutional reform topics rests with other departments; with the Scottish Office, Welsh Office and Northern Ireland Office respectively for devolution, Department of the Environment, Transport and the Regions for policy on the English regions, the Home Office on human rights, electoral reform and freedom of information. That dispersal of policy responsibility could change significantly post-devolution if the rump of the Scottish Office, Welsh Offfice and Northern Ireland Office all fell back into the Cabinet Office. Because devolution is such a large part of the constitutional programme, and for the next few years will continue to be so, the department that leads on devolution will be seen to lead on the programme as a whole.

This flies in the face of the traditional wisdom that the Cabinet Office centre should not take on executive functions which are better undertaken elsewhere in Government. But the time may have come to assert that for central government to manage effectively the new set of intergovernmental and other relations, central government itself needs a more effective hub. This might form part of the new 'corporate headquarters' following Sir Richard Wilson's review, although the review was completely silent about intergovernmental relations, either in Europe or within a devolved UK. More forgivably the review was also silent about the key ingredient necessary to strengthen the Cabinet Office, which is a strong ministerial lead. Cabinet and Cabinet committees have been weakened, under this administration as under its predecessors, because so many decisions ultimately are taken by the Treasury or Number 10. (The network of Cabinet committees supervising the constitutional reform programme and chaired by the Lord Chancellor is an exception to this: in the first year it was one of the few functional parts of the new Cabinet committee structure, holding frequent meetings with lively discussion).

What a stronger Cabinet Office would require is a strong set of Cabinet Office Ministers. Officials cannot operate without ministerial cover; a more proactive Constitution Secretariat would require a strong ministerial lead. This has come so far from the Lord Chancellor, whose role has been to chair all the

CRP committees, to lead the collective discussion which has helped to shape the policy, and to ensure that the programme as a whole achieves escape velocity. He could continue in this role, and seems likely to do so, since ministerial appointments are decided not simply for functional reasons, but by the Prime Minister endeavouring to achieve the best fit possible between the issues of principle, politics and personality that confront him. But in terms of the practicalities, it may become increasingly difficult for the Lord Chancellor to combine leading the constitutional reform programme with his other functions, and the demands of his department. Implementation of constitutional reform, and the conduct of intergovernmental relations may find its natural home in the Cabinet Ofice; but Cabinet Office Ministers have generally been low profile, and tend to be low in the Cabinet rank order.[18] The demands of the constitutional reform programme and a stronger Cabinet Office may require more non-departmental Ministers, and more senior ones, whose main functions would be to chair Cabinet committees, to conduct inter-governmental relations, and to handle inter-party negotiations with coalition partners.

CONCLUSION: IMPLICATIONS FOR THE CIVIL SERVICE

The conventions of a permanent, anonymous and apolitical service operating in a confidential relationship with whichever Government is in power have themselves been the product of a particular constitutional arrangement. The more that arrangement is altered, the more the conventions themselves come under stress. We have already noted how the unified civil service is likely to divide into a separate civil service in Scotland and Wales, similar to the Northern Ireland Civil Service. And in terms of the conventions mentioned above, civil servants no longer enjoy security of tenure; they are more in the public eye, in front of parliamentary committees and elsewhere; and as their role as negotiators increases, Ministers are likely increasingly to insist upon appointing officials in whom they have confidence.

In terms of workload, devolution and the other constitutional changes will initially increase the burdens on the civil service rather than lighten them. Intergovernmental relations will require more negotiation and meetings with the devolved administrations than currently take place under the Whitehall umbrella. ECHR will require a more deliberative and consultative policy process and will result in more litigation. So to a lesser extent will freedom of information. Coalition government will require more consultation. A more effective Parliament will increase the demands on the executive for information and will apply closer scrutiny to the legislative process. All these additional

---

[18] David Clark was not untypical in being ranked at number 20 in a Cabinet of 22. His successor Jack Cunningham ranks much higher at number 9.

demands will amount to a fundamental shift in the way that Whitehall works, and should provide the wider context for Sir Richard Wilson's next review.

9

Intergovernmental Relations in a Devolved United Kingdom: Making Devolution Work

RICHARD CORNES

Andrew Welsh MP: 'There will presumably be a need for co-operation between the Executive in Edinburgh and the Executive in London. One of our witnesses said that "the mechanisms which will facilitate Scottish–UK co-ordination are unclear". Would you agree?'

Henry McLeish MP (Minister for Home Affairs and Devolution, Scottish Office) : 'I would not agree that they are unclear, but I would accept that further work needs to be done ....'.

Minutes of evidence from the Scottish Affairs Select Committee, 1 July 1998.

INTRODUCTION

This chapter sketches the outline of what will be a significant new aspect of the study of government in the United Kingdom. In federal states intergovernmental relations refers to the interactions between the component governments. The topic is a separate discipline within law and politics. In Australia intergovernmental relations have been described as:

a major and intricate area of governmental activity ... [affecting] almost all operations of government. [They use] a wide and expanding variety of mechanisms ... [and are in] a constant state of flux, in the face of changing attitudes and practices of governments.[1]

A federal system highlights the interactions between component governments. The United Kingdom is a union state. A union state is a 'pact or compact, which since the parties [the constituent states or nations], have generally acceded on different terms, is often asymmetrical in origin'.[2] It is by

---

[1] Saunders, C. 'Constitutional and Legal Aspects' in *Intergovernmental Relations and Public Policy*, Galligan, B., Hughes, O. and Walsh, C., (eds) (Sydney: Allen & Unwin, 1991), 39, 54.

[2] Keating, M., 'What's wrong with Asymmetrical Government?', paper to Newcastle Conference, (February 1997); and *Nations Against the State* (1996).

definition made up of constituent nations; analogous to the component governments of a federation. The relationships established as a result of devolution, while not involving handing over absolute legal sovereignty over subject areas as in a federal system, do involve the handing over of effective political sovereignty. This is something which Westminster could only take back 'under pathological circumstances'.[3]

Devolution in the UK builds on the logic of a union state in order to accommodate the different nations and interests which constitute it. The devolution programme launched in September 1997 with the referendums in Scotland and Wales will progressively remove the unitary veil from the UK's union structure to make explicit the quasi-federal relationships between Westminster and the new governments in Belfast, Edinburgh, Cardiff, and in time possibly other English regions and major cities. Much of what is currently internalized within Whitehall consultative processes will be externalized in intergovernmental processes post devolution.

Previous research on intergovernmental relations in the UK has focused on territorial and local government issues in the context of a unitary state.[4] In the future, intergovernmental relations will take in a range of mechanisms from informal contacts between officials of the different governments, high profile summit meetings of the first ministers, equally high profile disputes between Westminster and devolved governments, to judicial challenges in which the senior law officers of UK governments[5] will argue against each other in the Privy Council and other courts. There will also be a new variety of agreements between UK governments, from political compacts to documents giving rise to enforceable legal obligations.

This chapter takes the position that devolution is establishing mainly shared, rather then divided competencies between Westminster and the devolved governments. This is clearly the case in Wales, where the Welsh Assembly will operate within a policy and legislative framework set by Westminster. It is less self-evident in the case of Scotland and Northern Ireland, which will have significant devolved legislative powers; but the legislative powers devolved down to the Scottish Parliament overlap significantly with the powers passed upwards in successive Treaties to the EC (agriculture, fisheries, industry, economic development, training, environmental protection, etc.). The UK Government will need to maintain residual executive competence in these subject areas in order to ensure compliance with EC obligations and to

---

[3] Bogdanor, V., 'Devolution: the Constitutional Aspects', in *Constitutional Reform in the United Kingdom: Practice and Principles* (Oxford: Hart Publishing, 1998), 12.

[4] e.g. Rose, R., *Understanding the United Kingdom: The Territorial Dimension to Government* (Harlow: Longman, 1982).

[5] 'UK governments' is used here to refer to all the governments (including Westminster) of UK post devolution: i.e. the Scottish Executive, Welsh Executive and Northern Ireland Executive.

represent British (including Scottish) interests at Brussels. The reality will be
that the UK Government retains a concurrent interest in many of the devolved
policy areas. Concurrency makes it imperative that effective intergovernmental
relations are established to avoid unnecessary overlap and duplication, and
destructive competition between governments.

Intergovernmental mechanisms are for the most part sub-constitutional. If
they are well designed they will help secure the working of the devolution
settlement over time. If they are inadequate, competition between the UK
governments could destabilize and ultimately threaten the remodelled Union.
The need to address intergovernmental relations was foreshadowed in the
Constitution Unit's first Briefing on devolution in June 1996:

For devolution to work it needs to be underpinned by co-operative machinery as well as
political will. The official level machinery should help maintain effective working
between central government and the devolved assemblies when the politics is under
strain. Whitehall will need to maintain the same level of contact with the devolved
assemblies as it currently does with the Scottish and Welsh Office and the Government
Offices for the Regions.[6]

The UK is not entirely unused to formalized intergovernmental processes. It
has dealt with them in the European Union (EU) from the summitry of Council
of Ministers' meetings to the technical discussions of official working groups.
The European Union, in addition to federal countries such as Australia,
Germany and Canada, will be a useful sphere to look to for comparative
guidance in designing intergovernmental arrangements within the UK over the
next decade.

In this chapter the Commonwealth of Australia is used as the primary
comparative touchstone, although reference is also made to Canada and
Germany. While Australia differs from the UK in population size and the
symmetrical nature of its constitutional arrangements, the powers of the states
are broadly similar to those devolved to Scotland in the Scotland Act 1998.
Further, one of the key driving themes in Australia, the fiscal dominance of the
federal centre, is likely to be mirrored in the UK where the devolved
governments will have no or very limited power of revenue raising.[7]

---

[6] Constitution Unit, Briefing: *Devolution in the Round*, June 1996, 3.

[7] The split in Australia of revenue raised is approximately 80 per cent Commonwealth, 20 per cent
states, while the approximate outlays are 51 per cent Commonwealth and 44 per cent the states. For
further discussion of devolution and fiscal matters, see Ch. 11.

COMPARATIVE STUDY—INTERGOVERNMENTAL RELATIONS IN AUSTRALIA
AND CANADA

Australian Intergovernmental Relations

The Commonwealth[8] of Australia, now comprising six states and two mainland
territories, was formed in 1901. Power is divided between state and federal
governments in the Constitution. The two mainland territories operate under
self government Acts, with powers like the states, but importantly (and
similarly to Scotland under the Scotland Act 1998 in relation to Westminster),
remain under the ultimate control of the federal Parliament in Canberra, which
can override any law the territories pass. In respect of the division of powers
between the federal Government and the states, specific powers are allocated to
the Commonwealth, with the residue being left to the states (as in the Scotland
Act 1998, which defines the powers reserved to Westminster, leaving all the
remainder to Scotland). There are also a limited number of exclusive
Commonwealth powers. Most of the Commonwealth's powers are exercisable
concurrently with the states; where there is inconsistency Section 109 of the
Constitution provides that the Commonwealth law prevails. The arbiter of
disagreements between governments is the High Court of Australia, which sits
at the apex of the Australian court system, and is the final court of appeal from
both state and federal courts.

To manage the relations between the federal and state governments there is
an elaborate network of conferences, councils and committees which is
summarized in Figure 9.1.

Figure 9.1. Australian intergovernmental institutions

- **Council of Australian Governments (COAG)**
Attended by the prime minister, the premiers of the states, the chief ministers of the
territories
Meets twice a year
A summit forum including all levels of Government attended also by President of the
Australian Local Government Association
- **Ministerial Councils**
Microcosm of the Premiers' Conference process
16 Ministerial Councils covering each subject area, e.g. the education Ministerial
Council is attended by education ministers
Mixture of politics and administration
- **Committees of Officials**
Made up of subject area officials from federal and state governments

---

[8] The term 'the Commonwealth' is also used in Australia to mean the federal government.

Meet more frequently than political bodies
Underpin the political bodies
- **Loan Council**
Established in 1927, the only intergovernmental body with constitutional status:
Section 105A of the Australian Constitution
Attended by ministers backed up by officials
Co-ordinates loan raising and servicing for Australian governments
Meets in secret
Decisions not reviewed by either federal or state governments
- **Commonwealth Grants Commission**
A Commonwealth body—not strictly an intergovernmental forum, but its deliberations
play a major part in financial intergovernmental negotiations
Not itself a ministerial council
Advises on the allocation of federal government funds between the states and territories
Works out the equalisation formulas for distribution of funds across the federation to
achieve equity between rich and poor states, sparsely populated and more heavily
populated

Other intergovernmental mechanisms in Australia include: co-operative
uniform legislation; intergovernmental agreements, varying from those ratified
in legislation, included in legislative schedules, authorized by legislation, or
just tabled in parliaments; joint administrative bodies; and *ad hoc* meetings of
ministers and of officials.

Fiscal Matters

Fiscal matters have dominated Australian intergovernmental relations. The
states in effect have very little revenue-raising power. The Commonwealth
stands as the tax collector, distributing revenue to the states.[9] The nature of the
transfers has '... [see-sawed] throughout Australian federal history ...'[10] from
general purpose grants to specific-purpose grants. Specific-purpose grants are
resented by the states because of the tight policy control retained by the federal
government; and because of the uniform regime which the federal government
seeks to maintain. In response to these concerns there has arisen increasingly
complex intergovernmental machinery in relation to specific-purpose grants
with overtones of subsidiarity; for example, while a range of governments may
participate in a programme, their roles may differ, the Commonwealth
providing broad policy guidelines with the states dealing with the detailed
managerial issues.[11]

---

[9] See above at note 7, and Ch. 11 for discussion of fiscal issues.

[10] Saunders, C., 'Constitutional and Legal Aspects' in *Intergovernmental Relations and Public Policy*, Galligan, B., Hughes, O. and Walsh, C., (eds) (Sydney: Allen & Unwin, 1991), 44.

[11] See discussion of the Supported Accommodation Assistance Programme in Saunders, note 10 above, 45.

The Commonwealth Government elected in March 1996 has pursued a policy of off-loading spending responsibilities to the states, without a consequent increase in fiscal transfers to the states. It is not uncommon for grant allocations to the States to be used as a 'balancing item' in the federal budget. The rhetoric of reducing Commonwealth involvement in 'states' affairs' can be used as one way of justifying reducing Commonwealth spending. This pressures states either to reduce services or find new revenue sources.

The following article (Figure 9.2.) from the national newspaper *The Australian* shows the sort of headlines to be expected over funding issues. The article concerns the Australian Medicare system, under which, with funds provided by the federal government, the states and territories provide health care.

Figure 9.2. 'Premier hopeful on health funding' *The Australian,* 11 June 1998[12]

A BREAKTHROUGH in the Medicare agreement row loomed last night after Victorian Premier Jeff Kennett predicted its resolution within weeks. But the development appeared to come too late for Victoria, NSW [New South Wales] and three other State and Territory governments holding out for extra funding to share in a $120 million bonus to slash hospital waiting lists. A deadline to get a share of the bonus expired last night with Queensland and the ACT [Australian Capital Territory] the only governments who have signed the agreement expected to share it. The Queensland Government, just days away from an election, is expected to get a windfall of $103.5 million, enough to perform 34,000 operations. The ACT will get the remaining $16.5 million. Hours before the bonus deadline, Mr Kennett revealed there had been a breakthrough in negotiations over the new funding deal. Mr Kennett said that to discuss details might jeopardize the talks, but he conceded the new arrangements fell short of the States' original demands. The States, which have until June 30 before the current agreement expires, are seeking an extra $5.5 billion over the five-year term of the new agreement, but the Commonwealth has offered only an extra $2.9 billion.

Enforceability of Agreements

Section 96 of the Constitution gives the Commonwealth the power to grant money to the states on such terms and conditions as it sees fit. While the terms of the Section have contractual overtones the High Court has held that Section 96 grants are voluntary, meaning that legally the federal Government may not be able to insist that states spend a specific-purpose grant on the purpose for which it was given.[13] The enforceability question arises in the other direction as well, if a state were to seek enforcement of payment of a grant.

[12] Hawes, R., Bachelard, M. and Kerin, J., *The Australian,* 11 June 1998.
[13] *Second Uniform Tax* case (1957) 99 Commonwealth Law Reports 575.

The issue has given rise to intricate legal debate, which will not be traversed in detail here;[14] it is notable though that an uncertainty arising from the legal formulation of the federal structure could remain controversial for a century after federation was achieved in 1901.

The legal answers to the enforceability of agreements between governments generally have been sought in two areas of law: public law and contract. The High Court of Australia dealt with the justiciability and enforceability of an intergovernmental agreement in 1962, and showed the court's reluctance to get involved:

the true substance of the agreement is that of a political arrangement defining the 'broad outlines of an administrative and financial scheme' of co-operation between governments and not of a definitive contract enforceable at law ...[15]

Accountability

A second theme is the impact of intergovernmental relations on parliamentary government and accountability. In Australia the issues have been:

- the paucity of information about the operation of intergovernmental relations, from the workings of ministerial councils, and conditions of grants to the detail of intergovernmental agreements;
- executive dominance of intergovernmental relations has sidelined parliamentary involvement and scrutiny;
- the dominance of the Commonwealth has meant, from a logistical point of view, that while the federal cabinet may discuss matters going to ministerial councils, the state cabinets have often been sidelined.

There are strong resemblances here to the debate about the democratic deficit in Europe. If the devolved assemblies and cabinets want to play a part in intergovernmental relations in the UK they will need to assert from the start the need for an effective flow of information and the right to be consulted in advance of intergovernmental meetings: exactly the same issues which have concerned the Westminster parliament in relation to meetings of the EU Council of Ministers (see Chapter 7).

Judicial Review

The provisions of the Australian legal system mean that only the general themes are of interest for the UK. First, issues arise as to the reviewability of

[14] See Saunders, C., 'Towards a Theory of Section 96: Part I', 16 *Melbourne University Law Review* (1987), 1; and Saunders, C., 'Towards a Theory of Section 96: Part II', 16 *Melbourne Medical University Law Review* (1988), 699.

[15] *Railway Standardisation* case: *South Australia* v. *Commonwealth* [1962] 108 Commonwealth Law Reports 130, 409.

decisions, of the decision maker in question and standing to seek review. Will third parties with an interest for instance in a grant agreement between the UK and the Scottish governments have a legitimate expectation such as to give rise to a right to be heard in relation to decisions under the grant agreement? In some cases governments have specifically sought to exclude certain intergovernmental arrangements from review, mostly for reasons of comity and avoiding the review by one level of government of the actions of another. In other cases there is acceptance of the need for review, and of the need for the reviewing body to have full jurisdiction. This arises not simply in relation to courts and tribunals, but also to ombudsmen: co-operative schemes have developed between Australian ombudsmen at State and Commonwealth levels.

Role of the High Court of Australia

From the beginning of the federation, cases decided by the High Court (Australia's Supreme Court) have highlighted the court's importance as ultimate referee between the states and the Commonwealth, and the important part played by the judges appointed to the High Court. The Commonwealth Attorney-General consults with his or her state counterparts prior to the appointment of High Court Justices, and since 1978 this has been a statutory requirement. But a number of states are still not satisfied, and some Premiers have called for a more formalized part in the process, including the possibility of a number of appointments being handed over to the states.

International Pressures

Increasing interaction between the domestic and international spheres, with domestic policy being strongly driven by international law in some areas has challenged the balance of power within the federation. In the *Tasmanian Dam*[16] case the High Court held that the Commonwealth's power in respect of external affairs included the power to legislate to implement international obligations within Australia. This included subject areas within the jurisdiction of the states; so that the federal government's responsibility for international relations can lead it to legislate on matters which are the responsibility of the states. Here too there are parallels with the UK membership of the EU, which will require the UK Government to enforce EU obligations even in devolved subject areas.

---

[16] *Commonwealth* v. *Tasmania, Tasmanian Dam* case (1983) 158 Commonwealth Law Reports, 1.

INTERGOVERNMENTAL RELATIONS IN CANADA

No minister in Canberra is specifically charged with the conduct of intergovernmental relations. This is one of the main differences in the institutional structure in Canada, where there is a special department in Ottawa to deal with intergovernmental matters, and similar departments in a number of the provincial governments. The federal department is headed by a minister of intergovernmental affairs. Figure 9.3. gives an introduction to the federal Department of Intergovernmental Affairs, extracted from the Canadian Government website.

Figure 9.3. The Canadian Department of Intergovernmental Affairs

Mandate

The Department of Intergovernmental Affairs is responsible for the management of federal–provincial relations. These are the ties that the federal Government maintains with the provinces and territories concerning all matters of federal–provincial significance.

The Department supports the Prime Minister and the Minister of Intergovernmental Affairs and works closely with other federal and provincial departments and the territorial governments to cover a variety of areas in which the federal Government, the provinces and the territories are involved. Areas dealt with include health and social programs, and agreements between the federal Government and one or more provinces, or constitutional issues.

In the constitutional field, Intergovernmental Affairs provides analysis and advice on constitutional and legal issues relating to national unity and the evolution of the Canadian federation.

Intergovernmental Affairs also has a mandate to co-ordinate the federal government's efforts to improve the federation and make it more efficient, by reducing overlap and duplication and eliminating inefficient administrative practices.

Organisational Structure

The Department has four secretariats:

Policy and Research: produces action plans, research reports and general advice on the conduct of intergovernmental relations. It is responsible for developing scenarios to guide the Prime Minister, the Minister of Intergovernmental Affairs and the Cabinet in decision-making, research on issues related to the evolution of the federation and national unity, and assessment of constitutional and legal issues which may affect relations between the federal Government and the provinces and territories.

Intergovernmental Communications: responsible for providing advice on the intergovernmental aspects of Government-wide communications activities and programs. It is also responsible for aspects of communication that concern intergovernmental relations, and supports the communication activities of the Minister of Intergovernmental Affairs. It also co-ordinates the federal government's communication efforts with respect to objectives relating to national unity.

Federal–Provincial Relations: provides advice to the Prime Minister and the Minister of Intergovernmental Affairs on the overall management of federal–provincial relations. It monitors and tracks social and economic developments in the provinces and territories and any other issues affecting the federation. It also has a lead role in the preparation and management of bilateral and multilateral meetings of first ministers and intergovernmental affairs ministers. The Secretariat also provides advice to make the federation more efficient, reduce overlap and duplication of services and programs between the federal Government and the provinces, and clarify the roles and responsibilities of each order of Government.

Aboriginal Affairs : provides advice and support on Aboriginal constitutional matters. It co-ordinates intergovernmental consultations on federal policy development and relations with Aboriginal associations. It also participates in tripartite self-Government negotiations by supporting the minister designated as the interlocutor for Métis and non-status Indians.

Intergovernmental Mechanisms

Liaison between intergovernmental affairs officials in each province
First ministers' conferences
Intergovernmental conferences of ministers and deputy ministers
Regional conferences

These conferences and informal exchanges have led to the signing of agreements, such as:

The Agreement on Internal Trade, the National Infrastructure Program (national agreements).
Canada-Quebec Economic and Regional Development Agreements—ERDAs (bilateral agreements).
The agreement on Improving the Efficiency of the Federation Initiative (IEFI).
Agreement on interprovincial trade among the Atlantic provinces (multilateral agreements).

Source: http://www.pco-bcp.gc.ca/aia

INTERGOVERNMENTAL RELATIONS IN A DEVOLVED UK

Introduction

Devolution, and the way it will build on the Union structure, is for the UK what
the structure of federalism is for Australia, Canada and the United States; it
provides the constitutional framework for the emergence and articulation of
intergovernmental relations. But the structures and processes will not be
prescribed by law: they will develop as and when the need arises. And it is
particularly difficult to forecast the machinery required to sustain a rolling
programme of devolution, in which the list of political actors is open-ended and
the devolution settlement is asymmetrical.

What will intergovernmental relations in the UK look like in ten years time?
To bring out the essential features they can be broken into four elements:

- actors
- subject matter
- structure and processes
- dispute resolution.

Actors

The main actors will be the political leaders of the UK, Scotland, Wales,
Northern Ireland. They are first in the field and represent three out of the four
nations in the Union. But they may be joined in time by the leaders of one or
more regional assemblies in England, and possibly by the Mayor of London and
of some of the other major cities. Whether the municipal leaders are included
depends on which form of devolution wins out in the English regions:[17] they
may be included in some intergovernmental forums but not in others (as in the
Council of Australian Governments, which is attended by the President of the
Australian Local Government Association).

The legislatures and devolved assemblies are unlikely to play much of a
role. Intergovernmental relations is precisely that: a relationship between
governments and not between parliaments. As we have seen, Australian
intergovernmental relations is marked by executive dominance, with the federal
cabinet in particular playing a central role in agenda setting. Given that much
of the day to day operations of intergovernmental relations concern policy
implementation, which will take place between civil servants, there will be an
ongoing operational link between the governments in the executive arena. The
stronger the devolved legislatures are, the more pressure there may be for
legislative involvement; but it is hard to see what form this might take, except

[17] See Ch. 3 on devolution.

possibly through reform of the House of Lords in which devolved assemblies gained representation in the second chamber.[18]

An embryonic proposal for interlegislative bodies may arise in connection with the proposed British-Irish Council (a body representing the governments of Ireland, the UK, Scotland, Wales, Northern Ireland, the Channel Islands and the Isle of Man). Comparison has been made to the Nordic Council, but its evolution was very different. The Nordic Council began as an inter-parliamentary body in the 1950s (not unlike the British-Irish Inter-parliamentary Body); and only developed an intergovernmental Council of Ministers twenty years later.[19] But the proposal in the 1998 Belfast Agreement is the other way round. The British-Irish Council is primarily intended to be an intergovernmental executive body. For the next decade at least, UK intergovernmental relations are likely to be dominated by executives. This is a familiar pattern in other federal systems which also have parliamentary government, with its associated characteristic of an executive dominated parliament.

Subject Matter: Shared not Divided Competencies

Despite the division of legislative competence which devolution entails, it is inevitable for there to be a significant degree of policy-making overlap between various levels of government in the UK. This is implicitly recognized in the Concordats being drafted during the passage of the devolution legislation in 1998 to regulate relations between Whitehall departments and the devolved governments. A conceptual framework for the Concordats could be strengthened by understanding the theory and the practice of concurrent and co-ordinate federalism. Classical federal theory[20] has characterized as ideal the co-ordinate model according to which each level of government has a quite separate area of responsibility, with very little overlap with any other level of government. Some recent observers of federalism argue that policy overlap is inevitable, and may even be beneficial. Concurrent federalism accepts that the federal and lower level governments will need to act in the same policy areas, but may carry out different functions: for example, the federal Government may set standards and the state governments implement them as they see fit (there are parallels between such framework legislation and the operation of EU Directives). While a pure co-ordinate model may not be feasible, it may assist in encouraging clear divisions of roles within policy areas. It may be that a more sophisticated approach is now required, which draws on co-ordinate theory to guide division of responsibilities within subject areas. The necessity

[18] See chs. 2 and 7.

[19] See the Constitution Unit, *The Nordic Council and the Council of the Isles* (October 1998).

[20] Sir Kenneth Wheare, *Federal Government* (London: Royal Institute of International Affairs, 1963).

of coping with policy making and implementation across several different levels of government is clearly the reality in a number of different fields, of which environmental policy is a good example, and one discussed further in Chapter 10.

The listing of reserved and devolved powers in, for example, the Scotland Act 1998 appears to follow a purely co-ordinate model. And while at least initially there may be political mileage for Scottish political parties in characterizing the Act in this way, it is misleading and mistaken to ignore the likelihood of concurrence once the system is operating. Overlap will still occur for a number of reasons:

- As important as reserved and devolved *legislative* powers is the division of *executive* powers. Here the UK Government retains huge responsibilities as the executive Government for England. Many of its decisions in relation to England will have knock-on consequences for the rest of the UK (especially in finance: see Chapter 11).
- The UK Government's EU responsibilities will require it to intrude upon the devolved subject areas in fields like agriculture, fisheries, industry, economic development, the environment, etc. In relation to EU matters there will be a complicated web of relations to manage between the devolved governments, territorial Secretaries of State, UK Government, UKREP and representation in the Council of Ministers.
- Other international obligations outside the EU (e.g. the UN Convention on Climate Change) will also intrude upon devolved subject areas, but it will be for the UK Government to ensure compliance.
- The UK Government's fiscal dominance and the constraints of the Barnett formula may mean devolved governments simply cannot afford significant policy variance from the central government position.

In legal terms Westminster retains the legal power to act directly in all subject areas.[21] In addition, as a result of the EU and foreign affairs power, the UK Government may act indirectly in devolved subject areas by entering into international obligations which it will have an international responsibility to implement. This leaves the way open for the same sort of intervention as occurred in the *Tasmanian Dam* case.[22] In respect of European Union obligations the UK Government cannot plead inability to implement an EU law

---

[21]For example, Section 27(7) of the Scotland Act 1998 makes explicit Westminster's residual power to make laws for Scotland.

[22] *Commonwealth* v. *Tasmania, Tasmanian Dam* case (1983) 158 Commonwealth Law Reports, 1.

on grounds that the EU law covers matters falling within a devolved government's competence.[23]

Concurrency will be even more evident in the executive model of devolution to be implemented in Wales. The Government of Wales Act 1998 sets in place a legislative process in which both Westminster and the Welsh Assembly will always play a part in legislative policy making, as Westminster passes the primary legislation under which the Assembly will then make secondary legislation. If this is to amount to more than Westminster dictating policy to Wales, it will be necessary for the UK Government and Welsh Executive to negotiate and co-operate over policy direction before Westminster legislates.

The Courts and Division of Subject Areas

The courts, and ultimately the Privy Council will have a central role in interpreting the devolution settlement; and in adjusting it in the light of changing circumstances and changing political values. This may go further than purely marginal adjustment: in the first century of the Canadian federation a series of decisions by the Privy Council in London turned the intended division of powers between the federal and provincial governments on its head.[24] The other court which may have some influence is the European Court of Justice. The European Court of Justice has jurisdiction in relation to Community law in every part of a member state, including devolved constituent elements. In the light of the ECJ's decision in *Commission* v. *Belgium* it will be necessary to put in place appropriate consultative machinery to ensure that a devolved government or assembly takes whatever action is necessary to implement Community law.[25] This is all the more necessary given the possibility of damages against a member state for breach of EU law, including failure to implement a directive.[26]

Structures and Process

The devolution Acts themselves, and the transfer orders which may accompany them, will provide the basic framework documents for the structures of intergovernmental relations—much as a written constitution divides competencies between levels of government in a federal country. But the

---

[23] *Commission* v. *Belgium* case 77/69 [1970] ECR 237, [1974] 1 CMLR 203.

[24] Zines, L., *Constitutional Change in the Commonwealth* (Cambridge: Cambridge University Press, 1991), ch. 3.

[25] On the consultative process concerning negotiation of EU matters and implementation of EU directives and liability for failure to implement EU obligations, see *Scotland's Parliament,* July 1998, (Cm 3658) ch. 5, paras 5.4 and 5.8 especially.

[26] *Francovich* v. *Italy* c–6/90 and c–9/90 [1991] ECR I 5357, [1993] 2 CMLR 66. In the Scottish White Paper the Government indicates that any penalties against the UK attributable to the conduct of the Scottish Administration will be paid for by the Scottish Administration (Cm 3658) para. 5.8.

legislation is silent about the machinery which will be required to make the intergovernmental arrangements work. The following are likely to feature amongst the mechanisms which will be required to ensure co-ordination and co-operation between the different levels of government in the UK.

Summit Conferences: First Ministers' conferences, which would be attended by at least the UK Prime Minister, the Scottish, Welsh and the Northern Irish First and Deputy First Ministers, and possibly the leaders of English regional assemblies and the elected mayors of the chief cities. In circumstances of political and constitutional flux these summits will be crucial. The impetus for such summitry will come from two directions. First, the political opportunities the occasion affords the assembled leaders, who can use the occasion to play to their 'domestic' audience in the way a Prime Minister may when attending world leaders' summits. Second, and more practically, such occasions provide a forum for the leaders to negotiate political settlements to issues between their governments which require solution by political, rather than policy bargaining; and to trade off one issue against another. This latter point also has its international comparisons: one use of the summit process being to allow for personal dealing between leaders, of the kind which cannot occur between lower level politicians or civil servants who lack the authority to strike one deal against another.

Ministerial Councils: In addition to the summitry of the First Ministers' conferences there may also emerge specialist meetings of ministers within particular subject areas: for example, health, the environment, education, etc.

Officials' Meetings: The Ministerial Councils are likely in turn to be mirrored by links between the civil servants from the subject departments.

Territorial Grants Commission: If the Barnett Formula collapses (see Chapter 11) new machinery may be required to devise a new formula and to monitor its operation.

British-Irish Council: A British-Irish Council, arising from the Belfast Agreement, might potentially be a useful body for negotiation between UK governments in respect of EU negotiations; especially where Ireland is similarly affected and might support the British line. The Nordic Council of Ministers has been used in this way since the accession of Finland and Sweden to the EU, to agree a common Nordic line in advance of EU meetings. But the British-Irish Council may also prove to be a forum in which the devolved governments make common cause against the British Government: for example, the Welsh, Northern Ireland and Irish Governments might combine to raise the question of nuclear waste in the Irish sea.

Inter-Parliamentary Links: The Nordic Council began as an inter-parliamentary body, and the interparliamentary Assembly is still the source of most Nordic Council initiatives. That is unlikely to happen in the UK, because the British-Irish Council is intended to be an intergovernmental executive body. But the Belfast Agreement envisages the establishment of some kind of inter-parliamentary body, stating that:

the elected institutions of the members [i.e. the assemblies] will be encouraged to develop inter-parliamentary links, perhaps building on the British-Irish Inter-Parliamentary Body.[27]

How such links might develop will depend initially upon whether the British-Irish Inter-Parliamentary Body invites members of the devolved assemblies to join it in an expanded Inter-Parliamentary Body. It might then include parliamentarians from two nation states (the UK and Ireland), three devolved assemblies (Scotland, Wales and Northern Ireland) and three Crown dependencies (the Isle of Man and the States of Jersey and Guernsey). The effectiveness of such a varied membership will depend on the leadership of the new body (crucial in the early years of the Nordic Council, which owed much to the vision of two men); the seniority of the parliamentarians who decide to join it; the subjects which they choose to focus on; and the attention paid by member governments to the body's debates and resolutions.

Co-operative Legislation: Where there are areas of subject overlap, or simply because it is convenient to adopt common standards across the Union, uniform legislative schemes may be adopted. These could be implemented by negotiation over a common text passed by one parliament and copied by the others, or the UK could look to the example of the directive in EU law, variants of which are also found in Germany and Spain.

The alternative to each parliament passing a common text would be for Westminster to enact uniform legislation for the whole country. It might adopt the form of a directive to enact framework legislation, leaving the means by which the legislation is implemented to the devolved governments. This might be particularly suitable in the case of international obligations (for example, a new convention on environmental standards, or child kidnapping) where all parts of the UK have to comply.

But it might also occur in domestic situations where all parts of the UK see the need for uniform legislation in a devolved subject area. Westminster still retains the legal power to legislate in devolved subjects, although politically it might choose to do so only at the invitation of the devolved governments. In such cases the devolved assemblies would save themselves the trouble of

[27] Belfast Agreement (Cm 3883) April 1998, Strand Three, Section 2.

legislating separately, and would in effect be pooling their legislative powers upwards to Westminster. They would be using the Westminster Parliament in the same way that the German Länder use the Bundesrat to come together and agree on uniform legislation, which they then enact not individually through their state parliaments but collectively through the federal Parliament (see Figure 9.4).

Figure 9.4. German intergovernmental relations[28]

The German federal system is characterized by interwoven institutions and overlapping competencies. The *Grundgesetz* (GG) gives the states the right to legislate, except when the powers are conferred on the Federation (GG Art. 70.1). The areas of legislative competence are divided into three categories; those where the federation has exclusive responsibility; those where the two levels have concurrent responsibility; and those where the Länder have exclusive legislative responsibility.

In certain areas the central government legislates in a manner similar to the European Union directive system. The federal minister drafts the Rahmegesetz (framework legislation) which is subsequently presented to a conference of Länder-ministers in the Bundesrat (the second chamber where the governments of the Länder are represented by the relevant ministers). The ministerkonferenz meets regularly in order to maintain a degree of unity in the areas regulated by framework legislation. As the Bundesrat is made up of representatives of state governments it is in effect an intergovernmental forum itself.

Division of legislative responsibilities in Germany

Federation (Bund)	Concurrent legislative responsibility	States (Länder)
Foreign affairs	Civil law	Culture
Defence	Criminal law	Broadcasting
Citizenship	Residence of aliens	Police
Currency	Nuclear energy	Health
Customs and trade	Law of association	
Post and telecoms	and assembly[29]	
Framework legislation		
Higher education		
Hunting		
Nature conservation		
Regional planning		

---

[28] My thanks to Mads Qvortrup for providing the information on which this table is based.

[29] Based on Laufer, H., *Das föderative System in der BRD* (Munich: Bayerische Landeszentrale für politische Bildungsarbeit, 1991).

Dispute Resolution

Experience in federal systems provides some guidance as to the types of dispute which might arise in the UK in relation to intergovernmental relations. Disputes will range from those which are primarily political and are played out solely in the realm of politics, through to those which result in judicial challenges, ultimately decided by either the Privy Council or the House of Lords. Disputes may arise in the following areas.

- **Finance:** quarrels over the total amount of funds transferred from central government to devolved governments, the methods used to work out changes to the annual block grants (see Chapter 11), and in time, challenges to central government's fiscal dominance as the primary revenue collector.

- **Enforceability of Concordats:** will the Concordats between Westminster and devolved governments, or between devolved governments themselves be enforceable as if they were a contract? They declare they are simply political documents with no legally enforceable obligations. In time something firmer may be required.

- **Rights under Intergovernmental Agreements (including Concordats):** if intergovernmental agreements are held to be enforceable in a particular case, who will have rights under them? Just the parties to the agreement? Or will third parties also have rights against a Government that fails to carry out its obligations under the agreement?

- **Foreign Affairs Negotiations:** what position the UK should take in international negotiations (including the EU), and the process by which the UK enters into international obligations, and then enforces them, especially in devolved subject areas.

- **The Right to Secede:** this will be a political question played out largely in the political arena; but there could be forays into the courts. If in time the Scottish National Party seeks to hold a referendum in Scotland on the issue of Scottish independence, there could be legal challenges to the validity of the referendum, and to the significance of the result. The Scotland Act clearly reserves constitutional issues to Westminster: the Scottish Parliament could not unilaterally declare independence. But it could probe the issue, or use litigation to make a political statement, or to throw down a challenge—as happened in the 1998 case brought before the Canadian

Supreme Court about the capacity of Quebec to secede without the assent of the rest of Canada.[30]

Mechanisms for Dispute Resolution

There are two main, formal types of dispute resolution mechanisms which may emerge, and one informal. First there are all the intergovernmental structures described above, which should allow for early warning systems, consultation and a range of political fora for compromising and resolving disputes. Only if these fail will the second, judicial mechanism come into play, with reference to the courts and the Privy Council as the final arbiter of devolution disputes.

Two problems may be noted about the role of the Privy Council. First, it is likely that there will be a significant number of legal disputes over the powers of the devolved parliaments, particularly in the early years. Even if governments are inhibited in their challenges, third parties will not necessarily feel so restricted; and many challenges will be raised by lawyers as collateral arguments in the course of other litigation. Not all these cases will go to the Privy Council; but even a small increase in its case load could be difficult to manage, particularly if they are big cases requiring urgent resolution.

The second problem is the split at the apex of the judicial structure, with the House of Lords continuing as the general highest court of appeal and the Privy Council as the highest court in relation to devolution matters. The supreme court in a federal system has a central role to play in working out the operation of a federal, or in the UK's case a quasi-federal settlement. Cases will inevitably arise in which there are a range of issues, with devolution matters intermingled with other areas of law. The common-law tradition is for a unified supreme court at the apex of the judicial system, enjoying a general jurisdiction over constitutional and other areas of law. The proposed bifurcation at the apex of the UK court system may lead to division and a lack of coherence in the case law. Added to all this there is the European Court of Justice which itself may influence aspects of the devolution settlement.

The third, and informal, mechanism for resolving disputes lies in the dealings which occur within and between political parties and their leaders (see Chapter 6). This mechanism is likely to flow around the others, and in particular around the intergovernmental meetings of ministers and the summits of First Ministers. The political parties offer a further channel for resolving disputes without recourse to the formal machinery, and without exposing the details in public; but they are better suited to resolving low level disputes or issues of patronage than major intergovernmental disagreements.

---

[30] Reference re Secession of Quebec at www.scc-csc.gc.ca/reference/hn.htm and www.scc-csc.gc.cal/reference/rea.htm

THEMES

Diversity of Actors

The UK's asymmetrical devolution process will create an environment for intergovernmental relations unlike that in symmetrical federations. There will be a range of different actors in different parts of the Union, with varying powers:

- three assemblies with varying degrees of legislative power in Scotland, Wales and Northern Ireland;
- three devolved governments constituted in different ways, from Scotland's Cabinet to the Welsh Assembly's Executive Committee and Northern Ireland's power sharing Executive;
- nine Regional Development Agencies in England, with some regions hoping to have directly elected Regional Assemblies, and others Regional Chambers;
- potential competition from directly elected mayors in some of the larger cities;
- some intergovernmental bodies which embrace the whole of the British Isles, such as the new British-Irish Council and the British-Irish Inter-parliamentary Body.

Diversity of Authority

It may be necessary to accommodate for these different levels of authority in intergovernmental processes. For instance, in relation to a particular subject Scotland may have full competence to act, while Wales may need the acquiescence of Westminster. Should these differences be recognized in multilateral meetings? Should a lesser empowered government speak as an equal with other governments?

Diversity of Power Balances

Flowing from the diversity of actors and associated with the diversity of authority possessed by those actors, a diversity of power balances may also emerge within the actors themselves. The balance between executives and legislatures is not necessarily going to be uniform throughout the Union, especially if the different units have differing electoral systems, powers, or internal structures. Also, the power balances may shift over time as the devolution process evolves. The consequence of this is that intergovernmental processes will have to be sensitive to the reality of power balances, as well as the formal allocation of authority.

Diversity of Motives

Motives for devolution vary widely at the outset of the devolution process. But once the devolved bodies are established there is the prospect that they may band together as a negotiating force against central government in a similar way to the Australian states in relation to their federal government. In Australia the states tend to co-operate with each other in their negotiations with the federal Government, regardless of their political colour.

Trend to Openness?

The operation of intergovernmental relations will lead to greater openness, as the negotiating processes which currently take place between Whitehall departments become externalized. This will not be a side-effect of freedom of information: information about state–federal relations is exempt under the FOI regimes in Australia and Canada, and the same can be expected here. Rather it is a direct effect of devolution: greater openness will come about because the First Ministers will fight much more openly with the UK Government than in the past, when they were part of the same Government and bound by collective responsibility.

Tension Over Finance

As discussed in Chapter 11, retention of the Barnett formula, without a fresh needs assessment, is likely to give rise to tension between poorer areas of the UK which receive less government expenditure per capita than parts such as Scotland which do very well. As the formula falls further out of date there will be pressure to spend outside of the block grant process, which is likely to lead to a lively lobbying industry between the devolved governments, Whitehall and the English regions. These tensions will remain as long as the Treasury remains the dominant revenue raiser. They are inevitable in any redistributive system of grants equalization, but may be the more intractable in the absence of a fresh needs assessment to provide a more up-to-date baseline.

CONCLUSION

The devolution legislation is only the start of the process. It lays down the division of powers between London and the devolved governments, but says nothing about how those governments then manage their continuing relations. In many policy areas they will discover that, whatever their initial expectations, there is a degree of continuing overlap; and hence the need to develop consultative machinery to manage those overlapping responsibilities.

In this respect devolution closely resembles the division of powers in a federal system, and will require machinery to handle intergovernmental relations, as is found in federal states like Australia, Canada and Germany. Failure to establish sufficient machinery could threaten the whole devolution settlement. It will require a major rethink of the way Whitehall conducts its relations with the devolved administrations (see Chapter 8); it might even require a special Minister for Intergovernmental Relations, as is found in Canada but not elsewhere.

The structures and processes will be largely determined by the UK Government, which will still be the dominant player in ten years' time. Devolution in the UK starts as a top-down process in a highly centralized state, and Whitehall will not lose its authority overnight. It also retains most of the trump cards; it provides all the finance, it retains primary legislative responsibility for the whole of England and Wales, and it retains responsibility for the whole conduct of negotiations in the EU, which gives it a lead in to many of the devolved subject areas in Scotland and Northern Ireland. But it will have to come to terms with the need for extensive negotiation and consultation with the devolved governments, and put in place adequate machinery to enable that to happen: summit conferences of First Ministers, sectoral meetings of Ministers in different subject areas, regular meetings of their officials.

A sophisticated system of intergovernmental relations requires machinery at all these different levels. Even then not all will be smooth. There will inevitably be disputes, but conflict *per se* will not be a symptom of the system failing. Relationships between UK governments may range from healthy competition and co-operation to conflicts and destructive non-co-operation over the next decade. The intergovernmental structures put in place will be the mechanisms which ensure that the administrative processes keep turning even when the politics is under strain, and secure the working of the new Union.

10

The Environment and Constitutional Change

RICHARD MACRORY

This chapter considers one sector of policy, the environment, and its relationship to constitutional change in this country. The last twenty-five years have seen an extraordinary development in the politics of the environment. Major international environmental treaties have been negotiated, the national legal framework has changed beyond recognition, and there have been significant developments to the structures of UK administration responsible for the regulation and delivery of environmental policy. Membership of environmental organizations in the early 1990s exceeded the total membership of political parties. A number of the themes discussed in previous chapters, such as the development of legal rights to information and participation, and the principle of subsidiarity, were first played out on the environmental stage. Elements of constitutional changes now under way, including devolution, an enlarged European Union, and the incorporation of the European Convention on Human Rights can be expected to influence profoundly the context in which environmental policies are negotiated and developed in the future. Paradoxically, however, the environment appears to have played little part in providing the rationale for constitutional change or in shaping the proposals now being implemented. Two broad questions therefore need addressing. To what extent are the major proposals consistent with the administrative and policy developments that have already taken place in the environmental field? Second, will the constitutional changes provide a framework that will assist in the effective development and delivery of environmental policies appropriate for the beginning of the next century?

The environment is a dynamic and complex policy field. This chapter will not attempt a comprehensive analysis of substantive aspects of environmental policy in all its guises. Instead, it will focus on four themes of constitutional change and how they are likely to impact on environmental policy: structures of national administration; the European Community; legal rights concerning the environment; and the role of Westminster and Whitehall. Nevertheless, there are a number of important general themes concerning the nature of the contemporary environmental policies which pose significant challenges for constitutional reform, and form a necessary backdrop to any discussion.

'Think Globally—Act Locally', which became a pervasive mantra in environmental politics after the Rio Earth Summit of 1992, hardly forms a firm basis for determining the allocation of environmental responsibility between different levels of government. Yet it reflects the pervasive nature of many environment issues and how the cumulative effect of local human impacts can affect the overall condition of the environment, on a national, regional or even global scale. Models of federal or quasi-federal government which attempt to identify a clear separation of powers in the environmental field are unlikely to reflect the physical and political realities of the issue. If the environment is not readily susceptible to a vertical disaggregation of functions, still less is it amenable to what might be described as horizontal compartmentalization of responsibilities, the traditional model of administrative structures. Differing perceptions of what constitutes the sphere of environmental concern have been a major source of tension between government and non-governmental organizations over the last two decades, with key issues of concern, such as agriculture, energy, and transport often falling outside the direct responsibility of more narrowly focused environment departments. The need to integrate an environmental dimension into nearly all aspects of the machinery of government is now widely acknowledged, and indeed given legal expression in the European Treaty.[1] Tentative experiments in new forms of co-ordinating and consultative mechanisms have been initiated, though progress remains slow.

The concept of sustainable development now pervades the environmental agenda, and introduces a new set of intellectual and political challenges. Previous chapters have identified minimalist and maximalist concepts of constitutional change. The implications of sustainable development are equally subject to competing visions, with the narrowest concerned with ensuring that contemporary decision-makers take a longer term view of the environmental impacts of existing trends than has been usual practice.[2] Others envisage a far more complex and politically unsettling picture incorporating notions of greater economic and social justice both within and between generations, and a revitalization of local and community identities.[3] There are inevitable tensions and contradictions involved—one criterion of success for constitutional change will be its ability to provide a political and legal framework for accommodating

---

[1] Under Art. 130r of the Maastricht Version of the Treaty, 'Environmental protection requirements must be integrated into the definition and implementation of other Community policies.' The Amsterdam Treaty strengthened the status of the integration principle by putting it at the head of the Treaty in a new Article 6, and including an express reference to sustainable development.

[2] Encapsulated in the phrase of John Gummer, former Secretary of State for the Environment of the previous Government 'We must not cheat on our children.' Reported in Hansard HC Col 994, 4/12/96.

[3] For a recent review see O'Riordan, T. and Voisey, H., *Sustainable Development in Western Europe: Coming to Terms with Agenda 21* (London: Frank Cass, 1998).

and resolving these concepts in the future. Yet, significant perhaps of a lack of coherent vision, the most recent government consultation paper on sustainable development, *Opportunities for Change*,[4] contains one reference to the constitutional changes now taking place.[5]

A final important element of the current debate concerns increasing public unease with the ability of governmental bodies to reach acceptable decisions especially in areas of scientific uncertainty, epitomized by the BSE crisis and contemporary arguments over genetically modified organisms. Expert judgment is no longer treated with the same unquestioning respect it might have been a generation ago. Understanding the mechanisms for improving trust in regulatory decision-makers, and appreciating the nature and role of public values will be a major challenge for those involved in public administration.[6]

STRUCTURES OF NATIONAL ADMINISTRATION

The Centralization of Environmental Control

Within the United Kingdom the trend of environmental administration has been to shift power away from local government towards Westminster or specialized public agencies. This was not due to some grand design or overarching theory about central–local government relations, but occurred incrementally over a lengthy period, with each shift being justified by the logic of the particular type of environmental problem at hand. The first major re-allocation of powers to a central authority took place well before more recent attacks on local government, with the establishment in the 1860s of a centralized government inspectorate to regulate emissions into the air from certain industrial processes. The political justification was that local authorities and local courts lacked both the technical competence and the political determination to ensure effective control. This initial concept of a largely technocratic and functional agency, not directly accountable to local political direction, has remained a powerful model which has continued to influence the shape of contemporary administrative structures. A similar but much more gradual pattern of the concentration of powers developed in the field of water management, where the traditional geographical jurisdictional boundaries of local government were seen as failing to reflect the physical realities of the water cycle and river systems. The pattern of centralization continued in 1995

---

[4] Department of the Environment, Transport and Regions, *Sustainable Development: Opportunities for Change. Consultation Paper on a Revised UK Strategy* (1988).

[5] The one reference is to the proposals that the Welsh Assembly and the Regional Development Agencies should have explicit responsibilities for developing policies on sustainable development.

[6] An underlying theme of much of the most recent report of the Royal Commission on Environmental Pollution, 'Setting Environmental Standards' (1998).

when the powers to regulate waste management and disposal were removed from local authorities in England and Wales to a newly established body, the Environment Agency.[7] The immediate cause of the loss of power was a series of critical reports questioning the commitment and competence of many local authorities in regulating what had become a highly technically complex industry. At the same time there was an increasing awareness that a medium-by-medium (air, water, land) approach to regulation which had characterized the development of administrative structures did not reflect the need to treat the environment as a whole. Waste, water, and many air pollution functions were therefore subsumed into the new Agency. This pattern of centralization of functions was reflected in Scotland with the creation of a Scottish Environment Protection Agency, though with a slightly different range of powers. An added pressure in recent years for centralization of responsibility has been the need for central government to demonstrate that it can ensure compliance with European Community obligations in the environmental field. As Nigel Haigh demonstrated over ten years ago this required central government both to preserve and threaten the exercise of reserve powers where local authorities were failing to achieve Community obligations.[8] More recently the model has been to translate Community environmental policies into binding national legislation as a mechanism for ensuring compliance.[9]

Local Authority Responsibility

Yet the allocation of environmental powers away from local authorities to specialized agencies of various types is not in reality as straightforward or inevitable as it might first appear. The environment is not amenable to clear boundaries of responsibility. Not every environmental regulation has been transferred to centralized authorities—local noise control, the control of site-specific statutory nuisances and air pollution from certain industries remain with local authorities, with the issue of contaminated land split between local authorities and the Agencies.

Above all, land-use planning controls have remained largely with local authorities, though with strong overall policy and appeal functions rest with central government. Land-use planning controls have never been exclusively concerned with environmental protection, but their importance as a mechanism for anticipating and preventing environmental problems has been increasingly

[7] Part I Environment Act 1995.

[8] Haigh, N., 'Devolved Responsibility and Centralization: the Effects of EEC Environmental Policy', *Public Administration* 64 (1986), 197–207.

[9] In a more recent study, Janice Morphet, Chief Executive of an English County Council, questions the extent to which Haigh's thesis now holds true, and suggests that the contemporary nature of European Community environmental policies with a greater emphasis on local and regional involvement has shifted the balance of influence in favour of local authorities. Lowe, P. and Ward, S., *British Environmental Policy and Europe* (London: Routledge, 1988).

recognized. This linkage was legally strengthened in 1988 with the introduction of requirements for environmental assessment procedures into the planning system as a result of European Community legislation on the subject. Nevertheless the role of local authority powers in the planning field, where they are dealing with a project which is also subject to specialized regulation by the Environment Agency, has proved a source of tension, especially where politically sensitive processes such as waste incinerators have been involved. Litigation has followed, with the courts attempting to devise principles which essentially recognize that while the environmental impact of a new project is a legitimate concern of local planning authorities they should not try to duplicate the regulatory functions of specialized agencies. But as the lengthy judgments indicate these are principles which are simple to state but less easy to apply in practice.[10]

Other major areas of contemporary environmental concern clearly do not fall within the remit of site-specific industrial control which historically dominated the development of regulatory structures. Transport, in particular, is now the most important source of most main pollutants in this country, with the exception of sulphur dioxide, with road transport predominating. Future projections, including those about carbon dioxide levels (the key contributor to global warming) indicate that the proportion attributable to road transport will rise considerably. Analysing the longer term effect of land use planning on transport patterns and the concomitant effect of transport infrastructure on the location and shape of development is complex, but it is clear that local authority influence on one of the most significant environmental challenges could be considerable.

But there remain a number of problematic challenges in existing structures. Leaving local authorities to make the difficult decisions may satisfy problems of local accountability but in the absence of clear national policies render authorities vulnerable to unruly competitive pressures, where local authorities are in effect played off against each other by larger economic interests—the development of out-of-town shopping centres in the 1980s being a clear example.[11] At the same time, the functional, and more technocratic model which underlies the specialized agencies sits unhappily with notions of political accountability, and may obscure the more ambiguous value and economic judgments inherent in environmental regulation. Moreover, the emerging policy objectives concerning sustainability call for decision-making structures that can encompass a broader mix of interests from environmental protection, economic consumption and development, to issues of equity. The enthusiasm

---

[10] See *Gateshead Metropolitan District Council* v. *Secretary of State for the Environment* [1995] Env.LR 37, *R* v. *Bolton Metropolitan District Council*, Court of Appeal, 5 May 1988.

[11] See the 18th Report of the Royal Commission on Environmental Pollution, *Transport and the Environment* (London: HMSO, 1984).

with which many local authorities have seized upon developing sustainable development policies can in part be attributed to the desire of a sector of government which lost so many powers in recent years to be associated with new policy areas which resonated positively with many sectors of the public. The significant role of local authorities is also recognized at international level with the launch of the Local Agenda 21 initiative at the 1992 Earth Summit and, according to the Secretary-General of the International Council for Local Environment Initiatives, it 'has engendered one of the most extensive follow-up programmes' to the agenda established at Rio.[12] The recent White Paper on local government[13] acknowledges the potential of local authorities to integrate concerns, and proposes a new legal duty to promote economic, social, and environmental well-being within their jurisdictions: this 'will put sustainable development at the heart of council decision making and will provide an overall framework within which councils must perform all their existing functions'.[14]

The Impact of Devolution

How will these patterns of administrative structure be shaped by constitutional change? There already exist asymmetrical patterns of responsibility between the specialized environmental agencies in England and Wales, Scotland, and Northern Ireland. To take one example, in England nature protection and the preservation of the countryside for amenity and recreational purposes have fallen to separate bodies, English Nature and the Countryside Commission, while in Scotland and Wales single bodies have carried out both areas of responsibility since 1990. Northern Ireland has frequently lagged behind in the development of environmental legislation, but the creation of the Environment and Agency Service in 1996 as an executive agency within the Northern Ireland Department of the Environment could provide a more radical integrating model. The Agency combines powers for countryside protection, nature preservation and pollution control in a way unseen in the rest of the United Kingdom. With pollution regulation increasingly concerned with effects on the natural environment as well as human health, the model has attractions. A minimalist view of the effects of devolution would see these distinctive patterns of administration being preserved and the asymmetry even perhaps growing over time. Alternatively, the opportunity for experimentation may

[12] Brugman, J., 'Local Authorities and Agenda 21' in Fodds, F., (ed.) *The Way Forward— Beyond Agenda 21* (London: Earthscan, 1997), 101–13. According to Tim O'Riordan and Heather Voisey (note 3 above). 'With slow progress so far at national level it is local government which is proving to be the most active and innovative in implementing sustainable development in the United Kingdom ...' (p.46).

[13] Department of the Environment Transport and Regions, *Modern Local Government—In Touch with the People* (1988).

[14] Ibid., para. 8.10.

provide pressure for successful examples to be adopted elsewhere. Precedent remains a powerful factor, and it is less easy for governments to resist changes which are already operating effectively in other parts of the country. Combining countryside and nature-protection functions in England along the lines in Wales and Scotland can be predicted. The more ambitious Northern Ireland model is unlikely to be adopted in Great Britain for some years but its very existence means that it cannot be readily dismissed as a concept. Asymmetric development also appears to underline the Government's recent proposals for local government reform with opportunities for experimentation and example—'The Government is clear that councils which perform consistently well will be able to acquire additional powers and freedoms that over time will be significantly wider than those available to councils which are performing less effectively.'[15]

Other effects of devolution on the current structure of environmental administration can be predicted. The devolved assemblies in Scotland, Wales, and Northern Ireland are likely to increase the political accountability of the specialized environmental agencies in those regions. In England, the minimalist approach to devolution is less likely to do so. Regional Development Agencies will hardly provide the appropriate forum for doing so. Similarly, if regional assemblies in England develop on an asymmetric model, it will be complex to develop lines of accountability for a body such as the Environment Agency with countrywide jurisdiction. The most radical model of devolution in England would eventually see regional assemblies in all areas of the country—that in turn could lead to pressure for a remodelling of existing structures, with the establishment of regional environmental agencies, perhaps on the Northern Irish model, more closely politically accountable on a regional basis.

The other significant area will be the development of mechanisms for discussion and co-operation on environmental policies between the different regions of the United Kingdom. In 1990 the Nature Conservation Council which has responsibility in Great Britain for nature protection matters was abolished in favour of separate agencies in England, Wales, and Scotland. A Joint Nature Consultative Committee which was established to retain a degree of co-ordination between the regional bodies has been criticized as lacking sufficient influence. The devolution model for Scotland proposes essentially that Westminster and Whitehall retain control over environmental policies which fall within the remit of international or European Community agreement with other aspects fully devolved.[16] This will not be an easy line to draw as the subsequent discussion demonstrates. But any re-emergence of agencies with environmental responsibility across the whole of the United Kingdom now

---

[15] *Modern Local Government—In Touch With the People*, para. 8.29.
[16] See Scotland Act 1998, Schedule 5.

seems unlikely. Yet experience of countries such as Australia indicates that there will be the need to develop new institutional mechanisms to discuss and co-ordinate the development of environmental policies and standards in the different regions.[17] Here the proposed Council of the Islands may offer an appropriate forum for handling discussion of environmental policies, and for allowing the further development of cross-border environmental initiatives that have already been developed between Northern Ireland and Eire.

THE EUROPEAN COMMUNITY

European Community Legislation in the 1970s and 1980s

Whatever the future distribution of environmental responsibilities, the United Kingdom no longer has a free hand in developing environmental policies whether at a national or strengthened devolved level. Only thirty years ago the national inspectorate responsible for regulating emissions from power stations could publicly doubt whether it had any jurisdictional responsibilities to consider the transboundary effects of atmospheric emissions from the industries they were controlling. Such an attitude could not be sustained today, either politically or legally. The European Community in particular has provided the base for developing a substantial body of legally binding environmental instruments over the last twenty-five years. For a country such as the United Kingdom where nationally binding environmental standards were resisted in favour of giving extensive discretion to regulators, the incorporation of Community legal requirements into the existing body of UK environmental law has been profound. Environmental emission and quality standards are now an accepted part of the legal landscape. The obligation to produce plans concerning various environmental objectives, and procedural rights including that of public access to environmental information are now enshrined in national law.

The 1970s and 1980s saw the rapid development of a range of environmental legislation at Community level encompassing such matters as water quality, air emissions, chemicals control, and environmental assessment. The first flush of enthusiasm has, however, now given way to a rather less confident and more measured approach, despite the European Parliament's continued promotion of green issues and increasing influence over the legislative process. There has been a growing appreciation that the early model of rigorously expressed environmental standards, often based on a confusing mixture of politics and science, is insufficient and too inflexible to deal with the range and breadth of environmental issues facing the European Community.

[17] See Ch. 9.

Until 1987 the Treaty contained no explicit legal powers concerning the environment, creating the need to look to other provisions in the Treaty as a legitimate basis for environmental legislation. Article 100, which permits harmonization to remove distortions of trade, was the preferred basis for many environmental directives, and in the case of product standards such as vehicle emissions standards and industrial pollution standards such use could be justified. The economic case for the need to harmonize, say, drinking water or bathing water standards on the grounds of potential trade distortion was intellectually far more dubious yet did not deter Member States from agreeing to such legislation.

With the Single European Act introducing explicit environmental provisions into the Treaty[18] this intellectual sleight of hand was no longer required. Nevertheless, the Treaty contained significant procedural differences for legislation based on trade-related Treaty provisions or environmental provisions, leading to a series of inter-institutional legal disputes between the Council, the Commission and the European Parliament. The Amsterdam Treaty has now largely removed such differences, with co-decision procedures applying equally to trade-related and the majority of environmental legislation. Fine legal arguments concerning the dividing line between environmental protection and trade harmonization are likely to disappear. But at the same time the legislative influence of the European Parliament will be substantially increased, requiring both Member States and the Commission to be more attuned to its approach to environmental issues. Non-governmental environmental organizations and other lobby interests are likely to pay increasing attention to securing influence with Parliamentarians at European level.

Subsidiarity

The environmental provisions of the 1987 Treaty were also significant in that they contained the first legal expression of the subsidiarity principle. The Treaty has never contained a clear division of competencies between the Community and Member States, not least in the environmental field where Laurence Brinkhorst, a former Director-General of DG XI, described the system as 'not so much a separation of powers but rather an intermingling of powers'. The subsidiarity principle contained in the Single European Act 1987 required the Community to act only if environmental objectives 'can be attained better' at Community level rather than at the level of individual Member States. As such it could be seen as suggestive rather than a formal expression of competencies, and appeared to have had little real influence. Many argued that it said little more than had already been expressed in the Community's First Action Programme on the Environment some fourteen years earlier, where it

---

[18] Art. 130r EC Treaty, now Art. 174 under the Amsterdam version.

was clearly stated that the level of action, be it local, regional, national, Community or international, must be best suited to the type of pollution issue at hand.

The Maastricht Treaty saw the transformation of the principle into one of general application which was positioned at the head of the Treaty,[19] signifying at the very least its political significance. Lawyers have argued over whether the principle is truly justiciable in the courts,[20] but one of the few cases where the principle has been raised before the European Court of Justice, the United Kingdom's challenge to the Working Time Directive in 1996, suggests that the judiciary will be reluctant to intervene on those grounds alone: 'The Council [of Ministers] must be allowed a wide discretion in an area which as here involves the legislature in making social policy choices and requires it to carry out complex assessment.'[21]

Even if legal challenges on the grounds of breach of subsidiarity are likely to remain a rarity in the future, this does not mean that the principle is devoid of political effect. At the time of Maastricht, some Member States appeared to foster extravagant expectations with talk of rolling back the frontiers of Community environmental legislation. Certainly the introduction of the principle and its heightened significance since Maastricht resulted in both Member States and the Commission in setting out in more detail a set of principles and procedures concerned with ensuring that measures were tested against the concept of subsidiarity.[22] But there has been no major withdrawal from a substantive area of policy.[23]

The Division Between Community and National Interests

The nature of environmental problems, people's perceptions of their relationship with the environment, and the capacity for cumulative localized impacts to have significant regional or even global effects make it

[19] Art. 3b EC Treaty now contained in Art. 5 of the Amsterdam version.

[20] In one key collection of papers, three distinguished lawyers come to differing conclusions on this point—see O'Keefe, D. and Twomey, P., (eds.), *Legal Issues of the Maastricht Treaty* (London: Chancery Law Publishing, 1994).

[21] *United Kingdom* v. *EC Council* C-84/94 [1996] ECR I-5755. More recently, Advocate General Leger considered that in view of the importance of the principle of subsidiarity in allocating powers between Member States and the Community, it did not seem excessive for Community institutions 'in the future systematically to state reasons for their decisions in view of the principle of subsidiarity'. The European Court, however, did not consider that an express reference to subsidiarity need be made in justifying Community action: *Germany* v. *European Parliament and EU Council* [1997] 3 CMLR 1379.

[22] Inter-Institutional Agreement on procedures for implementing the principle of Subsidiarity [1993] 10 EC Bull.

[23] The only clear example being the Commission's decision in 1994 to substitute its proposal for a Directive concerning zoos with a Recommendation. Even this change caused concern in the European Parliament.

extraordinarily difficult to draw hard lines of substantive competence between the Community and national interests. A minimalist approach would confine Community interest to environmental issues where there was a clear transboundary physical impact (such as the movements of waste, or transfrontier air emissions) or a clear transnational economic impact. But this ignores concepts of a European environmental heritage, or what has been described as transboundary cultural interests where a citizen of, say, France could be said to have a legitimate interest in the protection of natural habitats in Spain, or vice versa.[24] The notion of European citizenship, and the increasing reference to certain environmental rights (discussed further below) adds further to the complexity of drawing substantive boundaries.

Nevertheless, even if there are few issues which can be definitively described as no-go areas, the concept of subsidiarity is likely to have continuing influence on the content of Community environmental policies. The notion of 'shared responsibility' has been pursued in the environment field under the Fifth Action Programme on the Environment, and the detailed provisions of Community environmental legislation are likely to contain a greater role for Member States. Already there are important signals. Recent environmental proposals are making more use of framework directives, and there is likely to be less use of Community-wide environmental standards expressed in numerate form. For example, Commission proposals to amend EC legislation concerning drinking water standards would mean that standards concerning aesthetics or smell would no longer be determined at Community level. Member States will be given more discretion in the designation of areas subject to Community environmental policies, or the determination of decisions, say, concerning the award of eco-labels, without the need for a further hierarchy of decision-making at Community level. These developments could imply a greater role for new devolved administrations within the United Kingdom, but it could also lead to tension. Will, say, aesthetic standards for Scottish drinking water in future be determined by the Scottish Parliament on the grounds that the relevant EC law permits a Member State to determine such standards? Or since it falls within the ambit of EC law, does the responsibility remain with Westminster as a reserved matter?

Such trends away from Community-wide environmental standards are likely to be strengthened with the likely expansion of the Community. Given the difficulty of many of the accession states in securing compliance with current Community environmental standards in fields such as air or water quality, sensitive political decisions will have to be taken concerning the possibility of time-limited derogations (as happened with East Germany) or substantial financial assistance to ensure compliance. And the moves towards greater

---

[24] Wils, W., 'Subsidiarity and EC Environmental Policy—Taking People's Concerns Seriously', *Journal of Environmental Law,* Vol. 6 (1994), 85–92.

degrees of discretion at Member State level, more variegated standards, and the reciprocal recognition of decisions taken within Member States (such as approval to market a new chemical substance) implies a considerable degree of trust in the capabilities of institutions within other countries. Even where existing environmental directives (such as those concerning bathing waters or shell-fish waters) permitted a degree of discretion in designation, there have been well-known examples of Member States abusing the process. The concept of shared responsibility is therefore not necessarily a panacea but one fraught with the possibility of misuse. But if, as seems likely, it is a trend that will continue, it follows that it will be all the more important to develop procedural principles such as the public right to information concerning the environment and the right of action before national courts which can go some way to check that governmental powers are exercised legitimately. At the same time, there will be a pressure to create more sophisticated Community-wide monitoring and reporting systems, using comparable databases, a task being led by the new European Environment Agency and one that will require increased co-operation and co-ordination amongst the devolved players. Yet such a task of identifying objective criteria of measurement is far from mechanical and value-free, and can reveal subtle and often deep-seated differences between local and centralized perceptions of the environment.[25]

PROCEDURAL RIGHTS

European Law

For the United Kingdom at any rate the environmental field provided an early example of broadly based legislative rights to information. The need to implement the EC Directive on Access to Environment Information in 1990 required the Government to introduce in 1992 regulations granting any member of the public legal rights to an extensive range of information concerning the environment held by public bodies. Both the Community and national legislation contained a wide range of exemptions which can be expected to continue to be subject to legal dispute, although case law to date indicates that the courts will interpret these restrictively, on the assumption that

---

[25] 'Since rationalization and standardization are among the most prominent tasks of the [European Environment Agency] these issues of local variability and the question of how to respect legitimate cultural differences while maintaining enough consistency across cultures to provide a comprehensive review are among the most difficult challenges facing this new institution.' Wynne, B. and Winterton, C., 'Public Information and the Environment' in Lowe, P. and Ward, S., *British Environmental Policy and Europe* (London: Routledge, 1988).

the general right to information is the grounding principle.[26] The effectiveness of the national regulations has, however, been weakened by the failure to establish a dedicated appeals tribunal, relying instead on judicial review as a remedy against refusal to supply information or the imposition of excessive financial charges for supply. New institutional mechanisms such as a specialized appeals tribunal for appeals, perhaps in the context of wider freedom of information legislation, can be predicted.

The concept of general legal rights to a 'healthy environment' or some similar phrase is one that is found in some written constitutions, both within Europe and elsewhere, the most recent being the 1996 Constitution of South Africa. In case law before the European Court of Justice Advocate Generals have promoted the idea of EC environmental legislation concerning, say, air quality or water quality, as granting public rights to a clean environment, though beyond justifying the requirement for Member States to transpose such Community standards into national binding legislation rather than by administrative guidelines, the implications of such concepts have yet to fully realized.[27] Certainly, in the absence of any implementing standards, the concept of a general right to a clean or healthy environment is extremely nebulous and so imbued with complex scientific and political choices as to make it almost devoid of substantive legal meaning in terms of the actual environmental quality to which individuals are entitled.[28] Moves to insert such a general right into the European Treaty have been resisted to date and are likely to continue to be so.

The European Convention on Human Rights

Moves to insert explicit environmental rights into the European Convention on Human Rights have similarly been resisted. But accession to the Convention is likely to require national courts to handle disputes raising Convention rights in the context of environmental disputes. The Convention contains no express individual or collective rights concerning the environment, but other articles in the Convention have been invoked as implicitly relating to the environment, though more often with lack of success to date. The Article 2 protection of right to life has been restrictively interpreted to mean physical life rather than quality of life—in contrast, say, to the Indian High Court which has built up extensive environmental case law from a similarly worded constitutional provision.

---

[26] See the decision of the High Court in *R* v. *British Coal Board* ex parte *Ibstock* (21 October 1994) and the first decision of the European Court of Justice on the Directive, *Mecklenburg* v. *Kreis Pinneberg—Der Landrat* (C-321/96, 17 June 1988).

[27] Macrory, R., (1996) 'Environmental Citizenship and the Law: Repairing the European Road', *Journal of Environmental Law*, Vol. 8, No. 2 (1996) 219–36.

[28] For a valuable comparative survey see Brandl, B. and Bungert, E., (1992) 'Constitutional Entrenchment of Environmental Protection', *Harvard Environmental Law Review,* Vol. 16, No. 1 (1992).

Similarly, environmental claims concerning the right to the peaceful enjoyment of property under Article I of Protocol 1 have been unsuccessful. But in 1994 the European Court of Human Rights found against Spain in a case concerning the authorization and building of waste treatment plants near the applicant's home on the grounds of breach of Article 8 giving a right to respect for private and family life: 'severe environmental pollution may affect individuals' well-being and prevent them from enjoying their homes in such a way as to affect their private and family life adversely without, however, seriously endangering their health.'[29] A large award of compensatory damages was made. Though the facts of the case were extreme, it is predictable that the principles may be invoked in environmental disputes before UK national courts in the future. As Paul Craig indicates in Chapter 5 the most likely source of litigation is likely to be in the context of judicial review actions against bodies such as the Environment Agency or local planning authorities relying upon Section 6 of the Human Rights Act. Human rights, though, even if interpreted with an environmental gloss, are inherently anthropocentric, and cannot satisfactorily protect all environmental interests—the requirement under Section 6 of the Human Rights Act that a litigant be a 'victim' of an unlawful act means that non-government environmental organizations are unlikely to have standing.

Other Sources of Procedural Rights

Other procedural rights concerning participation in decision making may be further developed in the future. Both existing national laws and EC Directives such as that concerning environmental assessment grant considerable rights of public participation. The European Convention on Access to Information, Public Participation in Decision-Making and Access to Justice in Environmental Matters, proposed by the United Nations Economic Commission for Europe, can be expected to come into effect in around five years, and it seems unlikely that the United Kingdom would find it politically acceptable not to ratify. Many of the provisions build upon or reflect existing rights, but detailed changes to certain current national provisions may be required to secure compliance.

Recent years have seen a proliferation of judicial review actions in the environmental field, often brought by non-governmental organizations. Liberal interpretation of standing rules now appears to mean that there is little real difficulty in bringing such actions, but other procedural issues are likely to require far greater attention in the future. Examples include strict time-limits which often fail to reflect the reality of the complexities involved for organizations in deciding whether to proceed with a legal action; the problems in securing interlocutory injunctions where sites of high environmental value are threatened; and the whole question of costs. These are all the more

---

[29] *Lopez Ostra* v. *Spain* App. No. 16798/90, 9 December 1994.

important in the context of Community environmental obligations where the Commission has recently emphasized the importance of the role of national courts as the first line of defence in securing compliance.[30] The Commission has acknowledged the significance of these types of procedural differences within Member States but is equally aware of the political sensitivities in proposing Community measures to address them. As other chapters indicate, the current developments in constitutional change in this country imply a greater role for the courts, yet they have failed to address critical procedural issues concerning environmental litigation. The pressure to do so will increase.

WESTMINSTER AND WHITEHALL

The Role of Committees

The 15 per cent vote to the UK Green Party in the 1989 European Parliamentary elections hugely sensitized mainstream political parties to public dissatisfaction with the effectiveness of existing environmental policies. But although electoral reform may increase the chances of some Green Party representation at national or regional level, it seems unlikely that the mainstream parties will allow themselves again to be marginalized on environmental policies. Within Parliament the House of Commons Select Committee on the Environment performed a critical role in the 1980s and early 1990s in exposing inadequacies in environmental policies. But the departmental basis of the Committee was ill-suited to handling the cross-department nature of key contemporary environmental problems, with substantial issues such as transport and agriculture falling outside its remit. The 1997 restructuring of the Department of the Environment to re-incorporate Transport permitted the Committee to expand its terms of reference, but there will be increasing pressure to sensitize other Committees to the environmental aspects of their work. Further development of Joint Committees inquiries may be expected.[31] The new Environment Audit Select Committee established by the Government clearly reflected the peculiarly horizontal nature of environmental policies, but it has yet to define fully a distinctive role which does not create turf-battles with others.   Initially, the Government proposed that this Committee be called a Sustainable Development Audit Committee but it was renamed in order to be more understandable to the public. Whether this change

---

[30] Communication from the European Commission, Com (96) 500 final, 22 October 1996, *Implementing Community Environmental Law.*

[31] Reflecting the experiments made at European Community level with Joint Council of Ministers on issues such as energy/environment and transport/environment, and a particular feature of the recent British Presidency. The Committee structure of the European Parliament remains heavily sectorally-based, and pressure for new initiatives can be expected.

of name will encourage the Committee to avoid the more radical implications of the sustainable development agenda remains to be seen, but it will be a lost opportunity if it does. The House of Lords Select Committees have provided a consistent focus for inquiry into proposed European Community environmental legislation at a time when its significance was little recognized in the House of Commons, and its body of reports has generally commanded respect both in this country and other parts of the Community, including the European Commission. Furthermore, since it lacks the departmental structures of the Commons Committees, it has shown more flexibility in establishing particular select committees on issues such as sustainable development.[32] Similarly, the Science and Technology Committee has addressed a number of critical areas of environmental concern. The role of such committees in a reformed House of Lords, and their effective co-ordination with the functions of their counterparts in the Commons appears to have been little addressed as yet.

Devolution, Westminster and Whitehall

The relationship between the new devolved administrations and Westminster and Whitehall will be crucially influenced by the nature of Community and international environmental obligations. A division of powers which preserves international and Community affairs for Westminster sits uneasily with the nature of contemporary environmental politics, where there is a dynamic linkage between international, regional, national and local action. International environmental treaties continue to develop in importance. The relationship between environmental protection and the liberalization of world trade underpinned by the General Agreement on Trade and Tariffs and new initiatives such as the proposed Multi-lateral Investment Agreement is of equal significance, and potentially inhibits the capacity of nation states, let alone regional administrations, to promote unilateral environmental policies. Despite the development of an environmental division of the International Court of Justice, in the past many international environmental treaties have probably been more honoured in their breach than obeyance. But more recent environmental treaties have paid far more attention to developing more sophisticated administrative mechanisms for monitoring compliance, increasing the pressure on signatory states to demonstrate good faith. Furthermore, contemporary international obligations such as those under the Climate Change Convention and its Protocols potentially have immense significance for the internal policies of countries, and achieving, say, carbon dioxide reduction obligations can involve a range of sectoral areas such as

---

[32] *Report from the Select Committee on Sustainable Development*, HL Paper 72, Session 1994–5 (London: HMSO, 1995).

transport, energy production, building standards, and domestic energy conservation. Potential areas of conflict between Westminster and the regions can be predicted. Suppose the Welsh Assembly fails to introduce policies restricting business parking. Could a Secretary of State invoke his powers under the Government of Wales Act to direct the Assembly to take action in order to give effect to Climate Change obligations?[33] Or, as Paul Craig notes, the demarcation of reserved functions under the Scotland Act bristles with potential ambiguities. Could the Scottish Parliament legislate to prohibit the disposal of radioactive waste or the field testing of genetically modified foodstuffs in Scotland on environmental grounds, or does this clearly fall within one of the areas reserved for Westminster?[34]

CONCLUSIONS

Environmental policy has moved well beyond a model of public administration where problems were clearly identifiable as discretely environmental, amenable to scientific or technical analysis, and soluble by classical regulatory intervention. Uncertainty and risk pervade many areas of the environmental challenge, and competing visions of what is implied by an environmentally sound, let alone a sustainable, society abound. Some important institutional changes have been initiated, yet, as other chapters indicate in relation to constitutional change, no one really knows the outcome. As O'Riordan and Voisey have noted in a recent study, 'Sustainable development is a socially motivating force where we are not at all sure where we will end up but we keep on trying because we perceive our long term survival is at stake.'[35]

Constitutional change is about altering the relationships of citizens with government and parliament, and of levels of government with each other. Some impacts of the current changes under way can be predicted. The courts will be more involved in environmental litigation, both in boundary disputes between levels of government and in developing principles of environmental and human rights. Devolution will lead to potentially variegated environmental standards in different parts of the United Kingdom, but with the concomitant

[33] Under s. 108 of the Government of Wales Act the Secretary of State may direct the Welsh Assembly to take action required for giving effect to international obligations or require it not to take action incompatible with such obligations.

[34] Environmental policies are essentially devolved to the Scottish Parliament, but Schedule 5 of the Scotland Act, 'nuclear energy and nuclear installations', are reserved matters for Westminster; but this reservation does not include the subject matter of the Radioactive Substances Act 1993, which regulates the disposal of radioactive waste. Product standards and requirements in relation to Community obligations and product labelling are reserved matters, but food and agricultural produce are exempted from the reservation.

[35] O'Riordan, T. and Voisey, H., *Sustainable Devlopment in Western Europe: Coming to Terms with Agenda 21* (London: Fank Cass, 1998).

need to develop new institutional mechanisms for co-operation and co-ordination. Other aspects of contemporary debate concerning the environment and sustainability appear to be scarcely addressed by the current proposals. The precise role and powers of local authorities in securing policy goals still remain uncertain despite the commitment to put sustainable development at the heart of their functions.[36] The degree to which current models of devolution will satisfy environmental demands for local empowerment set against the apparently contradictory internationalization of many economic and environmental issues is equally unclear. Other aspects of the current constitutional changes would appear to many involved in environmental and sustainability politics to be based on overly conventional models of divisions of power and representative democracy which will do little to progress the more radical agenda. Openness of decision making, new mechanisms for exploring and articulating public values, and imaginative means of securing cross-departmental co-operation are all likely to be important elements of future debates. It is perhaps asking too much of the current proposals to address them all. Constitutional change will undoubtedly shift conventional patterns of decision making in profound ways and with consequences that are uncertain. What is rather more predictable is that those involved in the current environmental and sustainability debate will fully exploit the new opportunities provided by the changes under way as a means for influencing the future direction of policy.

[36] *Modern Local Government—In Touch with the People*, para. 8.10.

11

Financing Devolution: the Centre Retains Control

ROBERT HAZELL AND RICHARD CORNES

In Chapter 2 we said that the greatest tensions in the devolution settlement would arise over finance. It is one of the main sources of friction between central and regional governments in other countries, and the same is likely to happen here. What is different about the British model of devolution is the extent to which the centre will retain financial control. There is to be extensive devolution of political power, particularly in Scotland and Northern Ireland, but the new governments will have little or no revenue-raising power. Does this mean that the promises of autonomy will turn out to be hollow, because in financial terms the devolved governments will remain puppets of London?

There are two central issues: who will raise revenue, and how will revenue be shared out around the Union? Neither issue has received much attention, apart from the prominence given to the tax-raising power of the Scottish Parliament by being singled out in a separate question in the Scottish referendum. In Wales the lack of revenue-raising power is seldom mentioned; in Northern Ireland the issue has not surfaced at all.[1] The Government's assumption that the financial arrangements should as far as possible continue the status quo seems to be accepted by many of the participants.

Currently Westminster is overwhelmingly the dominant revenue-raising government. It finances through block transfers the activities of the Scottish, Welsh, and Northern Ireland Offices, and also, by about 80 per cent, the expenditure of local government. These arrangements look set to continue, with few questions being raised about the underlying pattern of distribution, or the problems which may be stored up for the future. It is not widely known how much certain parts of the Union appear to gain (Northern Ireland, Scotland and Wales) and others to lose out (the English regions); nor is it known how much these gains and losses correspond to differences in relative need. These differentials will come into sharp relief as devolution proceeds and the information about regional transfers comes much more into the public domain.

---

[1] The Belfast Agreement, the nearest we have to a White Paper on the new Northern Ireland Assembly, is completely silent about the Assembly's funding. The funding provisions in Part V of the Northern Ireland Bill were different in form (with assignment of tax) but not in substance from Scotland and Wales: the Northern Ireland Assembly will be dependent on block transfers from London.

In addition to the amount of the transfers, there are questions about the degree of dependency built into the funding arrangements. With the exception of the Scottish Parliament's power to vary the basic rate of income tax by plus or minus 3 pence, each of the devolved administrations is to be wholly dependent upon central government grant. This raises questions about the degree of policy autonomy they will be able to exercise, and the lack of fiscal accountability they will have to their own electors.

HOW THE DEVOLVED ASSEMBLIES ARE TO BE FINANCED

The White Papers on devolution in Scotland and Wales, published before the 1997 referendums, were in part designed to reassure Scottish and Welsh voters that in financial terms little would change. Thus the Scottish White Paper proposed:

a continuation of the existing 'Block and formula' system of funding most of Scotland's public expenditure programmes which has applied continuously since the late 1970s ...

For many years most of the expenditure programmes which fall within the Secretary of State for Scotland's budget have been controlled through an arrangement known commonly as the Scottish Block. Under this arrangement a block of resources, the annual changes in which have been determined by means of a population-based formula, has been made available annually to the Secretary of State for Scotland, who has then had the freedom to distribute those resources between Scottish programmes as he has thought fit. He has not been bound to replicate the spending decisions of Whitehall Departments but has been able annually to determine a specific set of Scottish priorities ...

In practice these arrangements, based on the Block and formula, have produced fair settlements for Scotland in annual public expenditure rounds and have allowed the Secretary of State for Scotland to determine his spending decisions in accordance with Scottish needs and priorities. They have largely removed the need for annual negotiation between The Scottish Office and the Treasury. The Government have therefore concluded that the financial framework for the Scottish Parliament should be based on these existing arrangements with, in future, the Scottish Parliament determining Scottish spending priorities.[2]

The Welsh White Paper was couched in similar terms, and contained the same reassurance that these arrangements have produced fair settlements for Wales. Neither White Paper addressed the question whether the funding arrangements were fair to the rest of the kingdom. They were not intended to: they were addressed to Scottish and Welsh voters in the forthcoming

---

[2] *Scotland's Parliament*, (Cm 3658) July 1997, paras 7.1–7.4.

referendums. But the last published figures show that in 1996–7 identifiable
public expenditure per head in Scotland was 19 per cent and in Wales 14 per
cent above the UK average: while spending in England was around 4 per cent
below the UK average.[3] These differential levels of spending are seldom
publicized, but will become much more exposed post-devolution; and pressure
will grow for the differentials to be justified.

TREASURY'S NEEDS ASSESSMENT STUDY AND THE BARNETT FORMULA

The last attempt to assess the different spending needs of England, Scotland,
Wales and Northern Ireland was made 20 years ago, as part of the last Labour
Government's plans for devolution. The Treasury was asked to undertake a
study to calculate the relative amounts of expenditure per capita required to
provide the same range and levels of service as in England. Taking data from
1976–7, the Treasury assessed the relative levels of spending need as follows:[4]

Figure 11.1. Treasury Needs Assessment Study 1978				
	England	Scotland	Wales	Northern Ireland
Relative needs assessment	100	116	109	131
Actual spending levels 1976–7	100	122	106	135

It can be seen that actual levels of spending varied from the assessed levels of
need, being higher in Scotland and Northern Ireland, but lower in Wales. The
Government decided that, in future, changes in spending should be determined
by a formula, which became known as the 'Barnett formula' after the then
Chief Secretary to the Treasury, Joel Barnett. The formula allocated increases
or decreases in public expenditure to Scotland, Wales and England in the ratio
10:5:85, the rounded share of Great Britain's population for the three nations
in 1976. For every £85 *change* in planned expenditure on comparable English
services, Wales would receive £5 and Scotland £10. (A parallel formula
allocated 2.75 per cent of the change in equivalent expenditure in Great Britain
to Northern Ireland).

[3] Public Expenditure: Statistical Analyses 1998–9, (Cm 3901) April 1998.
[4] HM Treasury, *Needs Assessment Study Report*, para. 6.5, December 1979.

The history of the Barnett formula is instructive in revealing how difficult it is to re-allocate spending patterns once they are established. The Barnett formula does not determine total budgets and does not directly address actual needs.[5] The 1970s Government decided not to disturb the existing territorial blocks of expenditure, which were carried forward, but to adjust new expenditure at the margin. The hope was that over time these incremental changes would bring about a gradual convergence of levels of spending in Scotland and Wales closer to the levels in England. But when in 1997 the Treasury Select Committee conducted an enquiry into the Barnett Formula it received evidence that no convergence had occurred. The committee reported that in 1995-6 expenditure in Scotland had been 19 per cent and expenditure in Wales 12 per cent above the UK average: while spending in England was around 4 per cent below.[6] This suggested that expenditure per capita in Scotland was some 24 per cent higher than in England, and expenditure in Wales some 17 per cent higher. The figures must be treated with caution because they cover only identifiable public expenditure per head (some three-quarters of total public expenditure), and because of changes in the underlying definitions.

The committee probed hard for evidence of the impact of the Barnett formula on relative levels of public spending per head. In particular the committee sought currently available information on expenditure in England comparable to that in the Scottish, Welsh and Northern Irish blocks. The Treasury submitted further evidence to the committee in February 1998 which showed the following differentials in 1995-6 in per capita spending between the three blocks and England: Scotland 32 per cent higher than equivalent spending in England; Wales 25 per cent higher; Northern Ireland 32 per cent higher.[7] As the blocks differ in coverage, the relatives cannot be directly compared with each other. None of the witnesses before the Committee disputed that public spending needed to be higher in Scotland and Wales, because of a whole range of factors; but the Treasury offered no evidence to justify the existing differentials. Lord Barnett himself argued for a review of the formula, because:

the levels of spending per head between Scotland and other parts of the UK are now very different. Scotland has a higher income per head than some other parts of the UK—the north east, north west and Merseyside—and comparable levels of income per

---

[5] For a detailed explanation of the Barnett Formula and its history, see House of Commons Research Paper 98/8, *The Barnett Formula*, January 1998.

[6] Treasury Committee, *The Barnett Formula*, HC 341 para. 7, citing figures from *Public Expenditure, Statistical Analyses 1997-98*, March 1997, Cm 3601. Figures converted in the next sentence to direct comparison with England by rebasing from England = 96 to England = 100.

[7] Treasury Committee, *The Barnett Formula: The Government's Response*, Appendix 2, para. 9, HC 619, 10 March 1998.

head as compared to other parts of the country, other than perhaps London and the south east.[8]

The Treasury Committee divided between its Scottish and English members, and delivered a brief report of only four pages. But the Committee did express its disappointment that no government studies had been made in relation to the continuing appropriateness of the Barnett formula and how it related to needs. The Committee's report concluded:

We believe that it is time to bring the needs assessment up to date; this would help to show whether the Barnett Formula remains the appropriate method of allocating annual expenditure increases (or savings) to the four nations of the Union. There may be good reasons why this formula should continue to be used in the future as it has for the last 20 years, but it is an argument that cannot finally be settled until it is clear that total expenditure, not just the increase, is still being allocated according to relative need. It is important there should be maximum possible agreement on this in all parts of the UK.[9]

DOES THE BARNETT FORMULA OFFER AN ADEQUATE FUNDING BASIS FOR DEVOLUTION?

The Barnett formula has not delivered convergence in spending levels for two main reasons: formula bypass and changes in population, particularly in Scotland whose population is declining. The formula has been adjusted once, in 1992 to take into account population changes. The Government now propose that the population shares underlying the formula should be recalculated annually on the basis of the latest population estimates published by the Office for National Statistics.

This may prevent the formula getting further out of kilter; but the underlying difficulty remains that the starting point may seem 'fair' in Scotland and Wales, but will not necessarily be seen in the same way in the rest of the kingdom. The discrepancy is particularly marked in relation to Scotland, where spending remains significantly higher, at a time when Scotland has become wealthier. Few are likely to question the levels of spending in Wales and Northern Ireland, which remain the two poorest regions of the UK. But as Lord Barnett pointed out to the Treasury Committee, in terms of Gross Domestic Product (GDP) per capita Scotland is now the third wealthiest region, wealthier than six out of the eight standard regions in England.[10] As it becomes clearer that Scotland is benefiting from higher transfers from Westminster in

---

[8] Treasury Committee, *The Barnett Formula*, HC 341, 17 December 1997, p.1.

[9] Ibid., p.viii.

[10] Office for National Statistics, *Regional Trends 1998*, Table 12.2. These regional comparisons need to be treated with caution because of the poor data for the English regions.

comparison to these poorer regions in England and Wales there will be pressure for a review of the amount Scotland receives.

The point was brought home by Charles Clarke, Labour MP for Norwich South, during the Treasury Committee hearings:

According to the Government's expenditure [figures for] 1995–96, an average person in England had about £871 a head spent less on them than an average person in Scotland ... If one were to take a city like Norwich, which has about 120,000 people in it, it would imply that if Norwich were somehow looped into the Barnett formula, became part of Scotland by some treaty or whatever, we would be allowed to spend in Norwich ... something around £100–104 million a year more than is currently being spent ...

(*Mr Gieve, Treasury*) I think your underlying point is right ...[11]

Would-be candidates for the post of mayor in London are also starting to make direct comparisons between the funding treatment of London and Scotland; and similar comparisons are being made by leaders in other regions, such as the South West.[12]

The funding issue was debated in the Cabinet Sub-Committee on Devolution. The only concession which English Ministers were able to obtain was a sentence in the Scottish White Paper which acknowledges that: 'Any more substantial revision [of the formula] would need to be preceded by an in depth study of relative spending requirements and would be the subject of full consultation between the Scottish Executive and the UK Government.'[13] If eventually the Government is forced to concede a fresh needs assessment, as the Select Committee and others have argued, it seems highly unlikely that it could be conducted by the Treasury, because the Scottish and other devolved governments would have little confidence in the results. Either it would have to be entrusted to an intergovernmental commission, which might find it difficult to agree, or to an independent Territorial Exchequer Board of the kind for which Professor David Heald has long argued.[14]

Aside from the question of fairness, there are two other reasons why the Barnett formula does not offer a satisfactory long term basis for funding devolution. The first is that it is not generalizable for the purpose of regional government in England. It is driven by changes in total English spending

---

[11] Treasury Committee, *The Barnett Formula*, HC 341, Q156, p21

[12] *Financial Times*, 25 September 1998 reported the publication of a prospectus for the South West Regional Development Agency launched by South West Enterprise, representing business in Devon and Cornwall. 'The prospectus voices anger about the higher public spending that Scotland, Wales and some English regions receive. If the south-west was given the same amount per head as Scotland—already wealthier—it would receive an extra £1.4bn a year or £290 for every resident. The RDA, by contrast, is likely to have a budget below £50m.'

[13] *Scotland's Parliament* (Cm 3658) para 7.7.

[14] e.g. Heald and Geaughan, 'Financing a Scottish Parliament', in Tindale, S., (ed), *The State and the Nations: The Politics of Devolution* (Institute for Public Policy Research, 1996).

programmes—a notional 'English block'. As soon as that block is disaggregated the basis of the Barnett formula disappears. A new formula could be devised, but it would have to be based upon figures of relative need which included the English regions. That task will need to be tackled anyway. The Government has promised greater transparency in the operation of the Barnett formula. The English regions will take a closer interest in the overall allocation mechanism and will want to know how it affects them. Some rough figures are available from Treasury exercises which allocate some 85 per cent of identifiable public expenditure to the eight standard regions of England: see Figure 11.2.

Figure 11.2. Comparison of per capita GDP, tax receipts and public spending, 1993–4 *Index, Great Britain = 100*					
Region	*GDP per capita*	*Per capita tax receipts*	*Spending, including social security*	*Spending, excluding social security*	*Spending, excluding social security and local authority spending*
North	89	89	103	97	98
Yorks & Humber	91	91	96	95	96
E. Midlands	95	96	90	88	91
East Anglia	101	97	88	85	91
London & S. East	115	119	100	102	96
South West	96	100	90	87	88
W. Midlands	93	83	94	91	88
North West	90	89	103	99	97
Wales	84	82	114	113	119
Scotland	98	95	120	131	144

Source: Institute for Fiscal Studies, *Financing Regional Government in Britain*, Table 2.6

But these are figures of expenditure, not of relative need. It would be a useful step towards preparing for a long term devolution settlement to start collecting data on relative needs and on spending variations for all the English regions, on the same basis as data between England and other parts of the UK. That would help to provide some objective underpinning to a formula-based allocation of territorial public expenditure, and help to make the process transparent for all interested parties. The objective should be to encourage a more sophisticated understanding of regional variations in public expenditure and the reasons for it, and promote a political debate centred on notions of 'equity' rather than 'subsidy'.

Figure 11.2 provides a starting point for such a debate. It is a composite table compiled by the Institute for Fiscal Studies to show regional variations in wealth, tax revenues and public spending across the eight regions of England, and in Scotland and Wales. Wales comes out as much the poorest region, and Scotland the third richest in terms of GDP per capita. Wales benefits from higher levels of public spending than any English region; but on all three measures of public spending, Scotland appears to receive the highest levels of spending of all the regions of Great Britain. Amongst the English regions the one which appears to do well is London and the South East.

The second reason why the Barnett formula is not an adequate funding basis in the longer term is that it does not allow for policy variation. Policy diversity is the object of devolution—the freedom of the devolved governments to determine their own spending priorities. But the financial arrangements need to allow that to happen in practice. Problems will arise whenever English reforms are introduced with large expenditure numbers attached, because of their knock-on effects. A current example is tuition fees for higher education. Funding of the health service could be another. Suppose that a future government in London wishes to cut income tax, and introduces tax incentives for private health insurance which enable it to reduce spending on the health service in England. Under the Barnett formula this would lead automatically to a proportionate cut in the block grants for Scotland, Wales and Northern Ireland; but they might want to retain their levels of health spending. The funding formula should be able to allow for policy variation, and to cope with differing concepts of the public sector in different parts of the country. In the long run this must mean moving to a needs-based formula, not one driven by spending priorities in England.

Before leaving the Barnett formula, it is right to recognize the political realities. Funding formulae have an uncanny ability to live on long past their useful lives, because of the immense political difficulty in agreeing upon a replacement. Most Scots do not believe that they enjoy relatively generous levels of public expenditure, and would be incredulous at the figures presented in this chapter. In one sense their scepticism would be justified: many of the official figures are estimates based upon inadequate data. The selection of different factors and weightings to go into relative needs assessments is an inevitably subjective exercise. This point was made by Professor Arthur Midwinter to the Treasury Committee:

[T]he key point is that needs assessments are fraught with imprecision, and open to political manipulation. Political acceptability rather than fiscal equalisation is the test of such formulae. That political acceptability, in a zero-sum game, will not be easily achieved. The local authority grant distribution mechanisms are bedevilled by political disagreements ...

It is this inevitability of contesting interpretations over imperfect techniques that leads me to conclude in favour of retaining the Barnett formula, which has the highly practical benefit of being based on historic spending thus providing stability ....[15]

In terms of prediction he may well be proved right. In ten years' time the Barnett formula may still be with us, creaking on, because of the political difficulty of agreeing upon an alternative. The cost for the devolved governments will be limited autonomy, with policy changes forced upon them because of the knock-on consequences of English spending decisions. To get round this there may have to be increasing resort to formula bypass to accommodate differential patterns of spending. Barnett may survive, but in a patched-up version. But once the formula is significantly bypassed it loses its point. There may be growing pressure to attempt equalization by spending outside the Barnett process, including perhaps special grants to the poorer English regions. This would amount over time to spending decisions across the UK being made on an increasingly *ad hoc* basis, according to the lobbying strengths of local interests, rather than a relatively principled distribution according to a proper equalization formula.

THE NEED FOR A DEGREE OF FISCAL FREEDOM

In considering the consequences of the Government's decision to continue with the Barnett formula we have looked mainly at 'horizontal equity', and the extent to which it meets the principle of equalization according to need. The remainder of the chapter looks at vertical fiscal relationships, and the imbalance between taxes raised at the centre and in the regions.

Apart from the marginal tax-varying power given to the Scottish Parliament, the devolved governments will have no sources of revenue under their own control. Experts on the financing of devolution are unanimous about the loss of autonomy this will entail. The Institute for Fiscal Studies (IFS) has declared:

If regional governments are to function as genuine democratic units, with the power to make decisions concerning the level and pattern of public services, they will need to have access to some form of tax revenues under their own control. Reliance on fiscal transfers from central government will undermine the ability of regional government to make their decisions free from central influence.[16]

[15] Treasury Committee, *The Barnett Formula*, HC 341, Appendix 1, December 1997.

[16] Blow, Hall and Smith, *Financing Regional Government in Britain*, Institute for Fiscal Studies, June 1996, p. 62.

The IFS develop this argument by drawing a distinction between decentralisation of administration and decentralization of choice:

Where regional government is principally concerned with the efficient implementation and administration of policies determined by central government, it may be appropriate for regional government to be financed largely or entirely through financial transfers from centrally-collected tax revenues ...

In contrast, where regional government is intended to function as a more independent level of democratic decision-making, giving regional voters the power to make choices that differ from those in other regions or that differ from the choices that would be made by central government, there is a much greater case for assigning some taxation powers to regional government. Indeed, in this case, some independent power over revenue is essential if the opportunity for regional government to make independent choices is not to be a meaningless fiction.[17]

Policy autonomy is one reason for allowing devolved governments a degree of fiscal freedom. The second is fiscal accountability to their own electors. This second reason has been expressed with equal force by Professor David Heald:

The kernel of the argument for tax-varying powers is that—when differentials in needs and resources have been addressed—the marginal expenditure decided upon by sub-national governments should be self-financed from an economically appropriate and politically acceptable tax base ... The link between elected office and responsibility for revenue-raising is deliberate. All those who spend public money by virtue of elected office should have responsibility for raising some of that money through taxation and/or user charges. Just as 'no taxation without representation' was the battle cry of those who fought for American independence, so 'no representation without taxation' is a maxim which deserves equal priority.[18]

LIMITS ON FISCAL FREEDOM OF DEVOLVED GOVERNMENTS

Some have argued that fiscal accountability can only be achieved if devolved governments are made responsible for raising all the money that they spend. This is to push the principle too far. It would preclude needs and resources equalization, and is completely unrealistic in the modern global economy. In no country are state or regional governments fully self-financing, and in most there is a drift of taxes towards the centre. This is to avoid economic inefficiencies in tax collection, and to strengthen safeguards against tax

---

[17] Ibid, p. 35.
[18] Heald, Geaughan and Robb, 'Financial Arrangements for UK Devolution', *Regional and Federal Studies*, Vol. 8, 1998, pp. 23–52.

avoidance and evasion. There are also growing limitations on fiscal freedom as a result of European economic integration and monetary union.

Professor Heald has analysed the limitations on different regional taxes as follows:

- **Economic globalization and deregulation** have led to both capital and labour becoming much more mobile. Even national jurisdictions find it difficult to protect their corporate tax bases. These factors combine to preclude the use of corporate taxes at sub-national level, and to limit the use of progressive income taxes.
- **EU membership** involves the acceptance of strict limits on the extent of variation in consumption taxes. The use of such taxes as one of the revenue sources of the German Länder is covered by derogations in regard of pre-existing taxes which, even before the European Commission's big push for tax harmonization, would not have been extended to the UK.
- **Consumption and retailing changes** have strengthened the revenue protection arguments for keeping VAT as simple as possible, and for not complicating matters by introducing regionally variable rates and/or supplementary retail taxes. Reductions in real transport costs have lowered the costs of shopping in other jurisdictions (e.g. cross-Channel shopping). Effective distances in the UK are small in international terms, ruling out many of the revenue sources from consumption taxes which are used by states in Australia and provinces in Canada.
- **Macro-economic policy** gives central government a legitimate interest in the expenditure and financing of sub-national governments, which account for a significant proportion of general government expenditure and of GDP. In addition to its general concern for securing macro-economic balance, the Treasury now has a specific obligation under the Maastricht Treaty's Excessive Deficits Protocol to control the current deficit to GDP ratio and the total government debt ratio.[19]

The culmination of these different factors has been to favour most tax-raising being effected at higher levels of government. Professor Heald adds that the best taxes for variation at sub-national levels are highly visible ones such as personal income taxes (though the variation band has to be kept modest) and property taxes, supplemented by user charges. The Institute for Fiscal Studies concur in making regional income tax their first choice, because it is least likely to lead to major locational distortions (especially if the regional power to

---

[19] Ibid, pp.30–2.

vary tax rates is confined to the basic rate) and because it is more transparent in its burden and incidence.[20]

WHAT REVENUE-RAISING SOURCES ARE AVAILABLE FOR DEVOLVED GOVERNMENTS?

A regional income tax is to be the main additional source of revenue for the Scottish Parliament; but not for the Northern Ireland and Welsh Assemblies, which are to be wholly dependent on central government grant. If the Scottish income tax is judged to be a success, this limited fiscal freedom may in time be extended to Wales and Northern Ireland. But what is the likelihood of the Scottish Parliament exercising its tax-varying powers?

There are four main reasons why it seems unlikely that the Scottish Parliament will exercise its tax-raising power. First, it would not yield very much. The Scottish Parliament's tax-raising power is limited to a power to vary the basic rate of income tax by plus or minus 3 pence in the pound. The total product of a 3 pence rise in the basic rate in Scotland would be to yield additional revenue of around £400–450 million. This does not amount to much, when set against the annual cost of the health service in Scotland of almost £5 billion. It would represent an increase of only around 3 per cent on the total Scottish block of £14 billion. This seems little financial gain to set against the political pain.

Second, the costs of collection are quite high. The White Paper gave estimates of the costs for government and the compliance costs for taxpayers. The initial direct costs to government of establishing the mechanisms for tax variation in Scotland were estimated at £10m, and the running costs of collecting the tax at around £8m per annum.[21] Beyond government, the main costs would be the additional costs for employers of collection through PAYE. The White Paper estimated their setting up costs to be around £50m, and running costs at around £6–15m per annum. This may prove a greater hurdle for a Scottish government than the Inland Revenue's collection costs (which would be passed on to Scotland). In practice it may mean that the tax-varying power will amount to a hypothecated tax, which would only be exercised for a purpose of which employers approved.

Third, and most important, raising tax is electorally unpopular. Political parties nowadays do not lightly campaign on a platform of raising taxes. The Australian states have for decades had a power to raise income tax, but no state government has dared to use it. Tony Blair pledged before the 1997 election

---

[20] Blow, Hall and Smith, *Financing Regional Government in Britain*, IFS, June 1996, p.62. The alternatives considered by the IFS were regional business tax and regional sales tax.

[21] *Scotland's Parliament*, (Cm 3658) July 1997, paras. 7.18–7.19

that Labour would not raise the basic or higher rate of income tax during the term of the 1997 Parliament. Such a pledge does not necessarily extend to a Labour administration in Scotland, but the electorate may expect it to do so.[22] The new leader of the Conservative party in Scotland has made a pledge not to use the tax-raising power.[23] The only factor which might undermine this iron law of electoral competition is the possibility of coalition government arising from the new electoral system in Scotland (see Chapter 6). If no party wins an outright majority it is likely that initially administrations will be formed on the basis of post-election coalition agreements. In the longer term these coalition partners might develop pre-election concordats. With the risk of being undercut by close political rivals removed, a pre-election concordat might include joint plans to exercise the tax-varying power.

Finally there is the factor of inertia. The longer the tax-varying power remains unused, the less likely it is that it will be used; or that it will be introduced in Wales or Northern Ireland. The political obstacles to the use of the tax-varying power can only grow during an extended period of non-use, and the administrative and compliance arrangements originally put in place will atrophy. As the White Paper figures show, the tax collection arrangements are not cheap; no government will maintain them for long unless the tax power is used.

One circumstance which might upset this analysis is an external shock, such as a national disaster in Scotland, justifying a special fund. Another would be a change in the Barnett formula, or a future needs assessment which revised downwards Scotland's spending share. In the latter circumstance the Scottish government would negotiate for a phased introduction of the reduced payments, but it might come under pressure to use the tax-raising power as another means of absorbing the shock. It would also assist in overcoming the political barrier, because the blame for introducing the tax could be shifted to the British government.

PRECEPTING ON LOCAL GOVERNMENT

Wales and Northern Ireland will have no such buffer, because they will be wholly dependent on central government grant. In Scotland and Wales a large part of the grant is in respect of local government expenditure: in Northern Ireland less so, because of the lesser responsibilities of their local authorities.

---

[22] Before the 1997 election *The Scotsman* published an interview with Mr Blair which reported: 'Mr Blair also ruled out the use of a Scottish Parliament's tax varying powers, which he likened to those of an English parish council, in the first term of a Labour government by saying [that] his five year pledge of no rise in the basic and standard rates of tax applied to "Scotland" as well as "England".' *The Scotsman*, 4 April 1997.

[23] David McLetchie reported in *The Daily Telegraph*, 17 September 1998.

With devolution, responsibility for grant support to local authorities will fall to the devolved governments, and represent one of their largest heads of expenditure. If they find their budgets squeezed it may be tempting for them in turn to squeeze revenue support grant to local authorities, and rely on the local authorities' capacity to increase levels of council tax to make up the difference.

The capacity to do this may be limited because of the limits of the local authority tax base. Evidence to the Lords Select Committee on Central–Local Government Relations suggested that the proportion of local authority expenditure funded by the council tax could rise from 20 to about 25 per cent, but not much more.[24] But it does not invalidate the general point, that the devolved governments could levy taxes by proxy through the council tax by cutting their grant to local authorities. In Wales and in Northern Ireland, without any source of revenue under their own control, this could represent their only variable source of revenue.

The only other variable source of revenue will be non-domestic rates. Although in England these are not to be returned to local government, they could be elsewhere. There would then be a greater capacity for the devolved government to precept because local authorities would have a stronger revenue base. If non-domestic rates remain determined centrally in Edinburgh and Cardiff (as now), the devolved governments in Scotland and Wales could decide to increase business rates to compensate local authorities for a reduction in grant support. Here too there would be limited room for manoeuvre, because of the risk of an adverse reaction from the business community; but the possibility is there.

There is also risk of an adverse reaction from the British government, which is mentioned in the Scottish but not in the Welsh White Paper. Amongst its general powers over local government, the Scottish Parliament will inherit power to control local authority expenditure, through capping or other means. It will clearly be expected by the Treasury to exercise those powers strictly. The White Paper warns:

If growth relative to England were excessive and were such as to threaten targets set for public expenditure as part of the management of the UK economy, and the Scottish Parliament nevertheless chose not to exercise its powers, it would be open to the UK Government to take the excess into account in considering the level of their support for expenditure in Scotland.[25]

---

[24] Report of the Lords Select Committee on Relations between Central and Local Government, *Rebuilding Trust*, HL Paper 97, July 1996, para. 5.19.

[25] *Scotland's Parliament* (Cm 3658) July 1997, para. 7.24.

FUNDING FROM EUROPE

Finally there is the possibility of levering additional funds out of Europe. Northern Ireland is an obvious candidate to receive extra funds, as part of the peace process, and should receive strong support from the Republic for any bids that are made. Wales is currently pinning high hopes on a new bid to the EU structural funds for Objective One funding in the next round from 2000 to 2006. Objective One funding provides support from the European Regional Development Fund and European Social Fund for the development and structural adjustment of the poorest regions. Wales has recently persuaded EUROSTAT, the European Commission's statistical office, that west Wales and the valleys of south Wales can qualify for Objective One status since their GDP per head falls below 75 per cent of the EU average. Extrapolating from the current Objective One programmes in the Highlands and Islands (300m ECU) and on Merseyside (800m ECU) Wales hopes to receive £900m to £1bn in EC funds over the seven years 2000–6 should the Objective One bid be secured.[26]

But the European structural funds do not offer a reliable long-term funding basis for devolution. The total Welsh bid may seem large, but the annual amount (£130–140m) is not, when set against the annual transfer from London of the Welsh block of around £7bn. Brussels will insist on matching contributions from the recipient country, and the Treasury will expect the Welsh Assembly to find that from within its own budget, and not look for additional funding to the British Exchequer. Perhaps most important, this may be the last opportunity for major bids to the European structural funds from the countries of Western Europe. Already the funds are being reshaped to prepare for enlargement to the east, with regions far poorer than amongst the current members of the EU. The countries of eastern and central Europe are likely to be the major beneficiaries from the structural funds in the future.

CONCLUSIONS

The main conclusions of this chapter can be summarized as follows. First, the UK has chosen an extremely centralized model for funding devolution. Only the Scottish Parliament will have tax-raising powers, and those will be limited to some 3 per cent of the Parliament's total budget. The Northern Ireland and Welsh Assemblies will have none. As a consequence all the devolved governments will find that their room for manoeuvre is tightly constrained. It is

---

[26] Morgan, K. and Price, A., *The Other Wales—The Case for Objective 1 Funding Post 1999*, Institute of Welsh Affairs, July 1998.

true that they will retain discretion to determine the distribution of public expenditure within their respective blocks; but this apparent freedom to determine the nature and level of public services in their regions may turn out to be largely hollow. All the major decisions about public expenditure and the pattern of public services seem set to be made by the government in London, and with no independent sources of revenue the devolved governments will find themselves obliged to follow suit through the operation of the funding formula. It may not be the Government's intention, but the funding mechanism will ensure that the Treasury and the English spending departments retain control.

As a result the Barnett formula will come under a lot of pressure. It will come under pressure from both sides: from the devolved governments, who will want greater autonomy; and from the English regions, who will question its fairness. The UK government will be forced to publish more data about the operation of the formula, and will come under pressure to produce better data about the relative spending needs and public expenditure shares of all parts of the UK, including the English regions. Selective facts and figures will be deployed by all the participants, and the debate will be bitter and confused. As with the longstanding wrangle over local government finance, arguments over the funding arrangements for devolution will significantly exacerbate intergovernmental relations.

Once it is more widely understood that the Barnett formula does not determine the devolved governments' total budgets and that it does not relate to spending needs, pressure will grow for a fresh needs assessment. The Treasury Committee has fired the first shot in what is likely to be a long-running campaign. The differences in territorial per capita expenditure need new legitimization, which can only be provided by an updated needs assessment. That in turn can only be carried out by an intergovernmental or independent body: the Treasury will not be trusted to carry out the needs assessment on its own. There needs to be machinery which the participants are willing to trust, using data which are a lot more reliable than the statistics which are currently available. The Treasury and the Office for National Statistics will need to invest in systematic data collection and in research on the regions to supply such data.

Even with better data the needs assessment will be a highly political exercise; followed by hard bargaining between the potential winners and losers among the governments concerned. It will occupy a lot of time in meetings of the Joint Ministerial Committee on Devolution. It may lead to litigation, as it has done in Germany, where some of the Länder have challenged the operation of the distribution formula before the Constitutional Court.

Political and electoral calculations will play a part as well as argument over the figures. Scotland may play the nationalist or independence card, just as successive Secretaries of State used to play the devolution card whenever public investment in Scotland was under threat. All these are arguments which the British government and Treasury may seek to deploy in private when discussing alternatives to the Barnett formula; but they cannot be deployed in public. The only public defence which will command credibility is that Barnett still delivers a result which is broadly fair and acceptable to all the parties. That is a line which will be increasingly difficult to maintain; and without a fresh needs assessment, it is a line which the Government will be in no position to justify.

12

Citizenship and National Identity

ANN DUMMETT

In most countries, the concept of citizenship can be clearly explained by reference to a written constitution and subsequent legislation. The former will say what a citizen's rights and duties are; the latter will draw a line between citizens and non-citizens. In the United Kingdom we have no such clarity.

National identity is a more difficult concept to pin down: a compound of views of history, popular traditions and official promotions, political leanings and attitudes towards non-nationals. These elements change over time and there is often disagreement over which are the most important. Moreover, senses of national identity vary in strength: they may be highly important to an individual's sense of personal identity—as in the United States now and in Britain a century ago—or may be less powerful than identification with a region, class, family, religion or linguistic group.

MEANING OF CITIZENSHIP

For many people in Britain, citizenship means involvement with the community: good citizenship requires honesty, reliability, helping one's neighbour and working voluntarily for good causes. It is a social norm for all residents: nobody thinks it odd that foreigners should have recourse to a Citizens' Advice Bureau or be called 'good citizens' for their local activities. For some people, however, citizenship is seen more formally as the exercise of civic rights and duties established by law: jury service, voting for Parliament and the local Council, and so on. Neither of these two concepts of citizenship is closely linked to a sense of nationality. Nationals of Commonwealth countries and Ireland have long been able to vote and stand for election, and be called on for jury duty, just as British citizens can (see below, *Nationality and Civic Rights*).

This is all vastly different from other countries' ideas of citizenship. A French citizen is supposed to be guaranteed individual freedom, civic rights and duties, cultural identity and membership of a nation all in one unified, clear-cut, exclusive and powerful concept. In Germany, the sense of ethnic Germanness is combined with attachment to language and culture and a sharply defined set of rights which foreigners cannot share. Nationality and citizenship are at one: legal definition of civic rights and national self-consciousness are intended to go together.

British nationality is much vaguer. Remarkably, there is no such thing as a 'British national' in United Kingdom domestic law. Professor Clive Parry, the leading expert of his day on nationality laws in the Commonwealth and Ireland, wrote in 1957, 'there is not and never has been any domestic concept of British nationality as such'.[1] Even in 1981, attempts to amend the nationality legislation of that year by designating certain persons 'British nationals' were rejected by the Government.[2] Common law had retained the medieval distinction between two mutually exclusive groups: subjects and aliens. An alien was any person in the world who was not the king's subject. Subjecthood was used *as if* it were a nationality, its attributes being defined partly by common law and partly by statute. The term 'citizen' had first been introduced, as late as 1948, in legislation which attached no rights or duties to citizenship.

This peculiar situation could never have arisen if the United Kingdom had ever made a clean break with the past and established a single-document constitution designed all of a piece to deal with the structure of government, the principles underlying the activities of the state, the division of powers, and the rights and duties of the citizen. Written constitutions of this kind are generally drafted following successful revolutions, the grant of independence, or the collapse of the civil power, for example after a war. No such situation has arisen in Britain since the seventeenth century. We have continued to make *ad hoc* adjustments to selected questions by means of ordinary legislation devised with limited purposes. The collection of changes being made by the present Government is part of this familiar process. An unusually large number of constitutional issues is being dealt with in an unusually short time, but the changes do not add up to a new constitution: they will be patches on an old garment. There has been no question of entrenching citizens' rights, although some will be strengthened by incorporating the European Convention on Human Rights. The devolution scheme will alter voting rights, but not uniformly. Some voters will have more voting opportunities locally than others. As to nationality, the only current proposal for change is the Foreign and Commonwealth Office scheme (reported in the *Guardian* on 14 July 1998) for giving British citizenship to the inhabitants of the remaining dependent territories. At the time of writing, this is the subject of negotiation between the

---

[1] Parry, C., *Nationality and Citizenship Laws of the Commonwealth and of the Republic of Ireland* (London: Stevens, 1957), 5.

[2] Parliamentary Debates, House of Lords, 13 October 1981, cols. 270–1. Speech by Lord Trefgarne.

Foreign and Commonwealth Office (FCO) and the Home Office. If successful, it would be one step in the direction of sorting out the present confusion in nationality and citizenship law, for reasons that will be described below.

To understand this present confusion, one must look first at the national identity of the United Kingdom.

NATIONAL IDENTITY

The United Kingdom is a historical growth. The English people have been dominant in its development. English national self-consciousness goes back a long way: some historians place it before the Norman Conquest; others see it emerge in the thirteenth century, others again point to the fourteenth, when St George's cross became the badge of English soldiers.

Throughout this long history, two factors have been of overwhelming importance in Englishness. It has been defined by a territory, not by ethnicity, and until very recent times it was anchored in allegiance to the monarch.

Celts, Romans, Anglo-Saxons, Normans and subsequently a stream of immigrants from various sources—Flemish, French, German, Italian in the Middle Ages and an even greater variety thereafter—were to settle in England. The feudal rule of *ius soli* made their children English: anyone born on the territory of the king was a natural-born subject.

The Welsh already had their own separate history and identity (partly anti-English and partly cultural and legal) when Henry VIII formally annexed Wales. Scotland, which had been a distinct nation with its own kings for centuries, became part of the United Kingdom, not with the union of the English and Scottish crowns in 1603, but with a Parliamentary Act of Union in 1707. Scotland retained its own church, educational system, and Scots law. British subjecthood and a British nation date from 1707. The Act of Union with Ireland in 1801 extended the UK, replacing the English Crown's claim to lordship of Ireland, which for centuries had implied that the Irish were subjects, though until 1801 subjects of a separate kingdom under one ruler. In the overseas colonies, the rule for making subjects by birth on the king's territory was also applied. Britishness, the attribute of the United Kingdom since its formation in 1707, was *not confined to the United Kingdom* but was spread over a large part of the globe.

From 1789 onwards, other European countries began to abandon feudal rules and set up new constitutions defining citizenship in modern terms. The United Kingdom retained the concept of subjecthood as the nationality of the British empire. The sense of identity of people in the United Kingdom itself was strongly encouraged to be imperial in the late nineteenth and early twentieth centuries. The size and wealth of the empire were sources of pride: so was its Britishness. Britishness was imbued with a sense of power combined with responsibility, a pride in both ruling and guiding others. School text books and popular fiction emphasized this theme: politicians' speeches drew on it.

Underlying these developments were several different layers of national consciousness. 'Britain' was not merely the creation of union between England and other nations but the ancient Roman name for the whole island, and one full of significance. King Arthur had been King of Britain; Geoffrey of Monmouth's popular and influential history in the twelfth century had been the history of the kings of Britain. The Welsh held themselves to be the true people of Britain, ousted by the English from much of the land. The term 'Briton' became popular as a name for English, Welsh and Scots in the eighteenth century, and in 1740 James Thomson wrote 'Rule, Britannia'. But English national consciousness persisted. History books were histories of England; in the nineteenth century Walter Bagehot's great book was called *The English Constitution*. When Wordsworth invoked Milton, he wrote, 'England hath need of thee', and England was frequently called 'the mother country', notably mother of the empire in the popular song of the Second World War, 'There'll always be an England'. Nobody has ever written a popular song invoking the name of the United Kingdom. England, yes; Scotland for ever, yes; there'll be a welcome in the valleys when you come back again to Wales—but we are not asked to invoke the United Kingdom, except by Unionists in Northern Ireland.

From 1914 onwards, the picture has changed irrevocably because of the loss of empire. After 1945, an ideal of the Commonwealth was supposed to replace the imperial ideal, but, as newly independent countries became republics, the link of allegiance was broken and the United Kingdom was to be one among equals rather than a mother country. Rapid loss of status as a world power and accelerated economic decline removed the bases of a British/English sense of pride and prestige. The reaction to the change in Wales and Scotland found expression for some people in nationalism. In England, there was no corresponding growth of English nationalism, but rather a harking back to the great days of the past, expressed for example in innumerable television plays and documentaries about the Tudors, the Edwardian era, the North-west Frontier and British bravery in the Second World War. The imperial identity was hard to shake off, and burst out in a wave of jingoism during the Falklands war of 1982. But it no longer fitted the facts, and British/English identity had to rely on pride in the occasional sporting success and resentment of foreigners and immigrants from the Commonwealth, or simply on a refusal to face facts. This country (Britain/England/the UK) was the greatest country in the world; everyone wanted to come here; everyone envied us and looked to our example: these myths still persist.

In Northern Ireland two rival senses of nationalism had erupted in a new stage of their ancient conflict. The Unionists clung to a Protestant identity, which had been central to the British constitution and the official notion of British/English identity since the Reformation. But although some aspects of it linger in the British constitution (it is still unlawful for the monarch or heir to the throne to be or to marry a Catholic, for instance), the widespread abandonment of religious practice, the arrival of more non-Christian faiths and the growth of ecumenism in the last fifty years or more have destroyed its significance.

Hardly any young people today can be aware that the identification of Church and State was a powerful symbol of national identity well into the present century. The establishment (which used to mean only the established Church and not, as it has done since the 1960s, the secular ruling class) permeated everyday life in numerous practical ways.[3] As with so many British institutions, it was a muddle, for the Church of England followed one doctrine, the Church of Scotland another (the Presbyterian) and the Church of Wales, disestablished in 1920, got a new property settlement but remained (like the Church of Ireland) part of the Anglican communion. Muddle, indeed, used to be a source of pride in Britishness: we muddled through while more precise and organized foreign nations got things wrong. The constitution was vague, but we gloried in the fact: Burke remarked that 'It is in the nature of all greatness not to be exact.'[4]

Now, however, the greatness has gone, and the vagueness has become a liability. Tom Nairn says of the historical British identity:

I suspect the trouble may be terminal. Even as a trade-mark, 'British' seems to be on the skids. 'Britishness' has passed from being one of the soundest properties on the international ideas-mart (liberal, trustworthy, first-among-equals, 'Mother-of' this and that, progressive haven, etc.) to being a down-market left-over, not quite a slum, but heading in that direction.[5]

There are, however, some old and some new ideas of national identity to be invoked. The old ones have been seriously damaged in recent years: personal liberty and independence by an explosion of regulatory legislation; helping each other out by the doctrine of competitiveness; a slow and gentle approach to life by puritanical pressures to work ever longer hours; freedom to be eccentric and nonconformist by intense pressures towards conformity and regulation. Constitutional change *could* make a real difference to people's sense of personal liberty. But a government cannot create and then impose a

---

[3] Taylor, A. J. P., *English History 1914–1945* (Oxford: Oxford University Press, 1965 and London: Pelican Books, 1970) ch. 5 has some useful and entertaining comments. Ch. 4 of Dummett, A. and Nicol A., *Subjects, Citizens, Aliens and Others* (London: Weidenfeld and Nicolson, 1990) describes the importance of Protestant identity to nationality law and civic rights over a long period. See also Colley, L., *Britons—Forging the Nation 1707–1837* (London: Pimlico, 1992).

[4] Burke, E., *Speech on American Taxation*, 1774.

[5] Nairn, T., *De Facto Independence*, an outline of evidence to the House of Commons Scottish Affairs Committee, June 1998.

sense of national identity: it needs, if considering constitutional change, to make use of existing aspirations and beliefs.

Besides the Scots, Welsh, and Irish national traditions, there are strong regional traditions and regional identities within England. These would surely flower if a devolution scheme gave the regions democratic elections and control of funds. The present scheme of devolution appears to be hesitating about any effective transfer of power from the centre. But without such a transfer one cannot reasonably expect people to be enthusiastic about a new tier of government. Quangos do not arouse popularity or commitment. For citizens to feel like active citizens, there must be useful activities for them to pursue and to some degree control. There is a strong contrast between the powers of regions in Spain, Germany and other European Community (EC) countries and those in the UK, a contrast which delegates to the European Union's Committee of the Regions are now able to observe for themselves.

Citizenship in the sense of active involvement would also be promoted by a reform of the House of Lords which was based on regional representation in England and national representation in the rest of the UK. But here again, enthusiasm might not be warm unless such a reformed House had powers which the population saw as effective and responsive to their concerns.[6]

To the many to whom public institutions mean 'the welfare', the benefits office, the rent officer and the truant officer, the police and the long wait in a casualty department, constitutional changes will not bring a new sense of self-confidence and national identity unless they are seen to be part of an overall plan responsive to everyone's needs. National identity has to go beyond middle England: to embrace optimistic forms of Englishness and at the same time hold true for the whole UK.

Of the new ideas of national identity surely the most promising is that of a diverse, pluralist United Kingdom. First, it embraces without difficulty the English, Scots, Welsh and Irish together with the Indians, Jamaicans, Australians, Poles, Vietnamese, Africans and so on who inhabit United Kingdom territory. It allots to them all cultural freedom and diversity within the framework of a unitary state. It accepts the freedom to follow any religion or none. The great advantage of the idea is that it is already at work, and indeed can claim a long history. English, Scots, Welsh and Irish have been migrating between each other's territories for centuries, and are still doing so. Simon Partridge[7] quotes figures to show that there are nearly 5 million residents of Britain having or qualifying for Irish citizenship: many more have

---

[6] These questions are discussed in more detail in 'Reforming the Lords and Changing Britain', a paper by John Osmond for the Institute of Welsh Affairs and the Fabian Society, August 1998.

[7] Partridge, S., *The Implications of the Irish Diaspora and Devolved Democracy in the British-Irish Islands*, paper based on an address given in Dublin on 25 April 1998 to a Democratic Left seminar.

Irish ancestry and a quarter of British people have an Irish relative. Nearly 20 per cent of the population of Wales is English-born, as is 8 per cent of the population of Scotland. There were 743,000 Scottish-born residents in England, according to the 1991 census, but of course England holds a far higher proportion than this of people with Scots ancestry. Similarly, the figure of 545,000 Welsh-born people in England omits the descendants of the Welsh who moved eastwards during the great Depression in the 1930s or who have followed their professional ambitions in England over a far longer period.

Similarly again, census figures for the foreign-born give no adequate idea of the large numbers of British people with foreign ancestry, derived from immigrants over the centuries. London is today, and has long been, the most cosmopolitan city in Europe, but even outside London foreign immigration has been an important feature of life in major towns and a few rural areas since the early middle ages. It grew rapidly in the later nineteenth century, and despite the immigration controls of the twentieth has continued up to the present. We have already had, over a century ago, a Prime Minister of Italian Jewish descent, and several of our major corporations were founded by foreigners (e.g. ICI, formerly Brunner-Mond). The census does not classify people's legal nationalities, and so it is impossible to use the 1991 census figure of 3,991,000 people born outside the UK to indicate foreigners resident here, partly because this includes Irish and Commonwealth-country immigrants and partly because it also includes children born abroad to British citizens. But if we include children born here to foreign parents, both in this generation and in earlier ones, it is reasonable to guess that the census figure of almost 4 million (7.27 per cent of population) foreign-born is a serious underestimate of our total foreign-descended population.

British residents from the former empire are not foreigners but Commonwealth citizens. They have settled in the UK in small numbers since the eighteenth century.[8] Their numbers grew between 1945 and 1973 but were sharply curtailed by a series of immigration restrictions from 1962 onwards, and in the early 1970s, although persons of Indian ancestry continued to arrive, more West Indians were leaving the UK than arriving. Entry from the white Dominions was in practice much less controlled than entry from poor countries, and many Australians settled in the 1960s. The enormous variety of minorities in Britain (only a few have gone to Northern Ireland) has influenced national identity. Food, entertainment and sport have all been greatly changed, but so, less tangibly, have public attitudes. This is best seen by contrasting our situation with that in other countries. In Germany it would be unthinkable to have dark-skinned Muslims working regularly as TV newsreaders. In France, Muslim girls are excluded from school if they wear headscarves. Although

---

[8] See Fryer, P., *Staying Power* (London: Pluto Press, 1984) and Holmes, C., *Immigrants and Minorities in British Society* (London: Allen and Unwin, 1978).

racism is strong in Britain, and there are some who would deny real Britishness to ethnic minorities, others have accepted a mixed society.

There has been much intermarriage. Figures are not available for every group, but the Policy Studies Institute, in its 1997 report on 'Diversity and Disadvantage', showed that the proportion of children with one white parent to those with two non-white parents was among Caribbeans 39 per cent, among Chinese 15 per cent, among Indians 3 per cent, and among Pakistanis/ Bangladeshis 1 per cent.[9] (One can assume that 'white' here meant British for the most part, though some white parents may have been foreign.)

Religious diversity is evident in the number of mosques and Hindu and Sikh temples, as well as synagogues, established alongside Christian churches, while linguistic diversity is recognized in many public information leaflets published in several languages. What all this shows is a society in which most people (with the exception of some, like Lord Tebbit) do not have to worry about whether they call themselves 'British' or 'British and Scottish' or plain 'Welsh' or plain 'Indian' or 'British Indian'. They can choose, because national identity is diverse in fact and is beginning to be so in theory. The Northern Ireland agreement formalizes one such dual identity by recognizing 'the birthright of all the people of Northern Ireland to identify themselves and be accepted as Irish or British'. Their right to hold both British and Irish citizenship is accepted by both Governments.

A study by Anthony Heath and James Kellas[10] of the self-identification of English, Welsh and Scottish people living in the UK shows:

the coexistence of dual conceptions of national identity. People can feel both British and Scottish, or indeed both British and English (although it is questionable how far English people really distinguish between the latter two and they often appear to use the terms interchangeably).

77 per cent of respondents in England accepted a dual identity, 65 per cent in Wales and 69 per cent in Scotland. But 16 per cent in England, 29 per cent in Wales and 39 per cent in Scotland felt they were *more* English/Welsh/Scottish than they were British. These findings are perfectly consistent with the idea of a diverse, pluralist UK.

The 1991 census asked respondents for the ethnic group with which they identified and for their birthplaces. On the former criterion it showed that ethnic minority groups formed 5.5 per cent of the population of Great Britain. Ten categories were offered on the census form (Indian, Chinese, etc.): 178,000 chose 'Black Other' rather than a specific origin, and 58,000 of these chose to

---

[9] Modood, T. and Berthoud, R., *Ethnic Minorities in Britain: Diversity and Disadvantage* (London: Policy Studies Institute, 1997).

[10] Heath, A. and Kellas, J., 'Nationalisms and Constitutional Questions', *Scottish Affairs*, Special Issue (1998).

call themselves 'Black British'. Nearly half of all people from ethnic minorities had been born in the UK.

A successful pluralist society is an idea in which all the people of the United Kingdom could take pride—a modern concept to replace the old imperial idea.

NATIONALITY AND CIVIC RIGHTS

From medieval times onwards, the King's subjects had certain rights at common law, principally the right to hold real property in the kingdom. Statutes over the centuries have added to these rights or redefined them. By the time of the Second World War, a subject had the right to vote and stand for office in the United Kingdom, work in the public service, serve in the armed forces and be master of a British ship. Duties included jury service and liability for conscription. There was a general duty of allegiance to the monarch, and the monarch was entitled to give protection to subjects. The position of aliens was not wholly clear. Since the seventeenth century, aliens had been considered to have a general right of entry to the country, unless specifically prohibited under prerogative or statute, but were not allowed to vote or stand for office. In 1870 they acquired the right to hold property in the country. Until the nineteenth century they had a right to a 'half-tongue jury' with alien members, but aliens were barred from jury service in 1919. Within UK territory, however, they were able to have access to the courts, and to form and join voluntary associations. Most countries at the time were less liberal to aliens. In wartime, however, aliens suffered very severe disabilities under temporary legislation.

The rights of the subject belonged to subjects from anywhere in the empire when they were present in the UK. In their own countries, rights varied enormously. But in the UK, Indians, Africans, Australians, etc., could vote, stand for Parliament and local councils, sit in the Lords or Commons and work in the police or civil service just as UK-born subjects could. (Former MPs Joan Lestor, a Canadian, and Bryan Gould, a New Zealander, are just two examples.) This situation persists to this day for Commonwealth-country and colonial citizens, although the name and character of subjecthood have been altered by statute, and the public-service rights have been gradually curtailed.

After Ireland left the Commonwealth, the Ireland Act 1949 provided that Irish citizens would continue to be treated in the UK as if they were subjects: hence they retain civic rights here, including full voting rights. UK citizens have reciprocal rights in the Republic of Ireland.

European Community law in the Maastricht Treaty enfranchised those EC nationals who have resided in Britain for at least five years in local and European but not national elections. The change was made in the UK by a statutory instrument in 1995 using powers conferred by the European Communities Act 1972. There is no locality where these votes could be crucial to an election result, as the total number of qualifying residents is small, and they are scattered and most unlikely to form a voting bloc for a single party. The principle that they can both vote and stand for local or European office here is, however, constitutionally significant.

The Maastricht Treaty explicitly provided that the decision on who its nationals were should belong exclusively to each member state.[11] All EC nationals are European citizens and have the rights mentioned above in any EC country.[12] They also have the right to move freely and reside in any member state and to petition the European Parliament and its Ombudsman.

All the civic rights mentioned above are the creation of either UK statute law or EC law. The ancient common-law right of the subject to move freely in and out of the kingdom has been curtailed by UK immigration law since 1962, but this curtailment has been slightly modified by EC law (see below).

BRITISH NATIONALITY LAW

There is no single definition of British nationality. In 1914, major nationality legislation put the common imperial status of British subjecthood on to a statutory basis but left each Dominion to settle the rights and duties of subjects and aliens for itself. In 1948, a citizenship of the UK and Colonies (CUKC) was established but with no accompanying rights and duties: these were still to be attached to subjecthood, and subjecthood was to be the secondary status of all Commonwealth-country citizens including CUKCs. Although in theory subjecthood was then to continue throughout the Commonwealth as a common nationality, the theory rapidly broke down as newly independent countries drew up their own separate constitutions and created their own nationalities. The rights of subjecthood became relevant only to those Commonwealth and colonial citizens who came to the UK. From 1962 onwards, a series of Immigration Acts limited their opportunity to come.

In 1981, a major British Nationality Act created a new status of 'British citizenship' based on connection with the UK alone, with no rights attached except right of abode (exemption from immigration control). The old *ius soli* (by place of birth) was abandoned: a child born in the UK would need a parent who was a citizen or permanently resident to qualify. Four other categories of British nationality were created, none of which conferred right of abode anywhere: these were acquired by those existing CUKCs who had been left out of the main category (becoming either British Dependent Territories' Citizens or British Overseas Citizens), British Protected Persons (who retained that status) and British Subjects without Citizenship of any Commonwealth country

---

[11] Treaty on European Union, second Declaration annexed to the Treaty.
[12] Ibid., Article 8 EEC.

(who were re-named simply and confusingly 'British Subjects'). The old category of British subjects, embracing the former empire, was renamed 'Commonwealth citizens'—a legal term first introduced in 1948 which includes British citizens among others, though few British people are aware of the fact.

Falkland Islanders were made British citizens by a minor Nationality Act of 1983. Gibraltarians are still British Dependent Territories' Citizens (BDTC), but in practice have never been subject to UK immigration control. There is a special definition of British nationality for EC purposes, under which British nationals consist of British citizens, BDTCs from Gibraltar[13] and those 'British Subjects' (under the 1981 definition) who have the right of abode in the UK.

Any account of UK citizens' rights which ignored the considerable rights they have under EC law, to work or establish a business or service under conditions of equality with its own nationals in any European Economic Area (EEA) state,[14] would be incomplete. But not all the people who are 'British' in international law share these rights. BDTCs from the remaining colonies do not have them: they would acquire them if the FCO proposal mentioned above to make them all British citizens were to succeed. The numbers involved are uncertain: perhaps 100,000 or fewer.[15] Their incorporation into British citizenship would, however, leave the other remaining 'British' people in their present suspended situation.

The British Nationality Act 1981 produced a situation unique in the world: five categories of British nationality were defined and four of these carried no right of entry to the state of nationality. This anomaly urgently needs correction. To be in line with all other modern states, we should have a single nationality with rights attached to it. The numbers of British Overseas Citizens, British Protected Persons and new-style 'British Subjects' who are still in existence, and have acquired no other nationality, are not enormous. Many of them wish for a status which would help admit them to countries other than the United Kingdom: at present, having passports which do not show them 'returnable' to anywhere, they suffer many of the disadvantages, though not the name, of stateless persons. Regularizing their status would give us a clearer and juster law.

The question might then arise: should civic rights be attached to the newly extended British citizenship instead of to 'Commonwealth citizen' (old subject) status, and should the civic rights now enjoyed within the UK by anyone from

---

[13] Gibraltarians had to be included under Article 227(4) of the Community Treaty, as inhabitants of a European territory for which a Member State was responsible.

[14] The European Economic Area includes all EC states together with Norway and Iceland. It was established in 1992 by a Treaty signed in Oporto.

[15] The official population figure for the dependencies concerned is about 135,000. However, many residents are foreigners or British citizens engaged in business or tax avoidance.

the rest of the Commonwealth be removed? No—politically this would be highly inadvisable. There are no current problems in maintaining Commonwealth-country citizens' rights here, and there would be an outcry if they were removed. Such removal would be seen as a racist gesture within the UK and an anti-Commonwealth gesture outside it. It would in fact affect a number of local Councillors (one cannot compute how many, as ethnic-minority Councillors are in some cases British but in others not: Indian citizens, for example, have often chosen to retain Indian citizenship while resident here, for fear of losing property rights and re-entry rights in India). It could affect future candidates for the Commons and Lords. It would also disfranchise significant numbers of people from ethnic minorities scattered across Britain. The racial situation is quite sensitive enough, without Parliament's gratuitously adding to its tensions with such a change.

It is also unthinkable to revoke the current arrangements for Irish citizens, especially in the light of the Northern Ireland agreement.

The retention of the present system need cause no theoretical difficulty if the diverse, pluralist image of British national identity described above is accepted. The inclusion already of some alien (EC) voters is consistent not only with EC law but with the retention of Commonwealth voters within a diversified UK.

BRITISHNESS AND THE EUROPEAN UNION

Since joining the EC in 1973, the UK has alternated between rushing forward to claim a place at the heart of Europe, or even leadership within the Community, and pulling back to claim special exemptions or to veto or delay measures agreed by other members. Within the UK, Wales and Scotland are keen Europeans (as is the Republic of Ireland), but England's attitude is more ambiguous, while Ulster Unionism is downright hostile. Most London-based newspapers have been hostile to the EC, but even journals with a more favourable view have not consistently reported EC developments; as a result most people in the UK know little about the Community they belong to, and frequently talk about 'Britain and Europe' as though of separate entities. The political debate has not helped: it argues over 'sovereignty' as though we had not voluntarily surrendered a part of our sovereignty already on signing the Treaty of Accession over 25 years ago. A British/European national identity has not clearly emerged.

The policy area in which the UK has held back from the EC most strongly and consistently is immigration. Freedom of movement for nationals of Member States between each other's territories is a fundamental principle of the original Treaty of Rome (1957), and this the UK had to accept. But the original principle was extended by later Treaty amendments and by case law of the European Court of Justice. The set of amendments known as the Single

European Act (SEA) (1986) provided that border controls within the EC should be abolished, so that everyone, EC nationals and third-country nationals alike, would be able to travel freely across internal borders. Although Mrs Thatcher signed up to the SEA, she was unwilling to accept this particular consequence. With negotiations bogged down, a parallel move towards open borders proceeded under the Schengen Agreement 1990, originating in 1985 from a decision by France, Germany and the Benelux countries to dismantle border controls between themselves. Currently nine EEA countries are covered by Schengen, six have observer or associate status and the UK and Ireland remain outside.

As a result, we have here (as with the euro) a two-track Europe. The Amsterdam Treaty of June 1997 provides for the Schengen *acquis* to become part of EC law, but the UK and Ireland negotiated exemption from the rule on open borders.

The UK is, however, party to the Dublin Convention on asylum, whose provisions on asylum are very similar to those of Schengen. The general trend in Europe as a whole is now to limit entry of asylum-seekers and to clamp down on illegal immigration. Opportunities for legal immigration have been greatly reduced.

The Amsterdam Treaty further provides for bringing EC immigration and asylum policy under EC control within five years of the Treaty's coming into force, but only with the unanimous agreement of Member States. At present, the UK looks certain to veto the move when the time comes. Other states, for example, Austria, may also be unwilling to support it. Already, however, EC law has some say. EC nationals who move between Member States are entitled to bring to join them their spouses, dependent children under 21 and dependent parents and grandparents of *any* nationality. Moreover, as a result of the *Surinder Singh* judgment by the European Court of Justice in July 1992,[16] an EC national who subsequently returns to his or her own state may bring such relatives back. These rules override UK domestic law. One curious result is that a national of another Member State has superior rights to a British citizen within the UK, so far as family unity is concerned. Another is that a British person who has waited for years for reunion, or has been refused it, can travel to another EC state, bring relatives in and return here. Few can afford to do this, but some have done so.

EC law also provides—in Association Agreements or Co-operation Agreements with Turkey, Maghreb countries and some East European countries—for favoured conditions for their nationals either concerning entry or guaranteeing certain rights after entry, and the UK is already bound by these.

---

[16] C–370/90.

PROPORTIONAL REPRESENTATION AND FREEDOM OF INFORMATION

Proportional Representation could enhance people's sense of citizenship if the system eventually adopted persuaded voters that they could have a real influence on the outcome in any constituency. The closed party-list system proposed for the European elections is not very promising here, for it gives voters only one vote each and no choice of candidates within party lists.

Current proposals on freedom of information appear likely to exclude immigration matters from openness to the public. But the new openness in naturalization policy is to be welcomed. A Government White Paper in July 1998[17] proposed that, notwithstanding Section 44(2) of the British Nationality Act 1981, reasons for refusing citizenship should be given to unsuccessful applicants for naturalization.

HUMAN RIGHTS

The Human Rights Act will offer valuable new opportunities in developing case law and perhaps also in contributing to a rights-based sense of UK identity. (People used to take great pride in having more rights here than in other countries: this boast has not been heard for some time.) Where citizenship, immigration and asylum are concerned, however, the prospects are uncertain. The European Court of Human Rights at Strasbourg has been very cautious, particularly in recent years, in dealing with such cases, regarding them as matters primarily for national authorities, and setting only a lowest common denominator. In *Abdulaziz, Casales and Balkandali* (1985),[18] for example, a British citizen woman and two women permanently resident in the UK claimed that the British Government's refusal to let their husbands join them in the UK was racially and sexually discriminatory and infringed the right to family life. The Court upheld only the claim of sex discrimination, since husbands at the time were theoretically entitled to bring in wives under UK law. The Government was able to comply with the ruling by withdrawing the right of reunion from both parties to a marriage, thus avoiding sex discrimination. Thus British citizens have no right to be joined by their spouses. In 1987, five Tamils who alleged that they had suffered persecution in Sri Lanka after being refused asylum in Britain went to the Court, which ruled that only Article 13 of the Convention, requiring an effective remedy before a national authority, had been breached, and not Article 3 concerning inhuman and degrading treatment.

---

[17] *Fairer, Faster and Firmer—a Modern Approach to Immigration and Asylum,* (Cm 4018) Home Office, 1998.

[18] *Abdulaziz, Casales and Balkandali* v. *UK* (1985), 7 EHRR 471.

It is impossible to guess yet whether judges in the UK will take a more expansive approach.

But there will certainly be many challenges. The provision in the Immigration Act 1971 which allows indefinite detention and removal of suspected illegal entrants without due process is sure to be tested. The position of those British persons who are not British citizens will remain unaffected because the Human Rights Act 1998 excludes the provisions of the Fourth Protocol to the Convention, which hitherto the UK has refused to ratify. (Under this, a state is bound to admit its own nationals to its territory.) Article 14, prohibiting racial discrimination in the provision of any of the rights in the Convention, has, however, a large potential impact, going further than the Race Relations Act 1976 in that it would cover certain actions in the provision of services by a wide range of public officials, including the police and immigration service. At present, Section 41 of the Race Relations Act has an exception for discrimination done under statutory authority.

The UK has recently ratified the Council of Europe's Framework Convention on the rights of minorities. This is a standard-setting document and will do nothing to alter UK law directly, but it is possible that the courts will look more in future to international agreements of this sort, once the Human Rights Act is in force. The Framework Convention might be invoked politically, if not legally, by Scots, Welsh and other minorities: it upholds certain linguistic and cultural rights and the right to belong to, or not belong to, a specified minority.

LOOKING AHEAD

How will constitutional changes, working together, affect our national identity and our citizenship over the next ten years? Prophecy depends partly on whether a Labour Government is re-elected to complete its programme. This is not the certainty that most people take for granted: much can happen in three or four years to alter prospects. It depends also on the exact form, not yet known, of regional government; on European developments; on the type of case that will set precedents under human rights law; and on the character and public perception of House of Lords reform. One must also allow for unforeseeable crises in foreign and domestic affairs.

What will probably happen is that nationality law will be slightly amended but not fundamentally reviewed: we shall still not have a single British nationality. The sense of national identity may increasingly accept a diversified United Kingdom (if encouraged by public policy and persuasion to do so) or may lapse into a backward-looking isolationism tinged with xenophobia and racism. Much will depend here on people's general sense of well-being and confidence, and this in turn will depend less on the constitution than on economic security and a belief in fairness between economic groups. Extreme inequalities of wealth are damaging to people's belief in civic equality. Constitutional change could be beneficial in stimulating a new sense of active citizenship, but only if real power is seen to be diffused rather than further centralized.

If human rights legislation and freedom of information work well, they could stimulate everyone's pride in belonging to a fair United Kingdom. Devolution and a stimulus to local government in the big conurbations could help to develop more active citizenship within a total UK structure. It will be important for House of Lords reform to reflect the devolutionary pattern. A useful point here is that the new European Parliamentary constituencies based upon regional lists could coincide with the nations and regions in the devolution plan: the House of Lords could have some representation on the same bases.

The big question is: how will the UK's position in the European Union change? It seems at present most unlikely that the UK will abandon its position (on which Ireland is dependent, because of the interrelation of British and Irish immigration controls) on open borders or on shifting responsibility for immigration matters from intergovernmental machinery to the European Community. But to change policy would be a very important gesture towards Europe, a symbolic step indicating full British acceptance of the character of membership.

Even without this change, the UK's laws and policies will continue to be affected by developments in the European Union. It will be difficult or impossible to resist increased rights for European citizenship. The European Commission has been pressing for some years for improved rights for resident third-country nationals, including the right to seek employment or establishment in a member state other than the one of original settlement. This could both enhance the opportunities of settled non-British citizens in the UK and slightly increase settlement here by immigrants to other European Union countries. But in the framework of a society already highly diversified, this could reinforce rather than damage national identity.

Young people are already much more accustomed to European free movement than their elders, because of international study and training programmes like SOCRATES and LEONARDO DA VINCI, and it is likely that a sense of European identity will be added to the UK identity—gradually, if left to itself; more rapidly if encouraged by closer political involvement in Europe. There needs to be wider recognition that the European Treaties and the European *acquis* are already part of our constitution and not something separate.

One cannot isolate the development of a changing United Kingdom identity from happenings in the world at large. Britishness will be defined not only by internal events and policies but by our relationship with other countries and our position relative to theirs. Prophecy is especially difficult here, but at present the European Community—despite its difficulties—looks both politically and economically a strong force in the world. The United Kingdom is one among equals in the EC, whereas its relationship with the United States has long been that of a client. Identification with Europe should surely be encouraged.

Britishness is partly a matter of culture, values and national character, but perhaps the most obvious feature of Britishness is to be suspicious of any attempt to lay down what our culture, values and character are or should be. We like to be different. We do not have a single set of values. No doubt all British people would agree that a sense of humour is important, but this in itself makes any attempt at earnest definition of ourselves problematic. It is not a good idea for a government to try to define the culture of its people: rather it needs to provide the framework for free and creative activity from which many cultures can emerge and flourish within one state.

13

The New Constitutional Settlement

ROBERT HAZELL

This chapter is in two parts. First, it draws on the conclusions of the previous chapters to identify the main features of the new constitutional settlement. We are going through a period of unprecedented constitutional change. Once those changes have settled down, what will be the main features of the new constitutional settlement, and how will it be characterized by the textbook writers in ten years' time?

Second, the chapter identifies some of the gaps which are beginning to emerge in the constitutional reform programme. These are not policies which we are trying to add, in pursuit of a reforming agenda of our own; rather they are necessary elements of underpinning to make the current reform programme work. The Government is keen to promote joined-up thinking in its approach to social policy; constitutional change similarly requires a joined-up approach. It is not surprising, given the speed with which the Government has moved in its first year, that a number of the constitutional changes have been introduced with scant reference to each other. But as the changes bed down the interrelationships between them will become clearer, and the need for a coherent and integrated approach made more apparent.

TOWARDS A NEW CONSTITUTIONAL SETTLEMENT

What will be the key features of the new constitutional settlement? Any list is bound to be selective; but there are five themes which run through many of the chapters in this book. A highly centralized system of government is being replaced by a form of quasi-federalism; this and other changes will lead to more checks and balances on the UK executive; parliamentary sovereignty is likely to be further eroded; there will be tighter rule of law, with a shift of power to the courts; and our majoritarian, two-party system will be replaced by more pluralist forms of democracy. Each of these features will be examined in turn.

QUASI-FEDERALISM: REBALANCING THE UNION

The UK is not and never has been a unitary state in the way that a country like France is. It is a union state, whose component nations joined the union at different times and on different terms.[1] Like other union states, it was asymmetrical in origin, and still exhibits asymmetrical features today: but in many respects the political culture is that of a unitary state, because of our highly centralized system of government. That is about to change with devolution, which will decentralize but also reassert the asymmetry in the underlying arrangements.

Devolution will restore the four nations of the Union, giving them new national institutions.[2] Although the devolved assemblies will operate under the umbrella of the Westminster Parliament, devolution will introduce some of the elements of a federal system. That is why we characterize it as quasi-federalism. Its federal characteristics include the following:

- Formal division of powers between the two levels of government. The devolution legislation formally allocates legislative and executive power between Westminster and Whitehall on the one hand, and the devolved governments and assemblies on the other.
- Although it is not constitutionally entrenched, the list of powers reserved and devolved resembles the division of powers in a federal constitution. The Scottish Parliament is given open-ended residuary powers, quite unlike any grant of power to local government.
- Overlapping jurisdiction through exercise of the foreign affairs power by central government. This is expressly reserved in the devolution legislation, which allows the UK government to intervene in order to uphold the UK's international or European Union (EU) obligations. In federal systems it is a growing source of intervention by federal governments in the affairs of the states: one which is resented but with growing globalization is likely to increase.
- A new constitutional court in the form of the Judicial Committee of the Privy Council. The Scotland Act and the Government of Wales Act 1998 both provide

[1] Keating, M., *Nations against the State: the new politics of nationalism in Quebec, Catalonia and Scotland,* (London: Macmillan, 1995). See also 'What's Wrong with Asymmetrical Government?', paper presented to ECPR Standing Group on Regionalism, Newcastle (February 1997).

[2] Strictly Northern Ireland is not a nation. It is part of two nations. The Belfast Agreement identifies it as a place with two nationalities, British and Irish; and as the site of devolved government within the UK linked to both Great Britain, through the Council of the Isles, and to Ireland, through the North-South Ministerial Council.

for devolution disputes to be referred to the Privy Council; with a special procedure for ruling on the *vires* of legislation before it comes into effect. This is a new role for the Privy Council; and a new role for the courts in ruling on the *vires* of legislation pre-enactment (although in volume terms most devolution disputes will be decided subsequently, and by the ordinary courts in the course of other litigation).

- A new structure of intergovernmental relations. The Concordats being drafted in Whitehall to manage relations between central government departments and the new devolved assemblies are only just the beginning. Chapter 9 shows how a whole new structure will need to be created to manage intergovernmental relations within the UK: similar to the interlocking committees of the Council of Australian Governments set out in Figure 9.1, or the structures which have developed to manage intergovernmental relations within the EU. There will be periodic summits between the Prime Minister and First Ministers; regular meetings of Ministers sharing the same portfolio (Health Ministers, Education Ministers, etc.); and an array of official committees managing the day-to-day business.

- Dual national identity. As we saw in Chapter 12, the new political institutions will sharpen people's sense of dual identity, with people seeing themselves as Scottish, Welsh, Irish and English as well as being British. Many will have no difficulty with expressing dual loyalty, but devolution will expose the tensions and conflict when the loyalties pull in different directions: as they do not just between Quebec and Canada, but equally often between the western provinces and eastern Canada. Federalism brings these territorial differences out into the open.

At the same time there will be big differences from classic federal systems, which should not be ignored:

- No constitutional entrenchment. In federal systems the constitution defines and protects the powers of the states; and each state is the guardian of its own constitution. In the UK, Westminster can unilaterally rewrite the constitution of the devolved nations; as it did when it abolished the Stormont Parliament in 1972. Such protection as the new constitution of Scotland enjoys lies more in the realm of politics than of law; but it may come to be protected by strong conventions, as were the powers of the Dominion parliaments, even though they operated under the Westminster umbrella for over a century.[3] In the case of Northern Ireland there is the added protection of an international agreement; but it is well established law that Westminster can legislate in breach of an international agreement,[4] so here too the protection lies in the realm of politics (and international relations) rather than of law.

- Asymmetrical devolution instead of the uniform division of powers normally found in a federation. Many federations have slight elements of asymmetry; the territories in Australia and Canada have lesser powers than the states; Quebec has its own system of civil law and administers its own income tax. But in general all the units in a federation enjoy the same degree of power. In the UK, devolution is beginning as an asymmetrical process and is likely to remain so: even if regional government in England grows apace it is hard to envisage any English region enjoying the same legislative powers as Scotland.

- English dominance. England, with 85 per cent of the UK's population, will continue to dominate the whole. In federations as a general rule no state has more than one third of the total population. In the post-war German constitution Prussia, which had constituted two-thirds of the Weimar republic, was deliberately broken up into five different states.

- Lack of English political institutions. Scotland, Wales and Northern Ireland will have their devolved assemblies. England will have no corresponding national political institution, apart from the Westminster Parliament; which is not an English parliament, but the UK Parliament.

- Central financial control. In many federations the central government is dominant financially; it has often seized the best taxes, and the trend internationally is for tax-raising to drift towards the centre. But in no federation does central government retain such tight control as it will in the UK, where two out of the three devolved assemblies will be 100 per cent dependent on central government grants, and the third—the Scottish Parliament—has a marginal tax varying power which at the maximum could vary its budget by 3 per cent. Even in Australia, generally regarded as a highly centralized federation in financial terms, the states raise 20 per cent of their own revenue.

---

[3] Zines, L., *Constitutional Change in the Commonwealth* (Cambridge: Cambridge University Press, 1991).

[4] *Cheney* v. *Conn* [1968] 1 All ER 799. However, the attitude of the courts to parliamentary sovereignty continues to evolve, not least because of the continuing effects of British membership of the European Union. See Bradley, A.W., *The Sovereignty of Parliament—in Perpetuity?* in Jowell, J. and Oliver, D., *The Changing Constitution* (Oxford: Clarendon Press, 1994), 107 .

In sum, our present system of territorial government is to be replaced by a form of quasi-federalism. Much can be learned from the governing arrangements in federal states. There is no inherent reason why a quasi-federal state should be any more difficult to govern than a unitary state or a fully federal state. But three factors create tensions, at least initially: the speed of the transition; the continuation of a unitary political culture at the centre; and the management of asymmetry.

CHECKS AND BALANCES ON THE EXECUTIVE

Largely because we have never had to codify our constitution, the British constitution is notoriously free of the checks and balances which characterize written constitutions. It has become, in Lord Hailsham's famous phrase, an elective dictatorship.[5] With the rise of modern disciplined mass political parties, parliamentary sovereignty has become the sovereignty of the executive. This may not change much, in terms of executive domination at Westminster, without more radical parliamentary reform than is currently on the agenda; but other elements in the constitutional reform programme will significantly curb the power of the UK executive. In particular:

- Devolution will create strong alternative centres of power. The British government will no longer necessarily be able to impose its will in Scotland, Wales or Northern Ireland, either formally through overriding devolved legislation, or informally through arm-twisting behind the scenes. As we saw in Chapter 3, the devolved assemblies will have their own democratic legitimacy (as will figures like London's elected mayor); and Chapter 6 showed how they will be less susceptible to control through the political parties, which themselves will become more fragmented and autonomous.
- European Convention on Human Rights (ECHR) incorporation will be a significant check on the Executive. It is often portrayed as a shift in power from Parliament to the courts; but it is the Executive's legislation which is presented to Parliament; and it will be the administrative actions and procedures of the Executive which are challenged in the courts more often than its legislation. A deportation order, a parole decision, discriminatory tax treatment will more often be the subject of ECHR challenge than will be the parent legislation. Judicial review has become a significant constraint on the actions of the Executive; the ECHR adds one more twist which will further constrain

---

[5] Hailsham, Q., *The Dilemma of Democracy*, (Collins 1978).

executive discretion. Devolution will also give a stronger role to the courts; and although they will not be able to strike down legislation of the Westminster Parliament, they will be able to overrule actions of the UK Executive—whether for breach of the ECHR or breach of the devolution legislation.

- Freedom of information will be a lesser check on the Executive. It is not the panacea which its proponents sometimes suppose; but it is a small check on the efficiency, integrity and fairness of Governments. And through introducing a statutory requirement to give reasons for administrative decisions, it will make it easier to challenge those reasons in the courts.
- Europe will also reduce the Executive's freedom of manoeuvre. Although in some respects the pace of European integration has slowed or been halted, in others the EU's competence continues inexorably to expand. Economic and Monetary Union (EMU) will be the major constraint; whether the UK goes in or remains on the outside, its freedom to manage British macro-economic policy will be significantly curtailed.
- Parliamentary reform could improve parliamentary scrutiny, and give the Executive less of an easy ride; as could reform of the House of Lords. Reform will give the Lords a greater sense of legitimacy, and even with no further changes to powers or composition, they might be encouraged to make greater use of their existing powers. It might also prove a spur to more effective reform of the Commons. This might be seen in low-key ways, through joint parliamentary committees (on Human Rights, or Lords reform itself); or more overtly, if the Government seeks to head off pressure for further Lords reform by setting about reforming the House of Commons.
- Lastly, electoral reform would reduce the executive domination of Parliament. Most forms of Proportional Representation (PR) would reduce the chances of a single party forming a government with a confident majority, and increase the chances of coalition government. Governments would have to construct cross-party majorities, and would have to listen more to the views of territorial and minority parties.

In sum, the dominant position of the Executive in the British system may be reduced in half a dozen different ways: through devolution, the ECHR, freedom of information, the onward march of the EU, parliamentary reform and electoral reform. To those in government and their advisers in the civil service the business of government will become more difficult, with a loss in their executive authority and scope for discretionary action. To those outside it will seem like a long overdue taming of the Leviathan.

PARLIAMENTARY SOVEREIGNTY GIVES WAY TO POPULAR SOVEREIGNTY

Since the extension of the franchise in the last century and the introduction of
universal adult suffrage in this century there has been an uneasy coexistence
between these two fundamental principles of the British constitution. No
constitutional textbook now seeks to uphold the doctrine of parliamentary
sovereignty as expounded by Dicey; but in the minds of politicians the doctrine
lives on. In the White Papers on Scottish devolution and on ECHR incorporation
the Government sought to reassure the public (or were these passages addressed to
fellow parliamentarians?) that parliamentary sovereignty would remain unaffected.[6]

Technically this is correct: the legislation is not entrenched, and it is open to
Parliament at some future date to repeal the Scotland Act or the Human Rights Act.
(Just as technically Parliament could repeal the European Communities Act 1972
which took us into the European Community: and it is worth noting that the Heath
Government gave the same reassurances about parliamentary sovereignty before
introducing the 1972 Act).

But in practice both devolution and ECHR incorporation represent a further
important shift towards the sovereignty of the people. The Human Rights Act is a
small but significant shift in the balance of power between the citizen and the state
which future governments will find it impossible to reverse. And the referendums
in Scotland, Wales, Northern Ireland and London, held to underpin the legitimacy
of the new assemblies, will also make it impossible for Parliament to abolish those
assemblies without their consent. Nor may it end there. Further referendums are
promised on the electoral system, on EMU and on directly elected assemblies in the
English regions. There is no clear doctrine in the UK on when a referendum is
required to authorize constitutional change; but each referendum adds a precedent,
and as the use of referendums grows so could political and public expectations that
referendums should be used for certain kinds of constitutional change.
Parliamentary sovereignty would not suffice; the exercise of popular sovereignty
would be required as well.

But this should not be pushed too far. There are parts of the constitutional reform
programme which are being introduced without any public involvement. The
European Communities (Amendment) Act to implement the Amsterdam Treaty
went through without a murmur. Lords reform is being planned and is likely to be
implemented with little or no public consultation, at least in stage one. Some of the

---

[6] *Scotland's Parliament*, Cm 3658, July 1997, para. 4.2; *Rights Brought Home,* Cm 3782, October
1997, para. 2.13.

changes are being introduced simply by the Government asserting its parliamentary majority. And if the overall effect is further to erode parliamentary sovereignty, some may question the corollary: that it raises up the principle of popular sovereignty. Populist perhaps, the referendum remains a device to be used by the executive, on issues, timing and a question of its choosing, to appeal directly to the people over the heads of their elected representatives. Only when people have the power to initiate a referendum, the question is not determined by Government, and the conduct of the referendum is in the hands of an independent body, might the referendum be said to uphold the principle of popular sovereignty.

TIGHTER RULE OF LAW

British public administration has typically been characterized by a high degree of administrative discretion, with relatively light supervision by the courts. That has already begun to change with the steady growth of judicial review described in Chapter 5. We now effectively have an administrative court, in the specialist Queen's Bench judges who hear the judicial review cases in the Crown Office list. But the current constitutional changes will lead to a much more tightly law-based system, with the courts exercising significant new powers not only over the executive, but also over legislatures:

- ECHR incorporation confers new powers for the courts to enforce the new rights culture, to grant remedies, to quash delegated legislation, and in the case of the devolved assemblies to quash primary legislation which is inconsistent with the ECHR.
- Devolution will similarly give the courts an important role in adjudicating on devolution disputes. The courts will be far more important in the devolution settlement than most commentators realize; in Canada and Australia they have turned upside down the federal/state balance of power intended by the original framers of their constitutions.[7] Even if Governments are restrained and refrain from direct challenge many cases will be brought by third parties, or will arise by way of collateral challenge in the course of other litigation.
- Pre-legislative proofing for ECHR and jurisdictional compliance will have to improve if Governments want to reduce the incidence of court challenges and defeats.

---

[7] Zines, L., *Constitutional Change in the Commonwealth* (Cambridge: Cambridge University Press, 1991), ch. 3.

- Europe will continue to be a source of further legal challenges and, as Chapter 5 shows, the courts are gradually introducing European norms of rule-based administration.
- Other watchdogs apart from the courts will also help to ensure due process and reduce administrative discretion. The public sector Ombudsmen may help to enforce the ECHR by regarding breaches as instances of maladministration.[8] And new constitutional watchdogs will need to be created to police aspects of the new constitutional settlement: an Information Commissioner with order-making powers, and possibly a Human Rights Commission, Electoral Commission, House of Lords Appointments Commission, etc.
- Separation of Crown and State. Finally, the shadowy and confusing notions of the Crown and the Royal prerogative, which are still important sources of ministerial power (to make treaties, and to issue passports, to name but two), will gradually be replaced in the language and reasoning of the courts by sharper concepts of the State and the executive. These will both reflect the reality of greater judicial control, but in turn make them more susceptible to further judicial control.

PLURALIST INSTEAD OF MAJORITARIAN DEMOCRACY

The greatest single blow to the two-party majoritarian system would come from a referendum on the electoral system which replaced 'first past the post' with a form of PR. Chapter 6 shows how quickly the introduction of PR in New Zealand led to a fragmentation of the major parties and a proliferation of minor parties; but it went on to explain how the stranglehold of the two-party system is beginning to break in the UK, with or without PR. And even if the voting system for Westminster remains the majoritarian system of first past the post, devolution and other items in the constitutional reform programme will usher in a more pluralist, consensus building style of politics:

- PR in Scotland, Wales and Northern Ireland will make it harder for a single party to form a government. In Northern Ireland coalition government will be required by law, as a result of the power-sharing executive jointly led by the First and Deputy First Minister. In Scotland coalition governments will be a likely outcome of the proportional voting system.

---

[8] Constitution Unit, *Human Rights Legislation* (1996), 86–7.

- Coalition governments will see the development of more inter-party agreements: sometimes after the election, as in New Zealand in 1996; but also beforehand, as parties learn the rules of the new electoral game, and sign up coalition partners in advance. They will build on the items they have in common, as Labour and the Liberal Democrats have in their joint support for the constitutional reform programme.
- A more consensual approach will also be required by devolution, as the British government uses the new machinery of intergovernmental relations to broker agreement with the devolved governments in areas of overlapping responsibility. And devolution will be a further cause of fragmentation of the major parties, and the growth of minor, regional parties.
- Increased consultation and public participation will also result from the due process requirements of the ECHR; the opportunities offered by freedom of information; and from changes to the legislative process, in particular the introduction of pre-legislative scrutiny of draft bills.
- Lords reform could also lead to a more consensus style of politics, if stage two produces an effective second chamber where the government does not necessarily have a majority. It would then have to negotiate and to build up coalitions of support in both Houses to get its measures through.

THE NEW CONSTITUTIONAL SETTLEMENT: TOWARDS A WRITTEN CONSTITUTION

Taken together, all these changes amount to a series of steps towards a written constitution, rather like those taken by New Zealand in the last 20 years. New Zealand had a Westminster form of government with a strong two-party system which led to similar critiques of an elective dictatorship.[9] But in recent times New Zealand has introduced a whole series of checks and balances which include:

- entrenched legislation, in the Electoral Act 1993
- freedom of information, in the Official Information Act 1982
- a Bill of Rights, in the Bill of Rights Act 1990
- provision for referendums, in the Citizen Initiated Referendum Act 1993
- proportional representation, in the Electoral Act 1993.

---

[9] Palmer, G. *Unbridled Power? An Interpretation of New Zealand's Constitution and Government* (Wellington, New York: Oxford University Press, 1979).

In the UK a similar process is at work. In neither country is it likely to result in a written constitution, in the sense of a single codified document. But in both there is a systematic attempt to build in more checks and balances to curb the untrammelled power of the parliamentary majority; and in the process more of the constitution has been written down.

As a result many of the structures and processes of the UK's rather shadowy and silent constitution are becoming more sharply defined. This is most evident in:

- the Human Rights Act, which gives us for the first time a domestically enforceable bill of rights;
- the devolution legislation, which provides a constitution for Scotland and Northern Ireland, and which talks for the first time about the UK constitution (in the list of reserved powers which defines the competence of the Westminster Parliament);
- wider reform of the House of Lords, which may have to define the functions and powers of the second chamber as well as making further changes to its composition;
- regulation of political parties, which have not previously been formally recognized in public law, but which will now be subject to the Registration of Political Parties Act 1998, and to controls on party funding following the report of the Neill Committee.

Another characteristic of these changes is that most of them are irreversible, and some are effectively entrenched. It may be easier to make constitutional amendments with an unwritten constitution; but it is very difficult to unmake them. It would require referendums to undo the devolution legislation, and in the case of Northern Ireland it would require the consent of the Irish government as well. The Greater London Authority and its mayor, having also been established following a referendum, will enjoy a similar degree of entrenchment; as will any directly elected assemblies established after referendums in the English regions.

GAPS IN THE NEW CONSTITUTIONAL SETTLEMENT

The second part of this chapter asks what further changes will be required to make the new constitutional settlement work. In institutional terms, they are mostly changes required at the centre: in England, and in the institutions of central government in London. But there is also a need for public consent and support for the new constitutional settlement, which may be harder to remedy.

THE ENGLISH QUESTION

It is the English who have been least consulted about the constitutional reform programme. In Scotland and in Wales Labour campaigned on their plans for devolution; but in England during the whole 1997 election campaign they remained silent about their plans for constitutional reform.[10] As a result the English could be forgiven for being taken by surprise at the scale of Labour's constitutional reform programme, which has dominated the first session of the new Parliament, with a lot more to come. But their consent should not necessarily be taken for granted, especially in relation to the devolution settlement. The English regions are slowly beginning to learn about the higher levels of public expenditure in Scotland, Wales and Northern Ireland, and English MPs have questioned the Barnett formula and asked for an updated needs assessment.[11] For the devolution settlement to work there needs to be a sense of give and take, and a spirit of trust and generosity on all sides. Public opinion surveys have shown that spirit of generosity exists amongst the English towards devolution in Scotland;[12] but it may not last as the financial terms become clearer.

The English also need to be assured that devolution is not simply for the Celts, but is a programme in which they can participate if they wish. Here the Government gives out mixed signals. As we saw in Chapter 3, the formal position remains that in time English regions will be able to have directly-elected assemblies upon demand; but the first steps point in the opposite direction. Regional Development Agencies could have been made directly accountable to Regional Chambers, and appointed by them, as the first step towards accountable regional government in England; but instead they are to be national quangos, appointed by Ministers, and accountable through Ministers to Parliament. And regional assemblies may also be threatened by the Government's subsequent interest in directly-elected mayors; if the leading provincial cities decide to have elected mayors, they may become the voice of the region instead of any leader of the regional assembly.

---

[10] In the six-week campaign (twice the normal length) not a single frontbench speech by Labour was devoted to the constitution. In the manifesto the plans for constitutional change appeared at the end, under the heading 'We will clean up politics.'

[11] Report of the Treasury Select Committee on *The Barnett Formula,* 17 December 1997.

[12] Joseph Rowntree Reform Trust/ICM *State of the Nation* poll, Summer 1995.

THE HOLE IN THE CENTRE: PARLIAMENT

In institutional terms, the hole in the centre of the constitutional reform programme revolves around the rebalancing and the changes required in all three branches of central government—in Westminster, in Whitehall, and in the courts. At Westminster the House of Commons will need to rethink its committee structure and its procedures to become a quasi-federal Parliament post-devolution. It is easier to see what must go rather than what to put in its place. Chapter 7 suggested that the Scottish and Welsh Grand Committees would go, but that the Select Committees might remain so long as there are separate Secretaries of State; and if in time one or more of the territorial Secretaries of State are merged, the Committees might merge into a Select Committee on Territorial Affairs. But that Committee would scrutinize the devolution settlement in Scotland, Wales and Northern Ireland, and would not provide any answers to the English question.

For England Chapter 7 suggested reviving the Standing Committee on Regional Affairs and giving it some wide-ranging procedures, like those developed by the Scottish and Welsh Grand Committees; but starting with a focus on regional policy in England. Other Select Committees, such as the Education and Health Committees would become *de facto* English Committees. This is a far cry from an English Parliament, and would not necessarily meet demands for a clear English voice to match the demands coming from the Scottish Parliament, Welsh Assembly and from Northern Ireland; but it is worth experimenting to see to what extent the House of Commons can be the UK Parliament but also provide an outlet for opinion from England.

Just as important are the potential new roles for the House of Lords. In a quasi-federal Britain one obvious role for the Lords would be to represent the nations and regions, as second chambers in federal systems represent the states and the provinces. This could help to counteract the centrifugal political forces released by devolution, and to give the devolved governments and assemblies a stake in the institutions of the centre. How strong a stake would depend upon how they were represented. Direct election would do little to help bind together the devolved governments and assemblies into the Union, because it would be the people of Scotland, Wales, etc. who would be represented rather than their institutions. (It has been said of the Australian Senate that it does nothing for the federation.) Indirect election would give the devolved governments or assemblies a direct stake; and it is a nice question whether it should be the governments which are represented, as in the German Bundesrat, or the assemblies, as in the second chamber in India. The Bundesrat plays a highly functional and integrating role in the conduct of intergovernmental relations in Germany, but leaves the state parliaments rather marginalized. Finally there is the possibility of appointment, like the Canadian Senate. This could prove to be a useful option so long as there are no regional assemblies in England: representatives of the English regions could be appointed, while representatives of Scotland, Wales and Northern Ireland were indirectly elected.

Other roles have also been posited for the House of Lords; that it should integrate upwards as well as downwards, and strengthen links with the EU; or that it should be a human rights watchdog and guardian of the constitution. Not all these roles are necessarily compatible; different expertise would be required, and there is a risk of the House of Lords becoming overloaded with different wish lists. But there is also a risk of undershooting on Lords reform: it creates a unique opportunity to underpin other parts of the constitutional settlement, and would be a major opportunity missed if reform simply stopped at removal of the hereditary peers.

Before leaving Westminster, mention should briefly be made of the 'classic' parliamentary reform agenda: stronger Select Committees, more use of special standing committees, pre-legislative scrutiny, higher status and salaries for committee chairmen, etc. These may all be desirable reforms, but none is necessary to underpin the rest of the constitutional reform programme; except improvements to the legislative process, which will be necessary to scrutinize legislation for ECHR compliance. The new machinery and procedures which might be required are discussed in Chapter 7.

THE HOLE IN THE CENTRE: THE COURTS

Chapter 5 discussed the role of the courts, and the impact of the constitutional changes on legal doctrine. The courts will play a central part in shaping the new constitutional settlement; and will themselves come under much greater public scrutiny. They will be called upon to adjudicate in high profile political cases, whether devolution disputes or clashes of controversial human rights; and they will experience a significant increase in their workload, from ECHR incorporation and from devolution. Will the courts be able to take the strain?

The strain will be particularly great on the higher courts. Judicial review, which has been a major growth industry, will see another surge of activity; leading to an increase in the number of Queen's Bench judges who specialize in the 'new administrative law'. And in the Court of Appeal and the House of Lords the lack of

back-up for the judges will become more sharply exposed: they may decide to
follow the example of other Supreme Courts and institute a system of law clerks or
assistants to provide them with research support.

Inside government more thought has been given to the impact of ECHR than of
devolution. In terms of the workload on the courts that is probably right; but
devolution will impose a different set of strains. It will require a strong legal
system, and a system which commands confidence and respect on all sides, to hold
the Union together when the politics comes under strain. In this respect the choice
of the Judicial Committee of the Privy Council as the final arbiter of devolution
disputes looks rather odd. It is not the final court of appeal in the UK legal system,
but stands largely outside it; and its constitutional jurisdiction in the rest of the
Commonwealth has declined almost to zero. It may prove to be a temporary
arrangement which will be reopened when wider reform of the House of Lords
opens up the question of whether we now need a supreme court which stands
clearly at the apex of the legal system and outside the legislature.

The Judicial Committee of the Privy Council risks creating a dual apex for the
legal system in devolution cases (although the House of Lords has discretion not to
refer devolution issues across to the Privy Council). But it does offer flexibility in
providing a larger pool of judges which can be increased more easily than the
House of Lords to include some with connections with Wales, Scotland and
Northern Ireland (although it may be difficult to identify 'Welsh' judges, since
there is no separate judiciary in Wales).[13]

Finally, ECHR incorporation and devolution may revive interest in the idea of a
Judicial Appointments Commission, to make appointments to the judiciary more
transparent and less the exclusive preserve of the Lord Chancellor. Hitherto calls
for such a commission have been linked to the need for the judiciary to include
more women and ethnic minority judges and a broader spread of social and political
opinion. Those pressures will increase with ECHR incorporation; but devolution
may introduce the idea of territorial balance.[14]

---

[13] Other problems may arise if it is felt that Scottish, Welsh and Northern Irish judges should sit in every
devolution case, because the decision might have implications for the rest of the UK. This could reduce the
number of English judges to one or two, which might be politically unacceptable. One way out would be to
increase the size of the court to seven.

[14] There is an interesting balance in the Scotland Act (s. 95) over the appointment of Scottish judges.
The UK Prime Minister will continue to advise the Queen on the appointment of the two senior Scottish
judges (Lord President of the Court of Session and Lord Justice Clerk); the Scottish First Minister will
advise on all other judicial appointments in Scotland.

THE HOLE IN THE CENTRE: WHITEHALL

Responsibility for different items in the constitutional reform programme is currently divided between eight Whitehall departments: the Home Office, Scottish Office, Welsh Office, Northern Ireland Office, Department of the Environment, Transport and the Regions, Foreign Office, Lord Chancellor's Department and the Cabinet Office. The Cabinet Office provides the Constitution Secretariat which services the main Cabinet Committee on the constitutional reform programme (CRP), and all its sub-committees: on Devolution, the ECHR, freedom of information and Lords reform. The secretariat performs the classic Cabinet Office role of circulating the papers submitted by departments and briefing the chairman (CRP is chaired by the Prime Minister, and the sub-committees are all chaired by the Lord Chancellor). It does not lead on any of the policy save on Lords reform, where the lead minister (initially Lord Richard, and now Baroness Jay, the leader in the Lords) has no department to support her.

In time the need will develop for a stronger focus for the programme as a whole, and for a central unit which is responsible for the constitution in a more strategic and proactive way than the Cabinet Secretariat is normally allowed to be. The Constitution Secretariat needs to go on servicing the CRP network of committees, but it also needs to develop a capability to look ahead and to conduct or commission research in a manner similar to the specialist units in the other part of the Cabinet Office, like the Citizen's Charter Unit, the Social Exclusion Unit or the new Innovation and Performance Unit. This would fit in wih Sir Richard Wilson's wish that the Cabinet Office should develop greater strategic capacity to identify future opportunities and threats, as part of its new corporate headquarters role. But the Constitution Secretariat cannot do this without ministerial cover: there needs to be a strong central minister with a similar strategic role, who can lead the constitutional reform programme and give it coherence.

Another function which will fall to the Cabinet Office to lead on is the conduct of intergovernmental relations (IGR). The case studies in Chapter 9 on the organization of the Council of Australian Governments and the Canadian Department of Intergovernmental Affairs show how the machinery is likely to grow. The Whitehall structures needed to manage IGR with the devolved governments might be based initially around the rump offices of the three territorial Secretaries of State, but in time they must fall back into the Cabinet Office, where they will be managed by the Constitution Secretariat, just as the European Secretariat manages and co-ordinates all relations with the EU. The Constitution Secretariat has already been tasked with providing the British secretary for the proposed Council of the Isles, which suggests where the IGR support function will come from. And to lead it the Cabinet Office will need more ministers, and more senior ministers, than are normally assigned to it; intergovernmental relations is not something to be managed by someone towards the bottom of the Cabinet rank order.

A strong ministerial lead is necessary not only in Whitehall but outside, to explain the constitutional reform programme to the wider public. These are fundamental changes in our system of government which are being introduced with a minimum of explanation. For electoral reasons Labour was largely silent about their constitutional reform plans during the election campaign except in Scotland and Wales. In their first session of the new Parliament they have introduced twelve constitutional bills, listed in Chapter 1, with more to follow. Yet in the first year of the new Government the silence continued, apart from the referendum campaigns in Scotland and Wales, Northern Ireland and London. The English could be forgiven for thinking that devolution is some special deal for the Scots, the Welsh, and the Northern Irish, because no one has troubled to tell them otherwise. This matters because for devolution to work it requires goodwill on both sides. And it matters more widely because for constitutional change to take root it needs first to be understood and to be accepted before it can command public support.

The Government is silent because constitutional issues are not the top priorities in middle England, among voters generally, or even among Labour supporters. Voters' priorities are the bread and butter issues of the economy, jobs, the health service, as they have always been. But the delivery of those services would be hugely affected by the constitutional changes being set in train. The public need to be prepared for those changes, not all of which will necessarily be welcome. The bland theme of modernization is not a sufficient explanation. There needs to be a strong and coherent story about the benefits of bringing government closer to the people, and linking constitutional reforms to the delivery of the public services which people value.

To be strong the story needs to be consistent; but the Government's programme at present is shot through with inconsistency and hesitations. Despite the devolution programme much of the Government's language is centralizing in tone, and in major parts of the constitutional reform programme distinctly ambivalent. This brings us back to the minimalist and maximalist scenarios outlined in Chapter 2. At this stage the minimalist scenario looks more likely: the Government wants a Human Rights Act but no Human Rights Commission; devolved assemblies which cannot be trusted with tax-raising powers; a House of Lords which will not present a threat to the House of Commons. In a number of areas the reforms risk being broken-backed for lack of commitment or resources: two possible examples being regional government and freedom of information, where collective ministerial commitment is the key to successful implementation.

But this concluding chapter has also brought out how many of the constitutional changes will release powerful dynamic forces which will be beyond the Government's control. Where devolution takes us will depend now on the new political leaders in Scotland, Wales and Northern Ireland, and in time the regions of England. To come to terms with the new political culture the centre will have to relax and be willing to let go. It will have to treat the devolved governments as equal partners, not subordinates. The centre needs to understand and respect the political forces which have been unleashed, and to channel and direct them by working with the flow and not against. Constitutions alone cannot bind nations together: but constitutions embody values, and to work they need politicians who accept those values and can give force and expression to them.

Further Reading

DEVOLUTION

General

Bogdanor, V., *Devolution* (Oxford: Oxford University Press, 1979).

Cambridge University Centre for Public Law, *Constitutional Reform in the UK: Practice and Principles* (Oxford: Hart Publishing, 1998).

Norton, P. (ed.) *The Consequences of Devolution*, King-Hall Paper No. 6 (London: Hansard Society, July 1998).

Report of the Royal Commission on the Constitution (the Kilbrandon Commission), Cmnd 5460, HMSO, 1973.

Tindale, S. (ed.) *The State and the Nations: The Politics of Devolution* (London: Institute for Public Policy Research, 1996).

Tomkins, A. (ed.) *Devolution and the British Constitution*, Society of Public Teachers of Law (London: Key Haven, 1998).

Scotland

Leicester, G., *Scotland's Parliament: Fundamentals for a New Scotland Act* (London: Constitution Unit, June 1996).

Scottish Affairs Select Committee, *The Operation of Multi-Layer Democracy*, HC 460-ii, (London: The Stationery Office, February 1998).

Scottish Affairs, Special Issue on *Understanding Constitutional Change* (Unit for the Study of Government in Scotland: Edinburgh University, 1998).

Scottish Constitutional Convention, *Scotland's Parliament. Scotland's Right*, November 1995.

Scottish Office, *Scotland's Parliament*, Cm 3658 (Edinburgh: Stationery Office, July 1997).

Winetrobe, B., *The Scotland Bill: Some Constitutional and Representational Aspects*, Research Paper 98/3 (London: House of Commons Library, January 1998).

Northern Ireland

Belfast Agreement, *Agreement Reached in the Multi-Party Negotiations,* Cm 3883 (London, HMSO, April 1998).

Foreign and Commonwealth Office, *Frameworks for the Future*, Cm 2964 (London: HMSO, September 1995).

Northern Ireland (Elections) Act 1998.

Northern Ireland Act 1998.

O'Leary, B. et al., *Northern Ireland: Sharing Authority* (London: Institute for Public Policy Research, October 1993).

O'Leary, B., *The British-Irish Agreement: Power-Sharing Plus* (London: Constitution Unit, May 1998).

Wales

Government of Wales Act 1998.

Hazell, R., *An Assembly for Wales* (London: Constitution Unit, June 1996).

Institute of Welsh Affairs, *Making the Assembly Work* (Cardiff: The Stationery Office, November 1997).

Osmond, J, (ed.) *A Parliament for Wales* (Llandysul, Dyfed: Gomer Press, 1994).

Wales Labour Party, *Shaping the Vision: A Report on the Powers and Structures of the Welsh Assembly* (Cardiff: Labour Party, May 1995).

Wales Labour Party, *Preparing for a New Wales* (Cardiff, Labour Party, March 1997).

Welsh Office, *A Voice for Wales: the Government's Proposals for a Welsh Assembly*, Cm 3718 (London, The Stationery Office, July 1997).

Regional Government in England

Department of the Environment, Transport and the Regions, *Regional Development Agencies: Issues for Discussion* (London: DETR, 11 June 1997).

Department of the Environment, Transport and the Regions, *Building Partnerships for Prosperity: Sustainable Growth, Competitiveness and Employment in the English Regions*, Cm 3814 (London: The Stationery Office, December 1997).

Donnelly, K. and McQuail, P., *Regional Government in England* (London, Constitution Unit, June 1996).

English Regional Associations, *Regional Working in England: Policy Statement and Survey of the English Regional Associations*, English Regional Associations (Taunton: Somerset County Council, June 1998).

Labour Party, *A Choice for England* (London: Labour Party, July 1995).

Labour Party, *A New Voice for England's Regions* (London: Labour Party, September 1996).

Regional Development Agencies Act 1998.

Regional Policy Commission (Chairman Bruce Millan), *Renewing the Regions* (Sheffield: PAVIC Publications, Sheffield Hallam University, June 1996).

Select Committee on Environment, Transport and Regional Affairs, *Regional Development Agencies*, HC 415 (London: The Stationery Office, December 1997).

London

Department of the Environment, Transport and the Regions, *New Leadership for London: A Consultation Paper*, Cm 3724 (London: The Stationery Office, July 1997).
Department of the Environment, Transport and the Regions, *A Mayor and Assembly for London*, Cm 3897 (London: The Stationery Office, March 1998).

EUROPE

Bainbridge, T. and Teasdale, A., *The Penguin Companion to European Union* (London: Penguin Books, 1995).
Bernholz, P. et al, *A Proposal for a European Constitution* (London: European Policy Forum, 1993).
Edwards, G. and Spence, D. (eds) *The European Commission* (Harlow: Longmans, 1994).
Norton, P. (ed.) *National Parliaments and The European Union* (London: Frank Cass, 1996).
Schmidtchen, D. and Cooter, R. (eds) *Constitutional Law and Economics of the European Union* (Cheltenham: Edward Elgar, 1997).
Van Tuyll (ed.) *Europe: Your Choice.* (London: Harvill Press, 1995).
Vibert, F., *Europe: A Constitution for the Millenium* (Aldershot: Dartmouth, 1995).
Westlake, M., *The Commission and the Parliament* (London: Butterworths, 1994).
Westlake, M., *The Council of the European Union* (London: Carterhill, 1995).

ELECTORAL SYSTEMS

General

Dunleavy, P., Margetts, H., O'Duffy, B. and Weir, S., *Making Votes Count*, Democratic Audit paper No. 11, September 1997.
Farrell, D., *Comparing Electoral Systems* (London: Prentice Hall/Harvester Wheatsheaf, 1997).
Katz, R., *A Theory of Parties and Electoral Systems* (Baltimore: Johns Hopkins University Press, 1980).
Katz, R., *Democracy and Elections* (New York: Oxford University Press, 1997).

Norris, P., *Electoral Change in Britain since 1945* (Oxford: Blackwell, 1997).

Independent Commission on the Voting System, *Report,* Cm 4090 (London: The Stationery Office, October 1998).

Vowles, J. et al. (eds) *Voters' Victory—New Zealand's First Election under Proportional Representation* (Auckland: Auckland University Press, 1998).

Devolution and the Parties

Brown, A., McCrone, D. and Paterson, L., *Politics and Society in Scotland* 2nd edn (Basingstoke: Macmillan, 1998).

Brown, A., McCrone, D., Paterson, L. and Surridge, P., *The Scottish Electorate* (Basingstoke: Macmillan, 1998).

Dunleavy, P., Margetts, H. and Weir, S., *Devolution Votes—PR Elections in Scotland and Wales*, Democratic Audit paper No. 12, September 1997.

The Party System and Europe

Hix, S. and Lord, C., *Political Parties in the European Union* (Basingstoke: Macmillan, 1997).

Electoral Administration

Butler, D., *The Case for an Electoral Commission—Keeping Election Law up to Date*, King-Hall paper No. 5, Hansard Society, 1998.

Committee on Standards in Public Life, *Fifth Report, The Funding of Political Parties in the United Kingdom* Cm 4057 (London: The Stationery Office, October 1998).

Electoral Geography

Field, W., *Regional Dynamics—The Basis of Electoral Support in Britain* (Portland, Oregon: Frank Cass, 1997).

Johnston, R. J., Pattie, C. J. and Allsopp, J. G., *A Nation Dividing—The Electoral Map of Great Britain 1979-87* (London: Longman, 1988).

WESTMINSTER

House of Commons

Giddings, P. and Drewry, G. (eds) *Westminster and Europe* (Basingstoke: Macmillan, 1996).

Griffith, A. G. and Ryle, M., *Parliament* (London: Sweet and Maxwell, 1989).

Hansard Society Commission, *Making the Law*, November 1992.

Power, G., *Reinventing Parliament* (London: Charter 88, 1997).

Power, G., *Representatives of the People? MPs and their Constituents* (London: Fabian Society, October 1998).

Riddell, P., *Parliament under Pressure*, (London: Gollancz, 1998).

Select Committee on European Legislation, *The Role of National Parliaments in the European Union*, HC 51-xxviii, July 1996.

Select Committee on Modernisation, *The Legislative Process*, HC 190, July 1997.

Select Committee on Modernisation of the House of Commons, *The Scrutiny of European Business*, HC 791, June 1998.

House of Lords

Constitution Unit, *Reform of the House of Lords*, London: April 1996.

Constitution Unit, *Reforming the Lords: A Step by Step Guide*, London: January 1998.

Osmond, J., *Reforming the Lords and Changing Britain*, Fabian Society, August 1998.

INTERGOVERNMENTAL RELATIONS

Galligan, B., Hughes, O. and Walsh, C., *Intergovernmental Relations and Public Policy* (Melbourne: Melbourne University Press, 1991).

Leonardy, U., *Working Structures of Federalism in Germany* (Leicester: Centre for Federal Studies, 1992).

Malcomson, P., *The Canadian Regime* (Peterborough: Broadview, 1996).

ENVIRONMENT AND CONSTITUTIONAL CHANGE

Carter, N. and Lowe, P., 'The Establishment of a Cross-Sector Environment Agency' in Dodds, F. (ed.) *The Way Forward—Beyond Agenda 21* (London: Earthscan, 1997).

Gouldson, A. and Murphy, J., *Regulatory Realities* (London: Earthscan, 1998).

Gray, T. S. (ed.) *UK Environmental Policy in the 1990s* (London: Macmillan, 1995).

Haigh, N., 'Devolved Responsibility and Centralization: the Effects of EEC Environmental Policy', *Public Administration*, 64 (1986), 197–207.

Kramer, L., 'The Open Society, its Lawyers and its Environment', *Journal of Environmental Law*, Vol. 1 (1989), 1–9.

Lowe, P. and Ward, S., 'Britain in Europe: Themes and Issues in National Environmental Policy' in Lowe, P. and Ward, S. (eds.) *British Environmental Policy and Europe: Politics and Policy in Transition* (London: Routledge, 1998).

Macrory, R., 'Environmental Law: Shifting Discretions and the New Formalism' in Lomas, O. (ed.) *Frontiers of Environmental Law* (London: Chancey, 1991).

Macrory, R., 'Environmental Citizenship and the Law: Repairing the European Road', *Journal of Environmental Law*, Vol. 8, No. 2 (1996), 219–36.

Osborn, D., *'Some Reflections on UK Environment Policy 1970–1995'*, Journal of Environmental Law, Vol. 9,. No. 1 (1997), 3–22.

Voisey, H. and O'Riordan, T., 'Governing Institutions for Sustainable Development: The United Kingdom's National Level Approach' in O'Riordan and Voisey (eds) *Sustainable Development in Western Europe* (London: Frank Cass, 1998).

Wards, S., 'Thinking Global, Act Local? British Local Authorities and their Environmental Plans', *Environmental Politics*, Vol. 2, No. 3 (1993), 453–78.

Wilkinson, D., 'Towards Sustainability in the European Union' in O'Riordan, T. and Voisey, H., (eds) *Sustainable Development in Western Europe* (London: Frank Cass, 1998).

Wyatt, D., 'Litigating Community Environmental Law: Thoughts on the Direct Effect Doctrine', *Journal of Environmental Law*, Vol. 10, No. 1 (1998), 9–20.

FINANCING DEVOLUTION

Blow, L., Hall, J. and Smith, S., *Financing Regional Government in Britain*, (London: Institute for Fiscal Studies, June 1996).

Heald, D., Geaughan, N. and Robb, C., 'Financial Arrangements for UK Devolution', *Regional and Federal Studies*, Vol 8 (1998) 23–52.

House of Commons Library Research Paper 98/8, *The Barnett Formula*, (January 1998).

Public Expenditure: Statistical Analyses 1998–99, (Cm 3901), April 1998, London, The Stationery Office.

Regional Trends 1998, London, Office for National Statistics.

Scotland's Parliament (Cm 3658), July 1997, ch. 7.

Treasury Committee, *The Barnett Formula*, HC 341, 17 December 1998.

Treasury Committee, *The Barnett Formula: The Government's Response*, HC 619, 10 March 1998.

CITIZENSHIP

Bainbridge, T., with Teasdale, A., *The Penguin Companion to European Union* (London: Penguin, 1995, revised 1996).

Colley, L., *Britons—Forging the Nation 1707–1837*, (London: Pimlico, 1992).

Dummett, A. and Nicol, A., *Subjects, Citizens, Aliens and Others: Nationality and Immigration Law* (London: Weidenfeld and Nicolson, 1990).

Education for All: the report of the Committee of Inquiry into the Education of Children from Ethnic Minority Groups, Cmnd. 9453, HMSO, March 1985. See esp. ch. 1, 'The Nature of Society'.

Fransman, L., *British Nationality Law* (London: Butterworth, 1998).

Fryer, P., *Staying Power* (London: Pluto Press, 1984).

Halsey, A. H., *Change in British Society*, 3rd edn (Oxford: Oxford University Press, 1986).

Holmes, C. (ed.) *Immigrants and Minorities in British Society* (London: Allen and Unwin, 1978).

Jackson, J. A., *The Irish in Britain* (London: Routledge, 1963).

Parry, C., *Nationality and Citizenship Laws of the Commonwealth and of the Republic of Ireland* (2 vols), (London: Stevens, 1957).

Taylor, A. J. P. *English History 1914–1945* (Oxford: Oxford University Press, 1965 and London: Pelican Books, 1970).

Index